SOFTWARE TOOLS

SOFTWARE TOOLS

Brian W. Kernighan

Bell Laboratories
Murray Hill, New Jersey

P. J. Plauger

Yourdon inc.
New York, New York

ADDISON-WESLEY PUBLISHING COMPANY
Reading, Massachusetts
Menlo Park, California · London · Amsterdam · Don Mills, Ontario · Sydney

 Printed in the United States of America. Published simultaneously in Canada.

ISBN 0-201-03669-X
HIJKLMNOPQ-HA-79

This book was set in Times Roman and Helvetica Regular by the authors, using a Graphic Systems phototypesetter driven by a PDP-11/45 running under the UNIX operating system.

PREFACE

This book teaches how to write good programs that make good tools, by presenting a comprehensive set, each one of which provides lessons in design and implementation. The programs are not artificial, nor are they toys. Instead, they are tools which have proved valuable in the production of other programs. We use most of them every working day, and they account for most of our computer usage. The programs are complete, not just algorithms and outlines, and they work: all have been tested directly from the text, which is in machine-readable form. They are readable: all are presented in a structured language called Ratfor (for "Rational Fortran"), which can be easily understood by anyone familiar with Fortran, PL/I, Cobol, Algol, Pascal or a similar language. (Ratfor translates readily into Fortran or PL/I: one of the tools presented is a preprocessor to translate Ratfor into Fortran automatically.) Most important, the programs are designed to work well with people and with each other, and are thus more readily *perceived* as tools.

The book is pragmatic. We teach top-down design by walking through designs. We demonstrate structured programming with structured programs. We discuss efficiency and reliability in terms of actual tests carried out. We treat portability by writing in a language that is widely available, and by isolating unavoidable system dependencies in a handful of small, carefully specified routines that can be readily built for a particular operating environment. All of the programs presented here have been run without change on at least two different machines; the larger ones have run on an IBM 370, a Honeywell 6070 and a PDP-11. The code is available in machine-readable form as a supplement to the text.

The principles of good programming are presented not as abstract sermons but as concrete lessons in the context of actual working programs. For example, there is no chapter on "efficiency." Instead, throughout the book there are observations on efficiency as it relates to the particular program being developed. Similarly there is no chapter on "top-down design," nor on "structured programming," nor on "testing and debugging." Instead, all of these disciplines are employed as appropriate in every program shown.

The book is suitable for a "software engineering" course or for a second course in programming — more so, we feel, than the traditional dose of "assemblers, compilers and loaders," for the programs presented here are more of the size and nature that will be encountered by most programmers. It is also suitable as a supplementary text in any programming course. The only prerequisite is programming experience in a high-level language. Professional programmers will find it a guide to good programming techniques and a source of proven, useful programs. Numerous exercises are provided to test comprehension and to extend the concepts and the programs presented in the text.

Building on the work of others is the only way to make substantial progress in any field. Yet computer programming continues as a cottage industry because programmers insist on reinventing programs for each new application, instead of using what already exists. What we hope to instill is a feeling for how to design and write good programs that can be widely used, how to use existing tools, and how to improve a given environment with maximum effect for minimum effort.

Any book on programming owes a debt to pioneers who have worked to improve the programming process. We freely acknowledge the influence of E. W. Dijkstra, C. A. R. Hoare, D. E. Knuth, D. L. Parnas, and N. Wirth.

We are grateful to our friends and colleagues for careful reading, perceptive criticism, and continuous cheerful support far beyond any expectation. In particular, Dennis Ritchie read several drafts with great care; his suggestions have materially improved our code and exposition. The language C which he designed for UNIX provided the model for Ratfor, and our text editor is patterned after his. He also designed and implemented a prototype of the macro processor of Chapter 8. Finally, he exercised our programs with a remarkable eye for potential errors, and ferreted out a number of embarrassing weaknesses. We deeply appreciate his contributions.

Our thanks also to Stu Feldman and Doug McIlroy, who diligently read multiple drafts, to Al Aho, Brenda Baker, Rick Becker, Phyllis Fox, Dan Franklin, Tom Gibson, Paul Jensen, Steve Johnson, Lee McMahon, Ken Thompson, Tony Wasserman and Ed Yourdon for comments on the manuscript at various stages, and to Mike Lesk and Joe Ossanna for assistance with text formatting.

Finally it is a pleasure to acknowledge our debt to the UNIX operating system, developed at Bell Labs by Ken Thompson and Dennis Ritchie. We wrote the text, tested the programs, and typeset the manuscript, all within UNIX. Many of the tools we describe are based on UNIX models. Most important, the ideas and philosophy are based on our experience as UNIX users. Of all the operating systems we have used, UNIX is the only one which has been a positive help in getting a job done instead of an obstacle to be overcome. The widespread and rapidly growing acceptance of UNIX indicates that we are not the only ones who feel this way.

Brian W. Kernighan

P. J. Plauger

CONTENTS

All of the programs described in this book are available in machine-readable form from Addison-Wesley.

INTRODUCTION

We are going to discuss two things in this book — how to write programs that make good tools, and how to program well in the process.

What do we mean by a *tool?* Suppose you have to convert a 5000-line Fortran program from one computer to another, and you need to find all the **format** statements, to make sure they are suitable for the new machine. How would you do it?

One possibility is to get a listing and mark it up with a red pencil. But it doesn't take much imagination to see what's wrong with red-penciling a hundred pages of computer paper. It's mindless and boring busy-work, with lots of opportunities for error. And even after you've found all the **format** statements, you still can't do much, because the red marks aren't machine readable.

Another approach is to write a simple program to find **format** statements. This is an improvement, for such a program is faster and more accurate than doing the job by hand. The trouble is that the program is so specialized that it will be used once by its author, then tucked away and forgotten. No one else will benefit from the effort that went into writing it, and something very much like it will have to be reinvented for each new application.

Finding **format** statements in Fortran programs is a special case of a general problem, finding patterns in text. Whoever wanted **format** statements today will want **read** and **write** statements tomorrow, and next week an entirely different pattern in some unrelated text. Red penciling never ends. The way to cope with the general problem is to provide a general purpose pattern finder which will look for a specified pattern and print all the lines where it occurs. Then anyone can say

> **find** *pattern*

and the job is done. **find** is a *tool:* it uses the machine; it solves a general problem, not a special case; and it's so easy to use that people will use it instead of building their own.

Far too many programmers are red pencillers. Some are literal red pencillers who do things by hand that should be done by machine. Others are figurative red pencillers whose use of the machine is so clumsy and awkward that it might as well be manual. One of the purposes of this book is to show how to build *tools* — programs to help people to do things by machine instead of by red pencil, and how to do them well instead of badly. We're going to do this, not by talking in generalities but by writing real, working programs, programs that we know from experience are useful tools. *Every* program in this book has been run and carefully tested, directly from the text itself, which is in machine-readable form. All of them have been run without change on at least two different machines; the larger programs have been run on three: a PDP-11, a Honeywell 6070, and an IBM 370.

The second concern of this book is how to write *good* programs. As we proceed, we hope to convey to you principles of: good design, so you write programs that work and are easy to maintain and modify; human engineering, so you can use them conveniently; reliability, so you get the right answers; and efficiency, so you can afford to run them.

There are a lot of terms being bandied about these days describing ways to improve the programming process: structured programming, top-down design, structured design, egoless programming — the list is long. For example, structured programming in a very narrow sense implies programming with a limited set of control flow statements, and avoiding **goto**'s. A broader interpretation encompasses the general process of programming so as to carefully control the structure of one's code — its control flow, data organization, and connection to the external world. Top-down design and successive refinement attack a programming task by specifying it in the most general terms, then expanding these into more and more specific and detailed actions, until the whole program is complete. Structured design is the process of controlling the overall design of a system or program so the pieces fit together neatly, yet remain sufficiently decoupled that they may be independently modified. Egoless programming means letting other people read your programs, without feeling wounded when they improve them. Each of these disciplines can materially improve programmer productivity and the quality of code produced.

But it is dangerous to believe that blind application of any particular technique will lead automatically to good programs. We don't think that it is possible to learn to program well by reading platitudes about good programming. Nor is it sufficient to study small and artificial examples. Rather than present ideas like structured programming and top-down design as abstract principles, we have tried to distill the important contributions of each and put them into practice in all our code. That way you can see what they mean, how to use them on real problems, and what benefits they are likely to produce. This is not a text on structured programming or on any of the other terms, but a presentation that happens to use them.

Thus we avoid writing **goto**'s, not out of reverence, nor in the hope of automatically producing good programs thereby, but because we have learned through experience that **goto**'s are often bad. We tend to design top-down because that leads to programs that are easier to get right, easier to change, and easier to keep right as they are changed. And as for egoless programming, this book contains more than 5000 lines of our programs for you to read.

We also try to show *how* we went about building the programs, rather than just presenting the finished product, or worse, pretending that we arrived at the final result by some mechanical process. Moreover, for each program we discuss its purpose, how it should be designed to be easy to use, what considerations affect its structure and implementation, and some of the alternatives that exist. We don't claim that these are the best possible programs, or that our way is the only way to design and write them. But even if you would do them differently, studying the development of a coherent set of well-written and useful programs should help you better appreciate the significance of some of these ideas, and ultimately to become a better programmer.

We have quite a few tools to show you. Most of these are programs of manageable size, programs that one person can reasonably write in an hour or a day or a week. Clearly we can't present giant programs like operating systems or major compilers; few of us have the time, training or need to delve inside such creatures anyway. Instead we have concentrated on the kinds of programs you *are* likely to become involved with, programs which help you to make most effective use of whatever operating system and language you already have. There is an important lesson in this: well chosen and well designed programs of modest size can be used to create a comfortable and effective interface to those that are bigger and less well done.

Whenever possible we will build more complicated programs up from the simpler; whenever possible we will *avoid* building at all, by finding new uses for existing tools, singly or in combinations. Our programs *work together;* their cumulative effect is much greater than you could get from a similar collection of programs that you couldn't easily connect. By the end of the book you will have been introduced to a set of software tools that solve many problems you encounter as a programmer. A few will be just skeletons, the basic minimum that is useful; the accompanying exercises will indicate how you can extend them in worthwhile directions.

What sorts of tools? Computing is a broad field, and we can't begin to cover every kind of application. Instead we have concentrated on an activity which is central to programming — *programs that help develop other programs.* They are programs which we use regularly, most of them every day; we used essentially all of them while we were writing this book. In fact we chose them because they account for much of the computer usage on the system where we work. Although we can hardly claim that our choices will satisfy all your needs, some should be directly useful to you whatever your interest. Studying those that are not should provide you with ideas and insights about how to design and build quality tools for *your* particular problems. Comparing our designs with related programs on your system may lead you to improvements in both. And learning to think in terms of tools will encourage you to write programs that solve only the unique parts of your problem, then interface to existing programs to do the rest.

Whatever your application, your most important tool is a good programming language. Without this, programs are just too hard to write and understand; you spend more time fighting your language than being productive. If you are lucky, your system already has a good language available and well supported. If not, you may have to build your own. That does *not* mean that you should go off and write a compiler, however; that is a job for experts. Instead, you should learn how to enhance whatever existing language you have with one or more preprocessors.

One of the problems with writing about programming is choosing a language for the programs. No single language is known to all readers, compilable on all machines, and easy to read. We must compromise: since Fortran is widely available and well supported, we will use it as our base in this book. Most programmers have at least a reading knowledge of Fortran, and it runs on almost all computers. The language is sufficiently well standardized that programs can be written to run without change on a wide variety of systems. In a real sense, Fortran is the *lingua franca* of computing, the closest thing there is to a universal language.

But bare Fortran is a poor language indeed for programming or for describing programs. So we have written all of our programs in a simple extension of Fortran called "Ratfor" (short for Rational Fortran). Ratfor provides modern control flow statements like those in PL/I, Cobol, Algol or Pascal, so we can do structured programming properly. It is easy to read, write, and understand, and readily translates into Fortran, PL/I or similar high-level languages. Except for a handful of new statements like **if-else**, **while**, and **repeat-until**, Ratfor *is* Fortran. If you have even a distant acquaintance with Fortran, you will adapt readily.

If you are used to other languages, you will still have no difficulty following our programs, for properly structured programs seem to read the same in most languages. We avoid the major idiosyncrasies of Fortran, and hide the unavoidable ones in well-defined modules.

Chapter 1 introduces most of the Ratfor language with examples and a concise summary. In Chapter 9 we build a Ratfor-to-Fortran translator. We also present tools which can enhance this translator, such as a macro processor in Chapter 8 and a file inclusion program in Chapter 3.

Preprocessing into Fortran is a convenient way to do business. We retain the advantages of Fortran — a language that is universal, portable, and relatively efficient — while at the same time concealing its worst drawbacks. You might say we treat Fortran as an assembly language that will run on any machine. If you work in a predominantly Fortran environment, you will find this approach rewarding. Even if you have a better language than Ratfor at hand, however, you can adapt the programs with the assurance that the code has been checked and does what it is supposed to.

A surprising number of programs have one input, one output, and perform a useful transformation on data as it passes through. Such programs are called *filters*. Some filters are so simple that you might hardly think of them as tools, yet a careful selection of filters that work together can be a tool-kit for quite complicated processing. Several smaller filters are collected in Chapter 2, including a powerful character transliteration program.

Not all programs are filters. Chapter 3 discusses programs which interact with their environment in more complicated ways, such as the file inclusion program mentioned above, a file comparator, a multi-file printer, and an archive system for managing sets of files. The major problem in moving programs from one environment to another is precisely this question of how a program communicates with its local operating system. We deal with this problem by specifying a small set of primitive operations for accessing the environment. All of our programs are written in terms of these primitives, so operating system dependencies are confined to a handful of subroutines. Programs that use them can move to any system where the primitives can be implemented.

Some filters are large enough to warrant separate chapters. The sorting program of Chapter 4, the pattern finding and replacement programs of Chapter 5, and the Ratfor-to-Fortran translator of Chapter 9 all fall into this category. The pattern finder uses most of the code of the transliteration program in Chapter 2 to recognize character classes, which are now just one of a larger set of patterns that can be specified. (The pattern finder is capable of a lot more than finding **format** statements, by the way.) Although these filters are biased toward program development, the filter concept is valuable in any application. It encourages the view that a program is just a stage in a larger process, and that stages should be simple and easy to connect. It also encourages the view that all files and I/O devices should be essentially interchangeable, so that any program can work with any file or device.

Chapter 6 contains a text editor which is rather more comprehensive than those normally found in time-sharing systems. The editor incorporates most of the code of the pattern finder of Chapter 5, so it recognizes the same class of patterns. When used with some of the other programs presented, it can do jobs that would otherwise require you to write a special program. Even if you are not working in an interactive environment, the editor will prove to be useful.

Chapter 7 contains a text formatter which is a (much smaller) version of the program used to set the type for this book. As we have already mentioned, Chapter 8 contains a modest but useful macro processor, which you can use to extend any programming language. Finally, Chapter 9 presents the Ratfor preprocessor.

It might appear from this outline that we stress text manipulation too heavily. Yet computing is not all number-crunching, nor is it the "compilers, assemblers and loaders" so hastily treated in many second courses in programming. A large part of what programmers do every day *is* text processing — editing program source, preparing input data, scanning output, writing documentation. These activities are at the heart of programming; as much as possible, they should be mechanized. Program development is the place where tools can have the most impact. And since text processing programs come in all sizes, they display at least as broad a spectrum of programming techniques as language processors or numerical programs.

As you can see, the book is organized in terms of applications rather than different aspects of the programming process. This is not a reference work on algorithms or data structures or any particular programming language. Nor will you find separate chapters on design, coding, testing, debugging, efficiency, human engineering, documentation, or any of the other popular themes. We are engaged in the business of building tools, and of building them properly. All of these aspects of programming arise, in varying degrees, with *every* program, and can only be kept in perspective by discussing them as we write the programs. In the process, we will try to communicate to you our approach to tool building, so you can go on to design, build, and use tools of your own.

Bibliographic Notes

One of the most influential proponents of good programming, whose name is most often associated with structured programming, is E. W. Dijkstra. You should read *Structured Programming,* by O.-J. Dahl, E. W. Dijkstra and C. A. R. Hoare (Academic Press, 1972). Dijkstra discusses the use of primitives in the construction of a hierarchical operating system in "The structure of the THE multiprogramming system," *Communications of the ACM (CACM),* May, 1968.

The programming language Pascal has had considerable impact on computing practice; it is especially suitable for structured programming and for control of data structure. Read *Systematic Programming: An Introduction* (Prentice-Hall, 1973) by N. Wirth, the designer of Pascal. The special issue of *Computing Surveys* on programming (December, 1974) also contains several papers well worth reading, including one by Wirth.

An excellent set of essays on the programming process and on the problems of developing big systems is found in F. P. Brooks' *The Mythical Man-Month* (Addison-Wesley, 1974). The term "egoless programming" was coined by G. M. Weinberg in his delightful book *The Psychology of Computer Programming* (Van Nostrand Reinhold, 1971).

"Structured design" was pioneered by L. L. Constantine. A summary of its basic principles can be found in W. P. Stevens, G. J. Myers and L. L. Constantine, "Structured design," *IBM Systems Journal,* April, 1974. Myers' book *Reliable Software Through Composite Design* (Petrocelli/Charter, 1974) discusses this topic in more detail. A later reference is *Structured Design* by E. Yourdon and L. L. Constantine, Yourdon, 1975.

The Elements of Programming Style, by B. W. Kernighan and P. J. Plauger (McGraw-Hill, 1974), contains an extensive discussion of how to improve computer programs, with numerous examples taken from published Fortran and PL/I code.

CHAPTER 1

GETTING STARTED

This chapter is an informal introduction to the programming language Ratfor and to some of the ideas and conventions used throughout the book. It also presents a handful of small but useful programs, to make the discussion concrete. We cannot present complete programs without occasionally using concepts before they are explained, so you will have to take some things on faith as we get started or we'll get bogged down explaining our explanations. Bear with us.

1.1 File Copying

The first problem we want to tackle is how a program communicates with its environment. Since many of our programs are concerned with text manipulation, one basic operation is reading characters from some source of input. To do this we invent a function **getc**, which reads the *next input character,* and returns that character as its function value; each time it is called, it returns a new character. For now we'll ignore where the characters come from, although you can imagine them originating at a card reader or an interactive terminal or some secondary storage device like a disk. We won't discuss what character set we have in mind. We'll also ignore all questions of efficiency, although we're fully aware that reading one character at a time at least sounds expensive. Temporarily we want to sweep as many details as we possibly can under the rug.

Next we invent **putc**, the complement of **getc**. **putc** puts a single character somewhere, such as a line printer, a terminal, or a disk. Again, we won't concern ourselves with the precise details, nor with the efficiency of the operation. The main point is that **getc** and **putc** work together — the characters that **getc** gets can be put somewhere else by **putc**.

If someone has provided these two basic operations, you can do a surprising amount of useful computing without ever knowing anything more about how they're implemented. As the simplest example, if you put the **getc/putc** pair inside a loop:

```
while (getc(c) is not at end of input)
        call putc(c)
stop
```

you have a program that copies its input to its output and quits. A simple task, performed by an equally simple program. Certainly, someone ultimately has to worry about the choice of character set, detecting the end of the input, efficiency and the like, but most people need *not* be concerned, because **getc** and **putc** conceal the details. (If you want to know how, there are simple versions of **getc** and **putc** at the end of this chapter.)

Functions like **getc** and **putc** are called *primitives* — functions that interface to the "outside world." They call in turn whatever input and output routines must be used with a particular operating system. To the program that uses them, **getc** and **putc** define a standard internal representation for characters and provide a general input and output mechanism that can be made uniform across many different computers. If we use primitives, we can design and write programs that will not be overly dependent on the idiosyncrasies of any one operating system. The primitives insulate a program from its operating system environment and ensure that the high level task to be performed is clearly expressed in a small well-defined set of basic operations.

The program shown above is written in a pseudo-code that resembles a computer language but avoids excessive detail by lapsing from time to time into ordinary English. This lets us specify quite a bit of the program before we have worked out all aspects of it. On larger programs, it is valuable to begin with pseudo-code and refine it in stages until it is all executable. This way you can revise and improve the design at a high level without writing any executable code, yet remain close to a form which can be made executable.

The next step is to write **copy** in precise Ratfor, ready to compile and run.

```
# copy — copy input characters to output
        integer getc
        integer c

        while (getc(c) ¬= EOF)
                call putc(c)
        stop
        end
```

Some explanations: The first line is a comment that names the program and briefly synopsizes what it does; this kind of comment will occur on every runnable program in the book. In Ratfor, a sharp sign # *anywhere* on a line signals the beginning of a comment; the rest of the line is the comment. This comment convention is more flexible than Fortran's "C in column one" because comments and code can co-exist on the same line, and it's easier to type than PL/I's /* ... */ though not quite as general. (There is a concise synopsis of all Ratfor statements and conventions near the end of this chapter.)

The two lines

```
        integer getc
        integer c
```

are ordinary Fortran statements that declare **c** and **getc** to be of type **integer**. We will declare *all* variables and functions in all of our programs, because we think it's a good programming practice — it enforces some discipline by making it harder to invent new variables at will, and it allows mechanical checking of declarations. (We will also be careful to separate function declarations from declarations for ordinary variables, to help you tell them apart.) We said earlier that **getc** is a function that returns a character, and **c** also contains a character, but since few implementations of Fortran provide an explicit **character** data type, integers will have to serve for now. PL/I does support characters, but for reasons we'll get to soon, they are not entirely adequate either.

The lines

```
while (getc(c) ¬= EOF)
        call putc(c)
```

are where all the work of **copy** gets done. The **while** is a Ratfor statement that specifies a loop; so long as the condition inside parentheses is true, the body of the loop (in this case, the single Fortran statement **call putc(c)**) is repeatedly executed. Eventually the condition becomes false, and the loop terminates, falling through to the **stop**. The condition being tested in the **while** loop is

```
getc(c) ¬= EOF
```

The notation ¬= is Ratfor shorthand for "not equal to," just as in PL/I. Fortran users will find **.ne.** more familiar, though less concise. Thus the loop continues while the character returned by **getc** is not **EOF**.

getc(c) returns the next character both as its function value *and* in its argument **c** so the value can be both tested and saved for later use, all in a single statement. This is an unconventional Fortran usage, but perfectly legal. It is so handy that we use it often.

EOF is a *symbolic constant* that stands for an integer value that is mutually agreed upon by **getc** and the users of **getc** to signal that the end of the input has occurred — that there are no more characters. We won't tell you what its value is, since the particular value doesn't matter; it may well be different on different machines. The only restriction is that **EOF** must be distinguishable from any possible real character that **getc** might return. We will consistently use upper case names for symbolic constants so they will stand out; all variables and functions will be in lower case.

There are a fair number of symbolic constants in our programs; they contribute a great deal to the readability of the code. You can see at a glance what the test

```
getc(c) ¬= EOF
```

means, because **EOF** is more meaningful than some magic number like **−1** would be. Chapter 8 describes a program that will let you define and translate symbolic constants, so that you can use them in programs and have the actual defining character strings written into the source code automatically before it is compiled. We use a program like this to process all the programs in this book.

To actually run a Ratfor program, the Ratfor source is passed through a program called a *preprocessor,* which translates the control statements like **while** into equivalent **if**'s and **goto**'s, replaces symbolic constants by their definitions, and converts shorthand like ¬= into **.ne.**. Everything else is assumed to be ordinary Fortran; it is copied through untouched except for being correctly positioned on the output line. The resulting Fortran statements are then compiled in the normal manner. So the processing sequence is

```
Ratfor source
        → Ratfor preprocessor
                → Fortran compiler
                        → runnable program
```

Still other preprocessors can be included in this chain. We will build a Ratfor preprocessor in Chapter 9.

The advantage of Ratfor is that it doesn't obscure what is going on with the syntactic peculiarities of Fortran, yet ensures that the program translates readily into Fortran or, with a bit more effort, into any similar language. It is a good practice to write first in an easy-to-read higher level language, then translate into whatever real-life language you happen to be working with — Fortran, PL/I, even assembly language. The programs in this book use only a few control structures like **while**, and a few data types like **integer**, so it's not hard to translate mechanically into the chosen target language.

One Fortran version of **copy**, for instance, is:

```
c copy — copy input characters to output
      integer getc
      integer c
10    if (getc(c) .eq. EOF) goto 20
           call putc(c)
           goto 10
20    continue
      stop
      end
```

The Ratfor **while** statement is a loop with a test at the top, which can be expressed with an **if** for the test and a **goto** at the bottom to close the loop. We indent the statements under control of the **while** for ease of recognition. We have also left **EOF** as a symbolic constant until we can decide what to write in its place. We shall continue to postpone such substitutions as long as possible, so that you will not be mystified by numbers of unknown significance.

copy is equally easy in PL/I:

```
/* copy — copy input characters to output */
    copy: procedure options (main);
    declare getc entry (fixed binary) returns (fixed binary);
    declare putc entry (fixed binary);
    declare c fixed binary;

    do while (getc(c) ¬= EOF);
        call putc(c);
        end;
    end copy;
```

The PL/I **do while** statement corresponds closely to the Ratfor **while**, so the translation is more straightforward.

Why is **copy** useful? Most operating systems permit you to specify what files or data sets or physical I/O devices correspond to the logical unit numbers or internal filenames you used when you wrote the program. This correspondence is established after the code is compiled, at the time it is actually run. That means you can have programs around, ready to run, and decide at the last moment what files or devices to use. It also means you can treat such programs like black boxes, and can pretty much forget about their innards. If you have the primitive **getc** read from a "standard input" — like Fortran logical unit 5 or PL/I file *sysin* — and have **putc** write on a "standard output" — Fortran logical unit 6 or PL/I file *sysprint* — you can connect them to the appropriate files or devices when the program is run.

By the way, the word "file" has different meanings on different computer systems. For now, we will use it colloquially to mean a place where information comes from (via **getc**, for example), or a place where it can be put (perhaps with **putc**). This might be a disk organized as a permanent "file system" or any I/O device.

Our program copies a stream of characters from any source to any destination. In an environment such as we just described, you can use it to read cards onto a disk file, list a file on a printer, replicate a file — to perform, in short, a host of utility functions.

Although there are other ways of doing many of these things, this method is general and you can build on it. You can improve it, if necessary, in any number of subtle ways, make it fancier or make it faster. **copy** is a basic *tool.* Useful in its own right, it can also serve as a base for constructing other, more elaborate programs. If you adhere to the design principle of pushing details as far down as possible, by writing in terms of basic primitives which read from an arbitrary source and write to an arbitrary destination, your new tools will be compatible with previous ones; you will be building a whole set that work together.

> *Exercise 1-1:* We explicitly declared **getc** and **c** to be of type integer; otherwise Fortran's default typing rules would have made them real variables. Why are integers preferable to reals? We could have avoided the declarations by naming the function **igetc** and the variable **ic**. Which names do you think are better? Would you prefer **nextc**? If you have to read someone else's code, would you rather have all variables and functions declared, or only those that absolutely have to be? □

Exercise 1-2: Why don't we declare all the data to be of type **character** in our PL/I version? What is a useful value to assign to **EOF** for the actual running program? Suggest some bad values. □

1.2 Counting Characters

There are times when all you want to know about a file is how many characters it contains, or how many lines, or how many words. If the file resides on permanent storage like a disk, you may be lucky enough to have an operating system that will tell you at least some of these things. If you are not lucky, or if the "file" happens to be a card deck, for instance, then the easiest thing is to pass the file through a program that counts what you want to know.

If you can't think offhand why anyone would want to merely count the characters in something, don't worry. This is a book on tool building, remember, and tools work best in combination with others. Applications will occur soon enough.

Counting characters is the most basic operation:

```
# charcount — count characters in standard input
        character getc
        character c
        integer nc

        nc = 0
        while (getc(c) ¬= EOF)
                nc = nc + 1
        call putdec(nc, 1)
        call putc(NEWLINE)
        stop
        end
```

In this program, **nc** is truly an integer, used strictly for counting. Accordingly its declaration is separated from those for **c** and **getc**, which are characters. This program also introduces the declaration **character**. Even though in most environments this will be synonymous with **integer**, we will henceforth distinguish the two types of variables in all our programs, so you can tell immediately what the usage of a particular variable will be. The same preprocessor that changes each occurrence of **EOF** to a literal number can also be used to alter each instance of **character** to **integer** just before the code is compiled.

To print the number it has computed, **charcount** calls **putdec**, which converts a number to a string of characters suitable for printing and outputs it with **putc**; this way it does not have to know how output is actually performed. (We will show you **putdec** in Chapter 2.) The second argument in the call to **putdec** is the minimum field width: the number will be right-adjusted in a field at least this wide.

In no case does **putdec** force the output device, whatever it might be, to end the current line, because we might want to put several numbers on one line with multiple calls to **putdec**. Thus we have to ask for a new line explicitly, with

```
        call putc(NEWLINE)
```

NEWLINE is an actual character in large character sets like ASCII or EBCDIC;

when sent to a typewriter-like device it typically causes a carriage return and line feed. We will use **NEWLINE** as a standard character for signaling end of line, regardless of the source or destination of information, so that our programs can have a uniform way of distinguishing lines.

You should observe that if the input file contains no characters, the **while** test fails on the first call to **getc**, and so **charcount** produces zero, the right answer. This is an important observation. One of the best things about the **while** statement is that it tests at the *top* of the loop, before proceeding with the body. Thus if there is nothing to do, nothing is done, even if this means that we never go through the loop body. Too many programs, particularly in Fortran, fail to act intelligently when handed input like "no characters." We will write ours so they do reasonable things with extreme cases; one of our basic tools for accomplishing this is the **while**.

1.3 Counting Lines

Suppose that instead of counting characters, we want to count the number of *lines* in some input. How do we tell that a line has been seen? An especially convenient solution is to have **getc** note the end of each line of input and return **NEWLINE** at the end of each line. (If your character set doesn't have a **NEWLINE**, then, just like **EOF**, it must be given some agreed-upon value distinct from all other characters.) Similarly, **putc** must accept a **NEWLINE** as a signal to put out a completed line of text.

We can thus make *any* device look like a "typewriter," with each line of text ending in a **NEWLINE**. **getc** and **putc** do whatever is necessary to hide the differences among devices. Programs do not have to know anything about record lengths on different devices (or even about variable length records on the same device); they process one character at a time until a **NEWLINE** is encountered. Treating **NEWLINE** as a character, even if it may not exist as such in your local character set, simplifies many programs; we will make extensive use of it.

If **getc** returns a **NEWLINE** at the end of each line, **linecount** is easy:

```
# linecount — count lines in standard input
        character getc
        character c
        integer nl

        nl = 0
        while (getc(c) ¬= EOF)
                if (c == NEWLINE)
                        nl = nl + 1
        call putdec(nl, 1)
        call putc(NEWLINE)
        stop
        end
```

This time the body of the **while** is a little bigger — it consists of an **if**, which in turn controls the assignment statement **nl = nl + 1**. The indentation shows what code is controlled by what, and unobtrusively but clearly draws attention to the logical structure of a program.

The double equal sign == is the Ratfor symbol for the comparison "is equal to"; we use it to avoid confusion with the assignment operator, which is a single = sign. The == translates into **.eq.** in Fortran or = in PL/I. As we said in the introduction, Ratfor *is* Fortran in most respects. In particular, if you don't care for notations like ¬= and ==, by all means use **.ne.** and **.eq.**; they are equally acceptable.

The idea that text information is just a string of characters, with arbitrary length lines delimited by explicit newline characters, seems pretty obvious when you think about how a typewriter or a terminal works. But for all its obviousness, it's still an uncommon concept in many computing systems, where text must often be forced into fixed length chunks reminiscent of cards.

If your system strongly encourages fixed length text formats, you can see how **getc** and **putc** must work. In Fortran, which is basically a card or record environment, we equate records and lines. **getc** reads a record whenever necessary and doles out characters one at a time, ending each record with a **NEWLINE**. **putc** saves characters in a buffer until called with a **NEWLINE**, then writes the entire record (less the **NEWLINE**). Buffers should be big enough to hold the largest possible records. Although there are drawbacks to such an implementation, it is enough to get started with. The versions of **getc** and **putc** at the end of this chapter work this way; they will serve temporarily in most Fortran systems.

This form of input is *not* identical to PL/I **stream** input, by the way. No information about record boundaries is passed back to the calling program on **stream** input, although it is possible to ignore characters up to the next line by means of the **skip** format specification. **getc** must therefore read records to be able to report **NEWLINE**'s, and is thus very similar in both Fortran and PL/I.

Of course the input might indeed be a stream of characters from a keyboard and the output might indeed be driving a typing mechanism, and all disk files might be maintained in this format, in which case **getc** and **putc** become trivial. But whatever the source or sink, we will usually *program* in terms of typewriter-like text, performing all necessary translations as early as possible on input and as late as possible on output, to match up with card readers, line printers, and other disk file formats. (Chapter 2 contains some examples of programs for matching up.) Having a uniform representation for text solves much of the problem of keeping tools uniform.

How should we test **linecount** to make sure it really works? When bugs occur, they usually arise at the "boundaries" or extremes of program operation. These are the "exceptions that prove the rule." Here the boundaries are fairly simple: a file with no lines and a file with one line. If the code handles these cases correctly, and the general case of a file with more than one line, it is probable that it will handle all inputs properly.

So we feed **linecount** an empty file. The **while** test fails the first time and the body is never obeyed. No lines are counted when none are input. Fine.

If we feed **linecount** one line, the **while** is satisfied for every character on the line; the **if** is satisfied when the **NEWLINE** is seen, and the line is counted. Then the test is repeated and the **while** loop exits. Again fine.

A multi-line file. Same behavior as for one line, only now we observe that after each line, the program ends up at the test part of the **while** — the proper place to begin handling the next line, or **EOF**. The program checks out.

This may seem like excruciating detail for such a simple program, but it's not. There are common coding blunders which could have caused any one of those three tests to fail, sometimes even while the other two tests succeed. You should learn to think of boundary tests as you code each piece of a program — try them mentally as you write and then physically on the finished product. In practice, the tests go much quicker than we can talk about them and cost but a little additional effort. It is effort that is well repaid.

Exercise 1-3: What happens if the last character of a file fed to **linecount** is not a **NEWLINE**? Does the program stay sane? Is its behavior a bug or a natural consequence of our definition of a "line"? □

1.4 Counting Words

The next counting program has applications in text processing — it counts the words in something. We use it to answer questions like "How many words are there in this book?" (About 80,000, excluding programs.) For our purposes a word is a sequence of any characters except blanks, tabs and newlines. Every time there is a transition from not being in a word to being in a word, that signals another word to count. The variable **inword** is used to record which state the program is in at any given time; initially it is "not in a word."

Writing this in Ratfor is succinct:

```
# wordcount — count words in standard input
	character getc
	character c
	integer inword, wc

	wc = 0
	inword = NO
	while (getc(c) ¬= EOF)
		if (c == BLANK | c == NEWLINE | c == TAB)
			inword = NO
		else if (inword == NO) {
			inword = YES
			wc = wc + 1
			}
	call putdec(wc, 1)
	call putc(NEWLINE)
	stop
	end
```

TAB is another symbolic constant, which must be made equal to the internal character code that **getc** returns for horizontal tab on your machine. The vertical bar **|** is the logical *or* operator. It will be familiar to PL/I users; Fortran programmers know it as **.or.**.

The symbolic constants **YES** and **NO** are probably one and zero, but it doesn't matter (nor do we care), so long as they are different and everyone agrees upon their values. They are far easier to read and understand than idioms like Fortran's **logical** values **.true.** and **.false.** or PL/I's **'1'b** and **'0'b**. For this reason, and because Fortran imposes some arbitrary restrictions on **logical** comparisons, we will stick to **integer**'s and use symbolic constants like **YES** and **NO**.

This example also shows several new and important aspects of Ratfor control flow. First, an **if** statement may include an **else**, to specify an alternate action if the condition of the **if** is not met:

```
if (condition)
        statement
else
        statement
```

says "**if** the *condition* is true do the *statement* following the **if**; **else** (otherwise) do the *statement* following the **else**." One and only one of the two statements is executed when the **if-else** is encountered. Either statement can in fact be quite complicated; in **wordcount** the one after the **else** is yet another **if**!

Second, we can replace any single statement in Ratfor by a whole group of statements enclosed in braces, a construction called a *compound statement*. Braces act like the **do** and **end** statements in PL/I or the **begin** and **end** of Algol and its derivatives: the statements within the braces are treated as if they were a single statement. Thus if **inword** is **NO** in the code

```
else if (inword == NO) {
        inword = YES
        wc = wc + 1
        }
```

both assignments are done. As in all of these languages, braces may in principle be nested to arbitrary depth.

We prefer braces to **begin-end** or **do-end** mainly because they are visually less obtrusive than spelled-out words, and a lot easier to type. We will consistently position our braces as shown: the left one on the line that controls the compound statement, and the right one on a line by itself at the same level of indentation as the group it terminates.

It is truly remarkable how much heated debate can result from such trivial questions as whether braces are better than **begin** and **end**, and where they should be placed. Rather than continue such a debate, suffice it to say that we find our style convenient and readable, but you are free to alter it as you see fit in your own code. We do recommend that you be consistent in applying whatever formatting standards you settle on.

Although the code that follows the **while** in **wordcount** is complicated, logically it is just a single **if-else** statement, not a compound, so it needs no surrounding braces. You may insert them if they make you feel more comfortable.

The **else if** construction occurs frequently in our programs, often as a longer chain of **if** ... **else if** ... **else**, to perform at most one of several alternatives. Chains are made longer by inserting more **else if**'s at the appropriate places. Three rules make such chains easy to read:

(1) Scan down the tests until you find one that is met — the first one encountered selects the case to be performed.

(2) If no test succeeds, the statement associated with the trailing **else** (if any) is performed.

(3) In either situation, execution resumes immediately after the body ot the last **else** (or the last **else if** if there is no trailing **else**.)

Some languages provide a "**case**" statement for expressing multi-way decisions directly. In a language without a **case**, a chain of **else if**'s is usually the clearest equivalent. We strongly favor this form of writing multi-way decisions, instead of arbitrarily nested trees of **if-else**'s, because it tends to be least confusing. We keep all the **else if**'s at the same level of indenting, to emphasize that the structure is really a multi-way decision.

How do we test **wordcount**? The best place to begin this activity is while the program is being written. The main assurance you have that a program is correct is the intellectual effort you put into getting it right in the first place. We wrote **word-count** with an algorithm based on two states — being in a word, and not being in a word. If we make the transitions between states correctly, set up initial conditions properly, and properly count the transitions for each new word, we can have confidence in the program. Testing is still necessary, however, to check that the algorithm is valid and that the program implements it correctly.

For a program of any complexity, you certainly can't test all possible inputs. As we said, programmers have learned from bitter experience that the boundaries of a program are the most fruitful places to examine, for they are where bugs most often appear. Besides, if you can show that a program works properly at its extremes of operation, you have a convincing argument that it works properly everywhere between as well. Thus a small selection of critical tests directed at boundaries is much superior to a shotgun-blast of random ones.

Although it's hard to give a precise definition, intuitively a "boundary" is a data value for which the program is forced to react differently from an adjacent value. For example, the case of "no input at all" is a boundary for most programs. In testing **wordcount**, if there is no input, the first call of **getc** returns an **EOF**, the body of the **while** loop is never executed, and the wordcount is zero, as expected. The analogous boundary, having input but no words, is also worth checking. If the input consists entirely of blanks, tabs and newlines, the first **if** is always satisfied, so **wc** is never incremented; again the result is zero, as it should be.

You should also verify that **wordcount** works when there is a single word of input, regardless of where in the input it appears, and when there are two input words at various places. If all of these cases are correct, you can be fairly confident that the program is right.

One final observation. In testing **wordcount** it was obvious what output was expected for each input. That is not always so clear in larger programs. Yet it is a fundamental principle of testing that you must know in advance what answer each test case is supposed to produce. If you don't, you're not testing; you're experi-menting. So part of the responsibility of writing a program is to prepare a comprehensive set of test inputs, and outputs against which to compare the results of test runs.

Exercise 1-4: Combine the functions of **charcount**, **linecount** and **wordcount** into one program. In what order should the three counts be printed? Is it better to have one program that does three things, or three programs that each do one thing? □

Exercise 1-5: Modify **wordcount** so it also counts sentences. (Choose your own definition of a sentence.) Is this program likely to be used often? Compare your solution to the program shown in Exercise 2.4 of *The Elements of Programming Style,* by B. W. Kernighan and P. J. Plauger. □

1.5 Removing Tabs

Suppose that you need to list a text file containing horizontal tab characters on a device that cannot interpret tabs. As a first approximation, you might be content with fixed tab stops at, say, every eight columns. A tab character is thus replaced by from one to eight spaces. Let us write a program **detab** to do this.

The program can have the same structure as **copy**, except that we must elaborate the **while** loop:

```
while (getc(c) ¬= EOF)
        if (c == TAB)
                output blanks until next tab stop reached
        else
                just put character
```

How do we know when the next tab position is reached? One possibility is to build into the main program the knowledge that tabs are set every eight columns; then an arithmetic test suffices to decide if the current column is a tab stop. The trouble with such an approach comes when we decide to change the program, perhaps to allow tabs to be set at positions which aren't related by a simple arithmetic formula. If the "every eight columns" decision is firmly wired into the program, it will be hard to cut it out.

A more flexible organization is an array of tab stops, initialized for now by the every eight columns rule. This will be a lot easier to change; in fact we haven't even said whether the array contains a list of stops or a **YES/NO** indicator at each column, like a typewriter. Representing the stops in an array, in whatever manner, leads to a program that will readily upgrade for more general applications.

However we do it, it is still worthwhile to write a separate function **tabpos** which tells the main program whether a particular column is a tab stop or not. This way we avoid muddying up the basic logic of the control loop with tab calculations, and conceal the representation of tab stops from the main routine.

It is clear that the program must also keep track of what column it is in, and it must recognize the end of each line of text so it can reset the column counter. The second cut at the tab remover is thus:

```
initialize tab stops
col = 1
while (getc(c) ¬= EOF)
     if (c == TAB)
          output (one or more) blanks and update col
           until (tabpos(col, tabs) == YES)
     else if (c == NEWLINE) {
          call putc(c)
          col = 1
          }
     else {
          call putc(c)
          col = col + 1
          }
```

This shows an **else if** chain with a trailing **else**, which is there to cover the "anything else" case, that is, neither a **TAB** nor a **NEWLINE**.

tabpos returns **YES** if column **col** is a tab stop, **NO** if it is not. In principle, this is an easy task. But wait a moment, and think over our discussion of boundary conditions. One obvious boundary is the *last* tab stop. What happens if the input contains a tab in a column after the last tab stop?

One solution is to outlaw tabs after some maximum column, but it's folly to write a program that blindly assumes that its input is legal. Or **detab** could abort or produce an error message (or both), but this is hardly desirable in a general-purpose tool. Why not do something intelligent instead? A program should produce reasonable output for reasonable input, and there is nothing unreasonable about a lot of tabs. Let us build **detab** so that when a tab is encountered after the last tab stop it is converted to a single blank.

Since the loop

```
output (one or more) blanks and update col
 until (tabpos(col, tabs) == YES)
```

will end only when it lands exactly on a tab stop, we must make sure that this always happens, even when lines extend past the last tab stop setting. A safe convention is to assume that there are tab stops set in *every* column after the last one set explicitly. **tabpos** must provide this feature.

All that remains is to spell out a few details and write **tabpos**. We have chosen a representation where each element of an array **tabs** contains a **YES** if there is a tab stop at that column, **NO** if there is not. Here is the final Ratfor version:

```
# detab - convert tabs to equivalent number of blanks
	character getc
	character c
	integer tabpos
	integer col, i, tabs(MAXLINE)

	call settab(tabs)	# set initial tab stops
	col = 1
	while (getc(c) ¬= EOF)
		if (c == TAB)
			repeat {
				call putc(BLANK)
				col = col + 1
				} until (tabpos(col, tabs) == YES)
		else if (c == NEWLINE) {
			call putc(NEWLINE)
			col = 1
			}
		else {
			call putc(c)
			col = col + 1
			}
	stop
	end

# tabpos - return YES if col is a tab stop
	integer function tabpos(col, tabs)
	integer col, i, tabs(MAXLINE)

	if (col > MAXLINE)
		tabpos = YES
	else
		tabpos = tabs(col)
	return
	end
```

detab uses **settab** to set up the **tabs** array initially, according to whatever representation is expected by **tabpos**.

```
# settab - set initial tab stops
      subroutine settab(tabs)
      integer mod
      integer i, tabs(MAXLINE)

      for (i = 1; i <= MAXLINE; i = i + 1)
            if (mod(i, 8) == 1)
                  tabs(i) = YES
            else
                  tabs(i) = NO
      return
      end
```

The **mod** function returns the remainder produced by dividing its first argument by its second. In this case, **mod(i, 8)** is used to produce the sequence 1, 2, 3, 4, 5, 6, 7, 0, 1, 2, ... as **i** increases. Thus a 1 is produced every eighth time, and this is used to set the tab stop. This is a standard use for the **mod** function.

It may seem silly to write a five-line function to be called only once, but the purpose of **settab** is to conceal a data representation from a routine that does not have to know about it. For a program the size of **detab**, this is not absolutely necessary, but it is vital to break larger programs into small pieces that communicate only through well-defined interfaces. The less one part of a program knows about how another part operates, the more easily each may be changed.

Most real programs are subjected to a steady flow of changes and improvements over their lifetimes, and many programmers spend most of their time maintaining and modifying existing programs. This is an expensive process, so one of the most important design considerations for a program is that it be easy to change.

The best way we know to achieve this is to write the program so its pieces are as decoupled as possible, so that a change in one does not affect others. We try to push down into separate modules those details which would degeneralize the program and commit it to some specific mode of operation. **getc** and **putc**, for instance, conceal all details of character set, lines, records, file assignments and end-of-file handling. Similarly, **detab** is organized so the main routine is not concerned with the representation of tab stops, only with counting columns.

Factoring the job into pieces also lets us concentrate on one aspect of a design at a time. We are more likely to get **detab** right, and make it understandable, by restricting it to counting columns. And we are more likely to get **tabpos** right by dealing only with tab stops and implementing just one function whose specification is easily remembered. The best programs are designed in terms of loosely coupled functions that each does a simple task.

detab introduces two more control structures, which pretty much complete our set. The **repeat-until** is a loop that is repeated one or more times **until** the trailing test is met. This is opposite from the **while**, which tests at the top whether to loop, before doing anything. The **while** seems to occur naturally more often, but each form has its uses. In **detab**, the **repeat** is necessary to ensure that each input tab causes at least one blank to be output.

The **for** statement compactly summarizes a frequently encountered pattern:

```
for (initialize ; condition ; reinitialize)
        body
```

is equivalent to

```
{
initialize
while (condition) {
        body
        reinitialize
        }
}
```

The idea of the **for** statement is to summarize all the loop control code in one line, much as in the conventional Fortran **do** statement. Unlike the **do**, however, the **for** is not restricted to specifying arithmetic sequences. This is important, for as we shall see, the vast majority of loops are not Fortran **do**'s, nor even PL/I **do**'s, but instead require a more elaborate test and more general initialization and reinitialization. *initialize* and *reinitialize* can be any Fortran statements; they are not limited to statements like **i=1** and **i=i+1**.

Exercise 1-6: Expand the **for** statement in **settab** by the formula above. Can it be replaced by a **do** loop? □

Exercise 1-7: Test **detab**. It must pass all the tests that **copy** must pass (except that tabs are replaced by one to eight spaces). In addition, there are several other boundaries involving the tab stops. You might consider testing rows of **x**'s, each with a tab in a different location. What happens if a tab occurs after the last tab stop? □

Exercise 1-8: What does **detab** do if the input contains a backspace character? Modify it so it does the right thing. □

Exercise 1-9: There are obviously several other ways to write **detab**. Implement the following variations and compare them on the basis of size, complexity and ease of subsequent change.

(a) Tabs are set every eight columns; the **tabs** array is unused.

(b) The **tabs** array contains a list of the columns which contain tab stops; the list is terminated by a zero entry.

(c) Each element of the **tabs** array contains the number of columns to the next tab stop; the last entry is a zero.

(d) Repeat (b) and (c) using an explicit count of tabs stops instead of an end-marker. □

1.6 Hand Compiling the Code

Translating **detab** into Fortran shows some of the advantages of writing in Ratfor:

```
c detab - convert tabs to equivalent number of blanks; Fortran version
      integer getc
      integer c
      integer tabpos
      integer col, i, tabs(MAXLINE)
c
c     set initial tab stops
      call settab(tabs)
      col = 1
10    if (getc(c) .eq. EOF)  goto 60
         if (c .ne. TAB)  goto 30
20          call putc(BLANK)
            col = col + 1
            if (tabpos(col, tabs) .ne. YES)  goto 20
            goto 50
c        else if
30       if (c .ne. NEWLINE)  goto 40
            call putc(NEWLINE)
            col =' 1
            goto 50
c        else
40          call putc(c)
            col = col + 1
50       goto 10
60    stop
      end

c settab - set initial tab stops; Fortran version
      subroutine settab(tabs)
      integer mod
      integer i, tabs(MAXLINE)
c
      i = 1
10    if (i .gt. MAXLINE) goto 20
         if (mod(i, 8) .eq. 1) tabs(i) = YES
         if (mod(i, 8) .ne. 1) tabs(i) = NO
         i = i + 1
         goto 10
20    return
      end
```

```
c tabpos - return YES if col is a tab stop; Fortran version
        integer function tabpos(col, tabs)
        integer col, i, tabs(MAXLINE)
c
        if (col .gt. MAXLINE) tabpos = YES
        if (col .le. MAXLINE) tabpos = tabs(col)
        return
        end
```

As you can see, it is harder to tell what the flow of control is, even with similar indentation and pseudo-code comments. All those statement numbers and **goto**'s obscure the intent of the code.

Writing the Fortran is purely a mechanical operation, once the Ratfor is specified. Each structure becomes a simple pattern; no ingenuity is required in the translation. Indeed, any ingenious use of **goto**'s in the final code, any use that does not make an easily recognized pattern, is going to be nothing but trouble for people who must understand the code. And that includes the original coder.

By now you are no doubt squirming over the inefficiency of this translation. There are **goto**'s that go to a **goto**; there are multiple tests like

```
if (col .gt. MAXLINE) tabpos = YES
if (col .le. MAXLINE) tabpos = tabs(col)
```

instead of the Fortran idiom

```
tabpos = YES
if (col .le. MAXLINE) tabpos = tabs(col)
```

And Fortran does provide the **do** statement to handle the initialization, incrementing, and testing of a loop control variable. Why not use it in **settab**?

There is no objection to the **do** where the translation is obvious, and in fact Ratfor provides a **do** statement (just leave out the statement number following the **do**). The initialization loop in **settab** goes over nicely since **MAXLINE** must be greater than zero. But we caution you that the Fortran **do** is highly restrictive: the index must typically run from some positive, non-zero value up to some positive limit, and in many versions of Fortran the loop is always obeyed at least once regardless of the limits, because the test is done at the bottom. The tremendous advantage of the **while** and **for** is that by testing the loop at the top they automatically test for the special case where there is nothing to do, and then do the right thing — nothing.

Moreover, *thinking* in terms of **do**'s rather than **while**'s encourages the notion that you should be counting something, or that your control variable must run from 1 to **n** in steps of **m**. But why should there always be a control variable? Even though there are many tricks for mapping arbitrary sequences into arithmetic progressions, remember they are *tricks*. They tend to obscure the actual logic and make a program more error prone. As we shall see from measurements presented in Chapter 9, program loops seldom fall naturally into the form imposed by the **do**.

You might argue that the **do** is more efficient than a **for** constructed out of **if**'s and **goto**'s. After all, the compiler knows about **do** loops and presumably worries over the code produced. In some cases this is true; matrix computations, for example, often benefit from the care a compiler takes with **do**'s. But surely the efficiency of **settab** is a red herring; it is only called once. Branching to branches, and the multiple tests in **tabpos** and **settab** are also irrelevant. Their effect on running time is so minuscule that we could not detect it.

Profiling the code — that is, measuring how much time was spent in each part of the program — revealed that **detab** spends about 60 percent of its time doing low-level input (in the routines called by **getc**) and an additional 20-25 percent doing low-level output (in routines called by **putc**). So even if the rest of the program could be rewritten to take *zero time* (which is hardly likely), the net speedup would be only 15-20 percent.

The moral should be obvious. By writing a program in a straightforward manner, you get it working correctly and minimize the chance of confusion. You can then *measure* how it performs to decide whether it works well enough and, if not, where to concentrate your attention. For a given algorithm, gains in speed are almost always obtained at the cost of readability. Sacrifice clarity for speed only when you know that you are solving the correct problem correctly and when you know that the sacrifice is worthwhile.

In PL/I, the program is:

```
/* detab — convert tabs into equivalent number of blanks */
      detab: procedure options (main);
      declare getc entry (fixed binary) returns (fixed binary);
      declare putc entry (fixed binary);
      declare c fixed binary;
      declare settab entry ((*)fixed binary);
      declare tabpos entry (fixed binary, (*)fixed binary) returns (fixed binary);
      declare (col, tabs(MAXLINE)) fixed binary;

      call settab(tabs);      /* set initial tab stops */
      col = 1;
      do while (getc(c) ¬= EOF);
            if c = TAB then do;
              loop:
                  call putc(BLANK);
                  col = col + 1;
                  if tabpos(col, tabs) ¬= YES then
                        goto loop;
                  end;
            else if c = NEWLINE then do;
                  call putc(NEWLINE);
                  col = 1;
                  end;
            else do;
                  call putc(c);
                  col = col + 1;
                  end;
            end;
      end detab;

/* settab — set initial tab stops */
      settab: procedure (tabs);
      declare (i, tabs(*)) fixed binary;

      do i = 1 to MAXLINE;
            if mod(i, 8) = 1 then
                  tabs(i) = YES;
            else
                  tabs(i) = NO;
            end;
      end settab;
```

```
/* tabpos — return YES if col is a tab stop */
        tabpos: procedure (col, tabs) returns (fixed binary);
        declare (col, tabs(*)) fixed binary;

        if col > MAXLINE then
                return(YES);
        else
                return(tabs(col));
        end tabpos;
```

This time we used a **do** statement in the translation because the PL/I **do** behaves much more like a **while** than the Fortran **do**. In particular, the PL/I **do** will be obeyed zero times if the upper limit is exceeded from the start. PL/I has no analog for the **repeat-until**, so it is necessary to build one with an **if** and a **goto**, much as in Fortran.

Exercise 1-10: Write out a translation of **if**, **if-else**, **while**, **for**, and **repeat-until** in Fortran. Use only the logical **if** and **goto**'s. Apply your rules to the Ratfor program **detab**, and compare your result with our Fortran version. What can you say about "optimizing" the **goto**'s you generate? How well does your Fortran compiler do? □

Exercise 1-11: Write out the rules for translating the **if**, **if-else**, **while**, **for**, and **repeat-until** into PL/I. Use **goto**'s only when you must. Apply your rules to the Ratfor program above, and compare your result with our PL/I version. What can you say about "optimizing" the translation of **while** and **for** loops? □

1.7 A Word on Structured Programming

You may be wondering why we make such an issue out of using **if-else** and **while** instead of **if** and **goto**. After all, you can do anything, and more, with the latter than you can with the Ratfor control statements. It turns out, though, that the extra freedom permitted by **goto**'s is just what you *don't* want. By restricting yourself to a small set of control flow operations, you tend to write code that is better thought out, more readable, and hence less error-prone. These benefits far outweigh any freedom of expression that you might sacrifice.

In the narrowest sense, this is what "structured programming" is all about: coding only with a restricted set of control flow structures. These include statement grouping with a construct like the Ratfor braces; **if-else** for decisions; loops like **while** or **for** or **repeat-until**; and subroutine and function calls.

It is sometimes claimed that merely using these structures somehow leads naturally and automatically to good programs. This is not true, for mechanical rules are never a substitute for clarity of thought. What is true is that a program which is well structured typically uses only these structures as its building blocks.

Our approach to structured programming is to stick to the basics. We invest extra effort in the design and coding process (which is fun) to minimize the much costlier testing and debugging phase (which is not). We put strong emphasis on clean, comprehensible code, saving efficiency considerations for the end. We check and test code as we write it, rather than relying on a final debugging binge to fix everything. We make extensive use of subroutine calls and statement grouping to modularize code, and we always write control flow in terms of **if-else** and the looping constructs.

But our primary tool for writing good programs is to strive to make them *readable.* In our experience, readability is the single best criterion of program quality: if a program is easy to read, it is probably a good program; if it is hard to read, it probably isn't good. From time to time we will call attention to matters of style as clear examples present themselves. We hope that you will learn from these observations, and keep readability in mind for every line of code you write.

1.8 Ratfor Synopsis

You have already been introduced to most of Ratfor; as the need arises we will introduce the rest and in each case show you how to hand-compile the code into Fortran and PL/I.

To assist you, here is a summary of Ratfor. Essentially, Ratfor *is* Fortran, except that several new statements have been added to make it easier to specify flow of control. At the same time, Ratfor provides some notational conveniences, so programs can be made more readable.

In the following, a *statement* is any legal statement in the Fortran you use: assignment, declaration, subroutine call, I/O, etc., or any of the Ratfor statements listed. Any Fortran or Ratfor statement or group of these can be enclosed in braces { } to make it into a compound statement, which is then equivalent to a single statement, and usable anywhere a single statement can be used.

The **if** *statement:*

```
if (condition)
        statement1
else
        statement2
```

If *condition* is true, do *statement1,* otherwise do *statement2.* The **else** part is optional. As in most languages, the construction

```
if (condition1)
        if (condition2)
                statement1
        else
                statement2
```

is ambiguous — the **else** could be associated with either **if**. Braces can be used to disambiguate this as desired. In the absence of braces, each **else** goes with the previous un-**elsed** **if**, just as in PL/I or the Algol family. The example above is indented to agree with the binding rule, but we will always use braces as well in such cases, to make our intent perfectly clear.

The **while** *statement:*

```
while (condition)
        statement
```

Test *condition.* If it is true, do *statement* once, then test again. If *condition* is ever false, resume with the first statement after the body of the **while**.

The **for** *statement:*

```
for (initialize ; condition ; reinitialize)
        statement
```

This is equivalent to

```
{
initialize
while (condition) {
        statement
        reinitialize
        }
}
```

with one exception listed below. The *initialize* and *reinitialize* parts are single Fortran statements. If either *initialize* or *reinitialize* is omitted, the corresponding part of the expansion is omitted. If the *condition* is omitted, it is taken to be always true, resulting in an "infinite" loop.

Although *initialize* and *reinitialize* may be any Fortran statements, as a matter of style they should always be directly related to loop control. And if two or more parts of the **for** are omitted, the statement is usually better written in terms of a **while** or **repeat**.

The **repeat-until** *statement:*

```
repeat
        statement
        until (condition)
```

The *statement* is done one or more times until *condition* becomes true, at which time the loop is exited. The **until** part is optional; if it is omitted, the result is an infinite loop, which must be broken some other way.

The **break** *statement:*

```
break
```

The **break** statement is one way to get out of an infinite **repeat** loop. It causes whatever loop it is contained in (which may also be a **while**, **for**, or **do**) to be exited immediately. Control resumes with the next statement after the loop. Only one loop is terminated by a **break**, even if the **break** is contained inside several nested loops.

We have not made use of **break** yet; we will in Chapter 2. There are two other Ratfor statements which we don't use at all in this book, but which sometimes provide the clearest way to express an operation. One is analogous to **break**.

The **next** *statement:*

```
next
```

causes whatever loop it is contained in to go immediately to the next iteration, skipping the rest of the loop body. **next** goes to the *condition* part of a **while**, **do** or **until**, to the top of an infinite **repeat** loop, and to the *reinitialize* part of a **for**. (This is why the **for** does not expand directly into a **while**).

The **do** *statement:*

```
do limits
        statement
```

sets up a standard Fortran **do** loop. *limits* must be a legal Fortran **do** specification, like i = 1, n.

Ratfor source statements may appear anywhere on a line; it is important to indent systematically so you can see what statements control what. Generally the end of a line marks the end of a statement, but constructions like

```
if (c == NEWLINE)
        nl = nl + 1
```

are obviously not finished after the line that contains the **if** and so they are continued automatically. This is also true of conditions which extend over more than one line, as in

```
while (c == BLANK
        | c == TAB
        | c == NEWLINE)
            i = i + 1
```

Lines ending with a comma are also continued.

Ratfor uses == for the equality test .eq. and ¬= for the inequality .ne.. The shorthands | and & stand for .or. and .and. respectively. <, <=, >, and >= have the obvious meanings of .lt., .le., .gt. and .ge. respectively. Except for ==, these notations are the same as in PL/I.

A sharp sign # anywhere in a line signals the beginning of a comment, which is terminated by the end of the line. Symbolic constants contain only letters and digits; they may be used anywhere, surrounded by non-alphanumerics.

To answer a frequently-asked question, an arbitrary Fortran program is not necessarily a Ratfor program. Blanks are significant in Ratfor in that keywords like **if**, symbolic constants like **NEWLINE** and relationals like >= must not contain blanks or they will not be recognized. Furthermore, keywords are reserved, and should not be used as variable names. Standard Fortran comments, continuation conventions and the arithmetic **if** are incompatible, but since Ratfor provides better alternatives for each, this is not a serious problem.

On the other hand, Ratfor is not far from Fortran. About twenty percent of the lines in our programs are Ratfor control-flow statements like **if** and **else**; everything else is Fortran. We have tried to stick to a subset of Standard (ANSI) Fortran that is portable without change between different machines. All of our programs have been run through a verifier that checks for adherence to this portable subset. Furthermore, to test our claim of portability the larger programs have been run on three machines, and all have been run on at least two, literally without change.

Our desire for portability is the reason for a few constructs that might seem strange. For example, ANSI Fortran prohibits complicated subscripts, so we occasionally need to invent temporary variables to avoid them. Similarly, variable names (but not symbolic constants) are limited to six characters. This leads to some rather strained mnemonics, for which we apologize in advance.

1.9 Simple Versions of getc and putc

getc and **putc** are sufficiently important that they should be provided by the local operating system, but often they are not. That doesn't mean you must do without them, however, since versions adequate for many purposes can be easily written. For example, here is **getc** as it might appear in a standard Fortran environment, taking input from cards. Reading it should clear up any residual confusion about what it does.

```
# getc (simple version) — get characters from standard input
        character function getc(c)
        character buf(MAXLINE), c
        integer i, lastc
        data lastc /MAXLINE/, buf(MAXLINE) /NEWLINE/
        # note: MAXLINE = MAXCARD + 1

        lastc = lastc + 1
        if (lastc > MAXLINE) {
                read(STDIN, 100, end=10) (buf(i), i = 1, MAXCARD)
                        100 format(MAXCARD a1)
                lastc = 1
                }
        c = buf(lastc)
        getc = c
        return

  10    c = EOF
        getc = EOF
        return
        end
```

getc reads an entire line and hands it out one character at a time. New lines are read as necessary, and newlines are added to the end of each line by putting a **NEWLINE** after the last actual card column. The symbolic constants **MAXCARD** and **MAXLINE** are the card length (probably 80) and the line length; they differ by one.

The **read** statement uses the construction **end=** to detect the end of file condition so **getc** can return **EOF**. When end of file is encountered, a branch is taken to the specified statement. This facility is widely available, but your system may require another form. **STDIN** is whatever unit number is used on your system for Fortran input; frequently it is 5.

putc is the obvious analog of **getc**, collecting characters into a line one at a time and flushing out the line, blank-padded if need be, when a **NEWLINE** is presented to it. **STDOUT** is the output unit number, often 6.

```
# putc (simple version) — put characters on standard output
      subroutine putc(c)
      character buf(MAXCARD), c
      integer i, lastc
      data lastc /0/

      if (lastc > MAXCARD | c == NEWLINE) {
            for (i = lastc + 1; i <= MAXCARD; i = i + 1)
                  buf(i) = BLANK
            write(STDOUT, 100) (buf(i), i = 1, MAXCARD)
                  100 format(MAXCARD a1)
            lastc = 0
            }
      if (c ¬= NEWLINE) {
            lastc = lastc + 1
            buf(lastc) = c
            }
      return
      end
```

There are some troublesome details in **putc**, primarily concerning what should happen if more than a full line of text comes along without a **NEWLINE**. The most reasonable solution seems to be to put out the line anyway if the buffer is full, as we did in our version. Silently truncating long lines is less appealing.

Another shortcoming with using a fixed length blank-padded representation is that trailing blanks can't be distinguished from padding. The best design in an environment that encourages blank padding is to have **getc** strip trailing blanks and **putc** reinstall them. Although some information is lost, the number of applications where this matters is quite small.

We have also assumed that when a line is written with **putc** (i.e., when a **NEWLINE** is passed to it), the output will actually appear if the program subsequently exits with a **stop** statement. If your system does not provide such a service **putc** must consider the problem of flushing any remaining output when the program terminates. One possibility is to modify **putc** so that

```
call putc(EOF)
```

is a signal to force out any accumulated characters.

The execution times of most of the smaller programs in this book are dominated by the character getting and putting mechanisms, even when these are efficiently implemented. You can be assured of a good return for your effort if you improve these simple versions.

Exercise 1-12: Modify **getc** and **putc** to strip and restore trailing blanks respectively. □

Exercise 1-13: Invent a general convention for signaling line boundaries within fixed-length cards, and modify **getc** and **putc** to handle it. This provides a way to gain the benefits of variable-length records even if the local system does not allow them. □

1.10 Prospectus

What have we done so far? We wrote several elementary but useful tools. We tried to structure them so they will be easy to understand, and easy to change if the need arises. We wrote them in a language which can be translated and run on almost any computer system without change. We wrote them in terms of primitives that conceal the differences among operating systems.

What we're going to do is repeat that process for a number of tools which we think will be useful to you, and which should teach you various lessons about programming. Most of these programs are bigger than the ones so far, some a lot bigger. Yet the basic approach of careful structuring and isolation of program from system will remain a constant theme. This is the only way to cope with big programs and real systems.

One thing you will notice is that programs often use code written in earlier sections or chapters. This is important. One way to achieve greater software productivity is to build on what has already been done, instead of endlessly reinventing the same things with minor variations. In a book, however, this organization does place a burden on the reader, since everything needed to run a given program isn't all in one place. We have tried to reduce it by carefully chosen names, reminders, back-pointers and an extensive index. Still, it will sometimes be hard to dive into the middle of a chapter and immediately appreciate what all the code does.

One of the best ways to learn good programming is to read and think about actual programs, to ask questions like "Why was it done that way?" or "Why not write it like this?" We believe that the amount of code in this book is an asset, not a liability, and we think you will profit from studying it, even if you would write things differently.

Bibliographic Notes

We assume throughout this book that you have a working knowledge of Fortran. If you need to know more, see D. D. McCracken, *A Simplified Guide to Fortran Programming* (Wiley, 1974). It provides an introduction that avoids unnecessary mathematics and concentrates on presenting just the good features of the language.

The Fortran verifier we used is described in "The PFORT verifier," B. G. Ryder, *Software—Practice and Experience,* October, 1974. This paper discusses the portable subset of Fortran in considerable detail. The article "RATFOR—a preprocessor for a rational Fortran," by B. W. Kernighan, *Software—Practice and Experience* (October, 1975) contains more discussion of the Ratfor language, especially its design considerations. There are many other Fortran preprocessors available besides Ratfor; the bibliography at the end of Chapter 9 indicates some possibilities.

CHAPTER 2

FILTERS

We are going to continue what we began in the previous chapter — writing simple programs that read a standard input and write a standard output. By obvious analogy to electronics (or plumbing) we call such programs *filters,* because they make useful changes to a stream of data passing through. You will find that many tools fall into this category, including most of those in this book.

2.1 Putting Tabs Back

Let us begin by writing the filter **entab**, to complement **detab**. **entab** replaces strings of blanks by equivalent tabs and blanks. Remember what we said earlier about the benefits of having all your files look as much alike as possible? You might use **entab** to read card images and produce typewriter-like text. That way, you could convert your files to a standard representation, one that has no wasteful imbedded blank strings. As an added payoff, your files are smaller and they all look alike; that makes it easier to write programs that talk and work together.

Another use for **entab** is to prepare output to be sent to a typewriter-like terminal. You might have a program that expects to drive a line printer. You would like to speed up the typing by tabbing whenever possible. Rather than rewrite a working program, you are better off with a separate program to filter the output just before it is typed. Thus **entab**.

The trick of getting most filters right is to find an orderly way of recognizing the components of the input stream, so that the order can be reflected in the flow of control of the program rather than in a collection of switches and flags. We got away with one flag in **wordcount**, for that is a small program, but anything larger quickly becomes confusing. If we think of the input to **entab** as a repetition of the pattern: zero or more blanks, followed by a non-blank character (or **EOF**), then this determines the control structure of the program:

```
col = 1
repeat {
        while (getc(c) == BLANK)          # collect blanks
                if (at tab stop)
                        output a tab
        if (any blanks left over)
                put them out
        # c is now EOF or non blank
        if (c == EOF)
                break
        call putc(c)
        if (c == NEWLINE)
                col = 1
        else
                col = col + 1
        }
```

col is the current output column.

break is a statement we haven't used before. It causes an immediate exit from an enclosing loop — a **while, for, repeat**, or **do**. A **repeat** loop without its trailing **until** clause specifies an "infinite" loop, i.e., one with no testing, just an unconditional branch from the bottom back to the top. Some other way is needed to terminate execution of such a loop; in this case it is the **break** statement, executed when an **EOF** is seen. Loops are written this way when we need one or more statements both before and after the test (or tests) controlling repetition of the loop.

break should *not* be used in an undisciplined way, as a substitute for a properly thought out **while** or **until** test. In particular, be wary of loops that exit from several places. When there are multiple **break**'s from diverse parts of a loop, it is difficult to ensure uniform behavior for all possible exits. You should always try to express the exit condition — be it from the test part of a **while** or **until**, or an **if** controlling a **break** — as a single logical expression.

An easy way for **entab** to keep track of the blanks is to use another variable **newcol** that moves away from **col** as blanks are encountered. Whenever a tab is output, **col** is made to catch up to **newcol**. Then, when a non-blank, non-tab character is encountered, if **col** is less than **newcol**, there are excess blanks accumulated (not enough to be replaced by a tab) which must be output before the character can be. The job is done:

```
# entab — replace blanks by tabs and blanks
        character getc
        character c
        integer tabpos
        integer col, i, newcol, tabs(MAXLINE)

        call settab(tabs)
        col = 1
        repeat {
                newcol = col
                while (getc(c) == BLANK) {        # collect blanks
                        newcol = newcol + 1
                        if (tabpos(newcol, tabs) == YES) {
                                call putc(TAB)
                                col = newcol
                                }
                        }
                for ( ; col < newcol; col = col + 1)
                        call putc(BLANK)          # output leftover blanks
                if (c == EOF)
                        break
                call putc(c)
                if (c == NEWLINE)
                        col = 1
                else
                        col = col + 1
                }
        stop
        end
```

tabpos and **settab** are, of course, the same routines used by **detab** in Chapter 1; again the program is organized so the representation of tab stops is hidden from the main routine. Note the use of a **for** statement with no initialization clause. In this case the code that went before provides all the initialization needed.

Exercise 2-1: Walk through **entab** with a file having two characters, one character, none. Try it with lines containing zero to ten blanks, followed by an **x**. Try zero to ten blanks followed by end of file. Under what circumstance will a file be restored to its original form after being filtered by **detab** and **entab** in turn? Can you think of any uses for such an operation? □

Exercise 2-2: What happens if **entab** reads a tab character? Make the simplest addition you can think of to the code to handle tabs correctly. How would you rewrite the code so that it maps an arbitrary string of spaces and tabs into the minimum number required to give the same appearance? What does **entab** do with text containing backspaces? □

2.2 Command Arguments

entab uses the same convention as **detab** does, a tab every eight columns. It would be nice, however, if there were an easy way to pass a list of tab settings as arguments to either of these programs at the time the program is run, so the normal settings could be temporarily overridden. Some operating systems make provision for you to access the command line or control card that invoked the program, so you can pick up arguments like options, parameters or other information. If such is the case on your system, you should provide the primitive function **getarg**, which does whatever is needed to make argument information available to a program. Most of the programs we present will benefit from having some (optional) arguments. For a few, arguments are mandatory. We will assume from here on that you can implement **getarg** in some form.

Our specific design for **getarg** is the following.

getarg(n, array, maxsize)

copies the characters of the **n**th argument into the integer array **array**, one character per array element. As before, we are going to use integers to hold characters. **maxsize** specifies the maximum number of characters that we are prepared to deal with; **getarg** will truncate the argument if necessary to fit it into the space provided. **getarg** returns as its value the length of the argument (the number of characters) if the **n**th argument exists; if there are less than **n** arguments, **EOF** is returned. This strongly suggests that **EOF** should be a negative value so it can be readily distinguished from a valid length. You might also consider making **EOF** a large number, larger than any conceivable value of **maxsize**, but this is less desirable.

Regardless of the choice, however, a program should always test the value returned by **getarg** for exact equality with **EOF**, and never take advantage of any secret knowledge about its value. If you fail to observe this principle, your code will be prone to falling apart mysteriously when its environment changes. The more a program depends on specific details of its host system, the less robust it is.

The argument that **getarg** places in **array** can now be used as a sequence of characters. The problem is that although we know the number of characters in the array, that information is separate, not part of the array, and this causes problems. It is much more convenient if the length information for an array of characters is carried along with it.

Two possibilities spring to mind. One is that the first element of the array, **array(1)**, could contain the number of characters that follow. The other organization is to mark the *end* of the array by some special value, one that is not any valid character. Each of these organizations has good and bad points (which you should think about for yourself). After some anguish, we decided on a mark-at-the-end representation. Every character string in our programs contains as its last element a special marker, which we call **EOS**. A string of one character has **array(1)** set to the character and **array(2)** to an **EOS**; an empty or *null* string has **array(1)** an **EOS**.

Thus one final thing that **getarg** must do is to ensure that the string it returns is properly terminated with an **EOS**, and this must fit within the limits of **maxsize** characters.

If you are able to design the interface from scratch, it seems most convenient for **getarg** to assume that arguments are separated by one or more blanks and/or tabs. (To provide for an argument with imbedded blanks or tabs, you might allow optional quotes around it, to be stripped off by **getarg**.) For supplying arguments to programs, we feel that commas and parentheses as argument separators merely add noise and keystrokes, and are better avoided.

Exercise 2-3: Write a program **echo** that copies its arguments onto the standard output. There should be one space separating adjacent arguments and a newline at the end. Can you think of any uses for **echo** besides testing your implementation of **getarg**? □

Exercise 2-4: Modify **detab** and **entab** to accept a list of tab stops as arguments, so users can call the program with commands like

```
detab 9 17 25 33 41
entab 10 16 33 73
```

Of course the code that interprets these arguments and fills the **tabs** array should be careful not to overfill the array. Both programs should do something intelligent and useful if there are no arguments. (Later on in this chapter there is a program **ctoi** for converting character strings to integers.) □

Exercise 2-5: Extend the programs to accept the shorthand

entab *m* +*n*

to mean tab stops every *n* columns, starting at column *m*. □

2.3 Overstrikes

You can overstrike characters on a typewriter by backspacing over what is already typed. This is how you underline words, for one thing; it is also a way to build additional characters from existing ones. If you send your output to a line printer, however, the result may be a hash, because a typical printer doesn't know what to do with backspace characters.

Many printers do, however, provide for overstriking entire lines. The Fortran convention for controlling this function is to provide an extra *carriage control* character at the beginning of each line: a blank means "space before printing," and a plus sign (+) means "do not space before printing," i.e., overstrike what has gone before.

The filter **overstrike** looks for backspaces in typewriter text and generates a sequence of print lines with carriage control codes to reproduce the effect of the backspaces. If we adopt a viewpoint similar to that for **entab**, that the input is an alternation of zero or more backspaces and non-backspace characters, the resulting code is very similar. If a string of one or more backspaces is encountered, the program ends the current line and inserts the appropriate number of spaces in the overstrike line.

This is not the only way to do it, of course, but it is one of the least complicated. Nasty behavior occurs if the text to be printed contains words underlined one letter at a time. Each sequence of *character, backspace, underline* causes a whole new line to be generated, which can be quite slow. So a better way would be to have two or more line buffers to build the overstrike images as they are needed.

But that is harder to code and get right. It is often better to get on with something that does most of the job well enough, then improve and add things as they prove to be worthwhile.

overstrike is useful even for text that contains no backspaces, for it converts the typewriter text produced by most of the programs in this book into lines with carriage controls, suitable for driving a line printer. It can serve as a final filter whenever printer output is desired, again encouraging you to keep as much as possible to a standard internal form for text for other programs.

```
# overstrike - convert backspaces into multiple lines
	character getc
	character c
	integer max
	integer col, newcol

	col = 1
	repeat {
		newcol = col
		while (getc(c) == BACKSPACE) # eat up backspaces
			newcol = max(newcol-1, 1)
		if (newcol < col) {		# start overstrike line
			call putc(NEWLINE)
			call putc(NOSKIP)
			for (col = 1; col < newcol; col = col + 1)
				call putc(BLANK)
			}
		else if (col == 1 & c ¬= EOF)	# start normal line
			call putc(SKIP)
						# else middle of line
		if (c == EOF)
			break
		call putc(c)			# normal character
		if (c == NEWLINE)
			col = 1
		else
			col = col + 1
		}
	stop
	end
```

max is a function, which we leave to you to write or obtain, for finding the maximum of its arguments. In PL/I, **max** is a built-in generic function. In Fortran, you can use **max0**, which finds the maximum of two or more integers and returns an integer result. **&** is the logical *and,* which in Fortran is **.and.**.

We used the symbolic constants **NOSKIP** and **SKIP** instead of **PLUS** and **BLANK** because the former are more descriptive of the function to be performed, and the latter are not universal. Besides, it is important to avoid confusion between a blank being put out to cause a line skip and one used to fill a line. The purpose of symbolic constants is to retain mnemonic information as long as possible.

We need no trailing **else** in the **else if** sequence in this example, since the third alternative (in the middle of a line) requires no action. But we stuck in a comment to make clear what the implied alternative is. We will frequently terminate an **else if** chain with an **else**, if only as a comment to spell out all the possible cases.

Exercise 2-6: What are a half-dozen test inputs that exercise critical boundaries of **overstrike**? Why did we write

```
newcol = max(newcol-1, 1)
```

instead of

```
newcol = newcol - 1
```

Give a test input and sample outputs that show the difference between the two cases. Our version of **overstrike** simulates the behavior of a terminal where backspaces are ignored once the left margin is reached. Rewrite the code to keep proper track of where characters should appear but print only those characters that occur in or after column one. □

Exercise 2-7: As we said earlier, if backspaces come one at a time instead of in long runs (for example, if each letter in a word is individually backspaced and underlined), **overstrike** is inefficient, in that it puts out a fresh line for each one. Modify it to put out fewer lines. □

Exercise 2-8: Another standard Fortran carriage control is a **1**, which causes the next line to be printed at the top of the next page. Modify **overstrike** to look for a special **FORMFEED** character and map each occurrence into a page eject. You might also consider adapting **overstrike** to look for long runs of empty lines and replace them by ejects when possible, since this is often faster on line printers. □

Exercise 2-9: **overstrike** in series with **detab** provides a general typewriter-to-printer conversion. Would it be worth combining them into a single program? Can you think of any other functions worth adding? □

2.4 Text Compression

Tabs and backspaces can be viewed in one sense as a shorthand; certainly typewriter encoded files tend to be shorter than card images or printer lines. But they are a very special form of shorthand. What we are going to consider next is a scheme suitable for compressing and expanding any text that has runs of repeated characters. The repeated characters are not necessarily blanks; they can be anything.

We emphasize that this is not the ultimate compression scheme. A file can have considerable redundant information that does not appear as repetitions of adjacent characters — consider a dictionary, for instance. But card images and print lines tend to have long strings of blanks, and computer output in general is often repetitious. So our naive approach should have a reasonable payoff for many of the things we have to deal with.

Certainly a file with no repetitions will end up no shorter after "compression"; in fact it gets slightly longer. All compression methods depend on having some knowledge of the structure of their input — otherwise there would be no redundant information to squeeze out. And so with every method you can always find a special case that gets worse when compressed. A file containing random information is a good test case, since on the average it has nothing to squeeze.

One measure of the *robustness* of a compression scheme is how bad it gets when it gets bad. We don't want things to blow up in our faces when a file is ill-suited, but we don't mind if the result gets slightly longer; that is inevitable and is thus only a little bit bad. Keep these thoughts in mind as we build the program. We will come back to them later.

The scheme we use is to look continuously for a run of any character. If we get one, we want to output something that says, "This is a run of *this* character, and it is *so* long." Between runs, we output chunks of stuff preceded by something that says, "Here comes a chunk of stuff, and it is *so* long." Big chunks, or long runs, can be output as a series of manageably smaller pieces. The output is an alternation of

repeat code
character to be repeated
repeat count

and

chunk count
that many characters

The important thing, as always, is to find a way of looking at the input data that makes it easy to lay out the program. In this case, we think of the input as a series of runs of *one* or more identical characters. We compare the length of each run against some threshold **THRESH**, left arbitrary for now. If the length of a run meets or exceeds **THRESH** it is output as an encoded run; otherwise it is appended to an internal buffer, eventually to be output as part of a chunk. Our first cut is:

```
for (lastc = getc(lastc); lastc ¬= EOF; lastc = c) {
        for (nrep = 1; getc(c) == lastc; nrep = nrep + 1)    # collect run
                ;
        if (nrep < THRESH)
                for ( ; nrep > 0; nrep = nrep - 1)         # append short run
                        add a lastc to buffer
        else {
                put out any chunk from buffer
                call putc(RCODE)
                call putc(lastc)
                put out repeat count
                }
        }
put out any chunk from buffer
```

Here are two ways of using the **for** statement that we have not encountered before. The outer **for** makes sure that each time the loop body is obeyed, **lastc** always holds the last character not processed. Nothing is being counted up or down, yet this is surely as valid a way of controlling a loop as any. It shows the greater flexibility of the **for** over the more traditional **do**.

The first inner **for** has no body except a semicolon. All the work is done in the test part, where **getc** returns a new character each time it's called, and in the reinitialize part, which increases **nrep**. The semicolon is used to mark the end of the **for**; otherwise the **for** would try to control the following **if**. A semicolon used this way is called a *null statement*. It is best to put the semicolon alone on a line, for it is otherwise easily overlooked and the code misread. While it can be used anywhere a Ratfor statement is permitted, the null statement should generally only be used as the empty body of a loop; other occurrences should be removed by revising the code.

We still have to figure out how to add characters to the buffer and how to dump them out. Since dumping occurs in two different places, we are encouraged to write a subroutine to do the job. Adding a character to the buffer not only involves incrementing an index and doing an indexed assignment, but also implies checking the index for a buffer full condition. If that occurs, there is a third occasion for dumping the buffer. A subroutine is definitely called for.

How big should the buffer be? There is no reason to make it bigger than the largest chunk we can output, which is limited in turn by the range of numbers we can represent as a character. That range also limits the number of repetitions we can represent with one encoding, because the count must be stored in a character.

This raises a second, more fundamental concern — how to represent counts as characters. So far we have avoided saying much about the internal or external representations of characters. So long as all characters have different codes and we only make integer comparisons for equality, just about any scheme will do. In fact, as we have written them, essentially all of the programs in this book are independent of the internal representation of characters.

compress is an exception. (The others are **expand**, the inverse of **compress**, and the encryption program **crypt**. These are discussed in the next two sections.) For **compress**, we could represent a count as a string of numeric characters and continue to avoid the problem, but this is wasteful when we are in the business of text compression.

The best thing is for **getc** to map all characters into a compact range of positive numbers, starting at zero or one. (In some Fortran implementations, the **r1** input format does this for you, but it is nonstandard.) Codes such as **EOF** and **EOS** can be given small negative values, for reasons we discussed earlier in this chapter. **putc** performs the inverse mapping from small positive integers to externally representable characters.

Under these circumstances, no special conversion is necessary when reading and writing counts. All we need to do is reserve some large character value for the repetition code **RCODE**, and set the maximum count to a smaller value. Or we could use zero for **RCODE**, since we never want to output a count of zero. On a computer with an eight-bit character representation, for example, **getc** could represent characters internally with integers in the range 0 to 255. Setting **RCODE** to 255 permits **MAXCHUNK** to be as large as 254. If **RCODE** can be set to zero, chunks can be 255 characters long.

You should convince yourself that this scheme works correctly even when the character **RCODE** itself occurs in the text to be compressed.

The final version of **compress** is:

```
# compress — compress standard input
        character getc
        character buf(MAXCHUNK), c, lastc
        integer nrep, nsave
        # must have RCODE > MAXCHUNK or RCODE = 0

        nsave = 0
        for (lastc = getc(lastc); lastc ¬= EOF; lastc = c) {
                for (nrep = 1; getc(c) == lastc; nrep = nrep + 1)
                        if (nrep >= MAXCHUNK)  # count repetitions
                                break
                if (nrep < THRESH)              # append short string
                        for ( ; nrep > 0; nrep = nrep - 1) {
                                nsave = nsave + 1
                                buf(nsave) = lastc
                                if (nsave >= MAXCHUNK)
                                        call putbuf(buf, nsave)
                                }
                else {
                        call putbuf(buf, nsave)
                        call putc(RCODE)
                        call putc(lastc)
                        call putc(nrep)
                        }
                }
        call putbuf(buf, nsave)        # put last chunk
        stop
        end
```

```
# putbuf — output buf(1) ... buf(nsave), clear nsave
        subroutine putbuf(buf, nsave)
        character buf(MAXCHUNK)
        integer i, nsave

        if (nsave > 0) {
                call putc(nsave)
                for (i = 1; i <= nsave; i = i + 1)
                        call putc(buf(i))
                }
        nsave = 0
        return
        end
```

A point of style: After appending a short string to the buffer, we tested whether **nsave** was equal to *or greater than* its maximum safe value. (We did the same with **nrep**.) And at the end of **putbuf**, we set **nsave** to zero even when it fails the test **nsave > 0**, an action that is only significant if **nsave** is negative. But from reading the code, we *know* that **nsave** can never exceed **MAXCHUNK** or go negative, so why bother?

This is what is known as "defensive programming." It costs next to nothing in source text or execution time, yet it reduces the chance of the program going wild should an important control variable somehow be damaged. You can't print out error messages *everywhere,* but you can and should take out insurance whenever possible.

It is much easier to debug a program if the output is not voluminous and if additional storage overwrites do not occur as a side effect of the original bug. The way to ensure saner behavior is to do the sort of things we did. Write your **if**, **while**, and **until** tests so they steer crazy situations back in a safe direction. Use the last **else** of a chain of **else-if**'s to catch conditions that should "never" occur, but just might. Never check for equality if it doesn't hurt to check for "greater than or equal to" or for "less than or equal to." In particular, don't let loops repeat when a variable is out of its expected range. Don't make your program a sucker for bugs.

Why did we write

```
for (nrep = 1; getc(c) == lastc; nrep = nrep + 1)
        if (nrep >= MAXCHUNK)
                break
```

instead of

```
for (nrep = 1; getc(c) == lastc & nrep < MAXCHUNK; nrep = nrep + 1)
```

This is a subtle question, which has nothing to do with null statements. In Fortran, as in most languages currently in use, there is no way to specify the order of evaluation of logical expressions connected by **&** and **|**. The compiler is free to make the tests in any order, and in fact to ignore some if it can deduce the truth value without making them. Most of the time this makes no difference. Here, however, the call to **getc** *must* happen, or **c** will not be set properly. If **nrep** is tested first, and **getc** is never called, the result is a particularly subtle bug. Thus we write two separate statements when one might seem adequate.

We always prefer to use a single logical expression to control a loop or an **if**; the resulting code is more readable. But whenever the order of evaluation is important, we write code that will work right without depending on the decisions made by any one compiler. That way the program can be run with another compiler without suddenly acquiring mystifying bugs.

Now let's go back to our earlier discussion of compression methods, to decide where to set the threshold **THRESH**. If **THRESH** is less than or equal to one, then every character is a candidate for being a repetition string. An input **abcdef** would be encoded as:

```
RCODE
a
1   (repeat count)
RCODE
b
1
RCODE
c
1
  etc.
```

The output would be three times as long as the input, which is not nice behavior. (The numbers are counts, not characters.)

A threshold of two would handle this case much better. Everything looks like a chunk, so there would only be one code output every **MAXCHUNK** characters. Still, a file like **abbabba** would be encoded as:

```
1   (chunk count)
a
RCODE
b
2   (repeat count)
1   (chunk count)
a
  etc.
```

This amounts to five characters output for every three input. Still not good. A threshold of three can also lose ground.

At four the threshold has us breaking even on nasty strings, and at five we always do better by encoding repetitions. Higher values discourage coding repetitions even when it would save space, so we want to avoid them. Of course, we can never escape the worst-case limit, when there are no repetitions, of one extra character for every **MAXCHUNK** characters; but we expected that. It seems best, therefore, to run **compress** with **THRESH** set to five.

Exercise 2-10: Describe precisely what combination of circumstances will produce what invalid output if the statement

```
for (nrep = 1; getc(c) == lastc & nrep < MAXCHUNK; nrep = nrep + 1)
        ;
```

is used in **compress**, as discussed above. □

Exercise 2-11: How would you take advantage of the redundancy in a dictionary (a sorted word list without definitions) to encode it in minimum space? Test your scheme by encoding the words on page 73 of your favorite dictionary. □

2.5 Text Expansion

Now that we have a way to compress text, we need a companion program to expand it once again so it can be used by other programs. We know what the input looks like: a sequence of repetitions and uncompressed chunks, each containing a code character telling which of the two follows and how many characters it represents. Our first impulse is thus to write

```
while (getc(code) ¬= EOF)
        if (code == RCODE) {        # it's a repetition
                c = getc(c)
                for (code = getc(code); code > 0; code = code - 1)
                        call putc(c)
                }
        else
                for ( ; code > 0; code = code - 1)        # it's a chunk
                        call putc(getc(c))
```

For valid input this works fine, but what happens if an **EOF** is encountered while reading into **c**? The program is unprepared for this, and so tries to send one or more **EOF** codes to **putc**. It may even make additional calls to **getc**. We have not defined what either of these primitives does under such circumstances. Although they should behave intelligently, it is important to make sure the program that calls them behaves sanely no matter what the input.

We could interpose another function, to be called in place of **getc**, which would remember an **EOF** and avoid further calls. With this would go a function that discards **EOF**'s, to be called in place of **putc**. Or we could modify **getc** and **putc** directly. Either choice would ensure correct behavior when reading or writing past end of file. It would permit less careful programming. Such a simple solution is not always possible, however, so we prefer to face squarely the basic issues of error checking.

We could also have the new input program stop when it finds **EOF**, since there is nothing else to do by way of wrapup. Sometimes this is the best, indeed the only, thing to do. But we try to avoid such solutions, convenient as they may at first appear, because they violate a basic principle of top-down design: every function should return to where it is called. This way, strategy is kept visible (and changeable) at the highest level of the code, and execution proceeds strictly from top to bottom.

So our working version of **expand** checks for **EOF** after every call on **getc**:

```
# expand - uncompress standard input
	character getc
	character c, code

	while (getc(code) ¬= EOF)
		if (code == RCODE) {	# expand repetition
			if (getc(c) == EOF)
				break
			if (getc(code) == EOF)
				break
			for ( ; code > 0; code = code - 1)
				call putc(c)
			}
		else {			# expand chunk
			for ( ; code > 0; code = code - 1) {
				if (getc(c) == EOF)
					break
				call putc(c)
				}
			if (c == EOF)
				break
			}
	stop
	end
```

Once again we have to spread a logical expression across multiple statements

```
			if (getc(c) == EOF)
				break
			if (getc(code) == EOF)
				break
```

to ensure correct order of evaluation. And in the **else** part, note that two **break**'s are necessary to get out of a doubly nested loop, the inner **for** and the outer **while**.

Error checking interferes with readability, no question about it, but it is necessary. With the best of languages, error checking obscures the main flow of events because the checks themselves impose a structure on the code which is different from that which expresses the basic job to be done. Programs written from the start with well thought out error checks, however, prove to be more reliable and live longer than those where the error checking is pasted on as an afterthought.

Exercise 2-12: Define what **getc** and **putc** should do on **EOF**, so as to simplify routines that call them. Rewrite **expand** to take advantage of this improvement. □

Exercise 2-13: What happens if you send an arbitrary (uncompressed) file to the first version of **expand**? To the final version? What happens if one character gets dropped from a valid compressed file? Can you think of any way to resynchronize reading with this encoding scheme? Can you devise a coding scheme that is easier to resynchronize? What is its worst-case expansion, and its behavior with files of random data? □

Exercise 2-14: The special code **RCODE** only conveys one bit of information: whether the next item is a repetition or not. If the full count range seldom occurred, there might be some advantage in halving the allowable range and including the code in the same character as the count. Describe a clean way of coding this and rewrite **compress** and **expand** to implement it. Does the range of counts have to be a power of two? A multiple of two? What should the value of **THRESH** be? □

Exercise 2-15: Prove that any compression scheme that is reversible, accepts any input, and makes some files smaller must also make some files *longer.* □

2.6 Encryption

One way to insure the privacy of computer files is to *encrypt* them, i.e., to store a representation of the original data that cannot be understood without the inverse process of *decryption.* True, many computer systems offer some degree of protection from other people reading your files, but there are almost always holes in the defenses, over which you have no control. By using the **crypt** program described here, you can provide your own protection for information you wish to keep confidential.

The scheme uses a text string **key**, which you specify, to determine how to alter each character from the standard input before writing it to the standard output. The first character of the key is used with the first input character, the second with the second, and so on. If the key is shorter than the input, which it usually is, it is reused from the beginning as often as necessary.

```
# crypt — encrypt and decrypt
	character getc, xor
	character c, key(MAXKEY)
	integer getarg, mod
	integer i, keylen

	keylen = getarg(1, key, MAXKEY)
	if (keylen == EOF)
		call error("usage: crypt key.")
	for (i = 1; getc(c) ¬= EOF; i = mod(i, keylen) + 1)
		call putc(xor(c, key(i)))
	stop
	end
```

error is a primitive that prints the message specified (up to but not including the period that marks the end) and stops. True, it violates the spirit of what we just said about error handling (or at least it does when called from anywhere other than the main routine), but there are times when things get just too messed up to continue processing. In some cases, no amount of high-level strategy will help us proceed further, at least not without completely obscuring the basic intent of the code. We will use **error** as a standard way of reporting fatal errors.

How is each key character used? There are any number of functions that can be specified to derive a valid output character from two other characters, but for binary encoded characters the most suitable function is the *exclusive-or.* It is also known as the *symmetric sum, half addition,* or *not equivalence.* There is no standard symbol for the *exclusive-or;* we will use ⊕.

In terms of Boolean algebra, *exclusive-or* is defined as:

$$a \oplus b = (a \ \& \ \neg b) \ | \ (\neg a \ \& \ b)$$

The value is true if **a** and **b** have different truth values, false if they are the same. To exclusive-or two characters together, we mean to perform the operation between corresponding bits of their internal binary representations. Standard Fortran has no provision for bit-wise logical operations, but many installations provide functions that perform **and**, **or** and **not**. If an exclusive-or function **xor** is not directly provided, you can write it in terms of the other logical functions:

```
# xor — exclusive-or of a and b
        character function xor(a, b)
        character and, not, or
        character a, b

        xor = or(and(a, not(b)), and(not(a), b))
        return
        end
```

Like **compress** and **expand**, this function requires that the internal representations for valid characters lie in a compact range. There is the further restriction that the representations form a complete set of n-bit numbers, for some n. That is, the number of characters must be a power of two. Otherwise, it might be possible for a key character to combine with an input character to form a code that cannot be output. If that is the case, some other less useful function will have to be substituted.

The advantage of exclusive-or is its symmetry:

$$a \oplus b \oplus a = b$$
$$a \oplus b \oplus b = a$$

The order of evaluation is irrelevant. This means that you can decrypt a file with *the same program* (and the same key of course) that you used to encode it, since applying the key twice gives you back what you started with. There's no need to figure out how to undo the effect of one program in order to write a second.

It also means you can *double encrypt* a file, then easily decrypt it. Let us say you first encrypt a file with the key **brillig**. Take the encrypted version and further encrypt with **frumious**. The information can be restored by decrypting with the two keys *in either order,* because of the symmetry of exclusive-or. The net effect is as if you had encrypted *once* with a key whose length is the least common multiple of the two key lengths, in this case 7 times 8 or 56 characters. Moreover, the resulting key is a string of characters that no longer looks like English text, and so is harder to guess. The resulting code is considerably harder to crack.

We emphasize, by the way, that there are far more effective encryption schemes than this one, which is in fact one of the earliest and best known. Unless the key is very long, you could expect the CIA or the NSA to decode your file overnight. And even if you are not bothered by those organizations, most computer centers have their share of puzzle solvers in search of a challenge.

For proof against casual probing or accidental display, however, **crypt** works nicely. If anyone decrypts your files, it will probably be because you left a copy of the key lying around! Until you can close that barn door, don't worry about anything fancier.

Exercise 2-16: What do you do with an encrypted file whose key you've forgotten? □

Exercise 2-17: If you know the clear-text version of the first line or two of a file, and you can read the encrypted version, how would you determine the key used to encrypt it? What tools would you use? □

Exercise 2-18: Write **xor(a, b)** for non-negative **a** and **b** using only standard Fortran operations, without using **and**, **or** and **not**. How fast is it compared to other available routines? How sensitive is it to the word size of the machine and to the type of arithmetic the machine does? □

2.7 Character Transliteration

One class of filters *transliterates* certain characters on their way through, passing all other characters through unmodified. We would like to have a program **translit** so that we can write

```
translit x y
```

and have all occurrences of **x** in the standard input be replaced by **y** on the standard output. Multiple translations are also handy:

```
translit xy yx
```

would change all **x**'s into **y**'s and all **y**'s into **x**'s. And it would be nice to have the shorthand

```
translit a-z A-Z
```

to translate all lower case letters to upper case, or

```
translit a-zA-Z A-Za-z
```

to do case reversal. Even good typists prefer

```
translit A-Z a-z
```

to

```
translit ABCDEFGHIJKLMNOPQRSTUVWXYZ abcdefghijklmnopqrstuvwxyz
```

Once the arguments have been expanded to eliminate any shorthand, the translation loop is straightforward:

```
while (getc(c) ¬= EOF) {
        i = index(from, c)
        if (i > 0)          # found a match
                call putc(to(i))
        else                # no match
                call putc(c)
        }
```

from holds the set of characters to be translated and **to** the corresponding translations. **index** returns the index of the character in **from** that matches **c**, or zero if **c** isn't in **from**. **index** is a built-in function in PL/I (for character strings, but not for our extended codes); it can be written in Ratfor as:

```
# index - find character  c  in string  str
        integer function index(str, c)
        character c, str(ARB)

        for (index = 1; str(index) ¬= EOS; index = index + 1)
                if (str(index) == c)
                        return
        index = 0
        return
        end
```

We will use the symbolic constant **ARB** for an array size declaration whose value is arbitrary because the array is passed in as an argument and its size is irrelevant to the routine. **ARB** would normally be given a large positive value.

There are times when we would like to translate a whole class of characters into just one character, and then to collapse runs of that translation into just one instance. For example, translating blanks, tabs, and newlines into newlines and then collapsing multiple newlines leaves each of the words in a document on a separate line, ready for further processing. Or we might want to convert all alphabetic symbols in a program text into **a**'s and all numbers into **n**'s. We specify this collapsing operation by giving a second argument that is shorter than the first:

```
translit a-zA-Z a
translit 0-9 n
```

The implication is that the last character in the second argument (the **to** string) is to be replicated as often as necessary to make a string as long as the first argument, and that this replicated character should never appear twice in succession in the output.

The main processing for **translit** then becomes:

```
lastto = length(to)
if (length(from) > lastto)
      collap = YES
else
      collap = NO
repeat {
      i = index(from, getc(c))
      if (collap == YES & i >= lastto) {       # collapse
            call putc(to(lastto))
            repeat
                  i = index(from, getc(c))
                  until (i < lastto)
            }
      if (c == EOF)
            break
      if (i > 0)              # translate
            call putc(to(i))
      else                    # copy
            call putc(c)
      }
```

length is a tiny routine that computes the length of a character string, excluding the **EOS**. We use it here to decide how to set **collap**, which indicates whether or not collapsing is to take place.

```
# length - compute length of string
      integer function length(str)
      integer str(ARB)

      for (length = 0; str(length+1) ¬= EOS; length = length + 1)
            ;
      return
      end
```

translit leaves open the possibility that some characters can be translated while others are collapsed, not so much because it is likely to be a heavily used option but so that the program behaves in a sane and predictable fashion no matter what the arguments. Esoteric cases should do something reasonable.

Only characters corresponding to the last translation character (or beyond) are subject to collapsing. The index **lastto** points at the last character in the **to** array if that array is shorter than **from**, otherwise it points at the **EOS** in **to** and never affects translations.

But there is a bug: if **to** is missing or empty, containing only an **EOS**, any translation will reference **to(0)**. (You might want to verify this.) We could give an error message when the second argument of **translit** is empty, but we could also take this condition as a request to *delete* all occurrences of characters in the first string, since that is a useful and sensible interpretation. The changes to implement this are straightforward if we keep firmly in mind that the condition **lastto==0** always calls for the matched character to be deleted. The matched character is one whose **index** is greater than zero.

One final capability is worth adding: sometimes we would like to be able to translate and compress *all but* a set of characters. For instance

```
translit ¬a−z −
```

would replace strings of non-letters with a dash (minus). The leading ¬ in the **from** string reads as a "not," just as in Ratfor source code. And

```
translit ¬a−z
```

would delete all but lower case letters.

The addition is once again easy because of the way the program is partitioned into functional modules. We need only introduce a flag **allbut**, set to **YES** when we wish to deal with *all but* a specified set of characters, and a new function **xindex** which interfaces between **index** and the rest of the program.

```
# xindex — invert condition returned by index
      integer function xindex(array, c, allbut, lastto)
      character array(ARB), c
      integer index
      integer allbut, lastto

      if (c == EOF)
            xindex = 0
      else if (allbut == NO)
            xindex = index(array, c)
      else if (index(array, c) > 0)
            xindex = 0
      else
            xindex = lastto + 1
      return
      end
```

When **allbut** is **NO**, **xindex** returns the value returned by **index**. When **allbut** is **YES**, however, **xindex** tells a lie: if **index** says the character was found, **xindex** says it wasn't; if **index** says it wasn't found, **xindex** says it was. Furthermore, we presume that the set of *all but* a few characters is so huge that it only makes sense to map them all into one character (or delete them), so if **allbut** is **YES**, **xindex** returns an index that is guaranteed to be collapsed if the character is in the set, zero if it is not, or the normal result of **index** if **allbut** is **NO**. **xindex** is also careful never to report **EOF** as a matched character.

With this organization, **index** remains simple, and so does the program that uses it through **xindex**. Imagine what the logic would be like if the equivalent decisions were scattered throughout the main routine instead of localized in **xindex**.

By the way, we could have written **xindex** as

```
xindex = index(array, c)
if (c == EOF | (allbut == YES & xindex > 0))
        xindex = 0
else if (allbut == YES & xindex == 0)
        xindex = lastto + 1
```

This is shorter but less clear. Logical decisions that intermix & and | or that require parentheses seem to be hard to grasp, so we avoid them. The version we used shows clearly that exactly one of four cases is to be chosen. When in doubt, try the "telephone test" — if you can understand a logical expression when it's read aloud, then it is acceptably clear. Otherwise, it should be rewritten.

All that remains is to add the argument-interpreting code and we have a powerful character translator:

```
# translit - map characters
	character getc
	character arg(MAXARR), c, from(MAXSET), to(MAXSET)
	integer getarg, length, makset, xindex
	integer allbut, collap, i, lastto

	if (getarg(1, arg, MAXARR) == EOF)
		call error("usage: translit from to.")
	else if (arg(1) == NOT) {
		allbut = YES
		if (makset(arg, 2, from, MAXSET) == NO)
			call error("from: too large.")
		}
	else {
		allbut = NO
		if (makset(arg, 1, from, MAXSET) == NO)
			call error("from: too large.")
		}
	if (getarg(2, arg, MAXARR) == EOF)
		to(1) = EOS
	else if (makset(arg, 1, to, MAXSET) == NO)
			call error("to: too large.")

	lastto = length(to)
	if (length(from) > lastto | allbut == YES)
		collap = YES
	else
		collap = NO
	repeat {
		i = xindex(from, getc(c), allbut, lastto)
		if (collap == YES & i >= lastto & lastto > 0) {  # collapse
			call putc(to(lastto))
			repeat
				i = xindex(from, getc(c), allbut, lastto)
				until (i < lastto)
			}
		if (c == EOF)
			break
		if (i > 0 & lastto > 0)		# translate
			call putc(to(i))
		else if (i == 0)		# copy
			call putc(c)
						# else delete
		}
	stop
	end
```

Notice, by the way, that the message printed out when there are no arguments is not just "no arguments." Instead, a prompt is given reminding the user how to use the program properly. Better to tell people concisely how to do things right than tell them only that they did something wrong.

Other than that, we wrote **translit** so that it produces few error messages. An unusual argument is given some reasonable interpretation whenever possible, and a harmless interpretation otherwise. For a general purpose tool, this is a good design principle. Otherwise, we might inadvertently head off a useful application we didn't think of at the start. It also minimizes the confusion introduced by a welter of error checks.

makset creates the **from** and **to** sets, by calling **filset** and **addset**.

```
# makset — make set from array(k) in set
      integer function makset(array, k, set, size)
      integer addset
      integer i, j, k, size
      character array(ARB), set(size)

      i = k
      j = 1
      call filset(EOS, array, i, set, j, size)
      makset = addset(EOS, set, j, size)
      return
      end
```

addset adds a character at a time to a specified position of an array and increments the index. It also checks that there's enough room to do so. We will use this function extensively in later programs.

```
# addset — put c in set(j) if it fits, increment j
      integer function addset(c, set, j, maxsiz)
      integer j, maxsiz
      character c, set(maxsiz)

      if (j > maxsiz)
            addset = NO
      else {
            set(j) = c
            j = j + 1
            addset = YES
            }
      return
      end
```

translit provides shorthand for consecutive lower case letters, upper case letters, and digits, and does so without making any assumptions about the internal representation of characters in integer variables. **filset** does all the work of building a translation set, expanding shorthand as necessary, with the help of **addset**, **dodash**, **esc** and **index**. We wrote **filset** in a general fashion, looking for an arbitrary delimiter and returning updated indices, because we expect it to be of use in our later dealings with sets of characters.

```
# filset - expand set at array(i) into set(j), stop at delim
	subroutine filset(delim, array, i, set, j, maxset)
	character esc
	integer addset, index
	integer i, j, junk, maxset
	character array(ARB), delim, set(maxset)
	string digits "0123456789"
	string lowalf "abcdefghijklmnopqrstuvwxyz"
	string upalf "ABCDEFGHIJKLMNOPQRSTUVWXYZ"

	for ( ; array(i) ¬= delim & array(i) ¬= EOS; i = i + 1)
		if (array(i) == ESCAPE)
			junk = addset(esc(array, i), set, j, maxset)
		else if (array(i) ¬= DASH)
			junk = addset(array(i), set, j, maxset)
		else if (j <= 1 | array(i+1) == EOS)	# literal -
			junk = addset(DASH, set, j, maxset)
		else if (index(digits, set(j-1)) > 0)
			call dodash(digits, array, i, set, j, maxset)
		else if (index(lowalf, set(j-1)) > 0)
			call dodash(lowalf, array, i, set, j, maxset)
		else if (index(upalf, set(j-1)) > 0)
			call dodash(upalf, array, i, set, j, maxset)
		else
			junk = addset(DASH, set, j, maxset)
	return
	end
```

The **string** declaration is a shorthand we use to avoid burdening programs with long initializations. In Fortran

```
	string id "xyz"
```

must be expanded into

```
	integer id(4)
	data id(1) /LETX/
	data id(2) /LETY/
	data id(3) /LETZ/
	data id(4) /EOS/
```

where **LETX**, etc., are symbolic constants for whatever internal representation is used for the corresponding letter. Chapter 8 contains a discussion of how **string** can be translated automatically with a macro processor.

The other new thing in **filset** is the set of calls of the form

```
	junk = addset( ... )
```

Since **filset** has no interest in the value returned by **addset** (final checking is done by **makset**), you might think we could throw away the value by writing instead

```
call addset( ... )
```

Although this is much more esthetic, regrettably some implementations of Fortran really distinguish between subroutines and functions, and get upset if a function is **called**. If our programs are to be truly portable, we must protect against this by always calling functions *as functions.* We will always assign unwanted function values to **junk** to show that they are explicitly discarded.

translit also provides an *escape convention* for writing tabs and newlines so that they are visible and cause a minimum of grief for any program that must inspect the arguments. We use the at-sign @ as an *escape character:* whatever character follows the escape character is in some way special. In particular, we define **@t** to be a tab and **@n** to be a newline, so we can write:

```
translit "  @t@n"  @n
```

to change all occurrences of "whitespace" (blanks, tabs, and newlines) to just one newline and leave one word per line. (Note the use of quotes, which we mentioned earlier, to include a blank in the first argument string.) Other special codes can be added easily, if need be. The escape character also turns off the special meaning of any character following, including blanks and quotes and the escape itself, so that special characters can be used literally. The example above could also be written

```
translit @ @t@n @n
```

provided **getarg** also knows about escapes.

The escape convention provides a clean and uniform mechanism for altering the meaning of special characters. Checking for an escape, and returning the appropriate character and the proper index is done by **esc**:

```
# esc - map array(i) into escaped character if appropriate
	character function esc(array, i)
	character array(ARB)
	integer i

	if (array(i) ¬= ESCAPE)
		esc = array(i)
	else if (array(i+1) == EOS)	# @ not special at end
		esc = ESCAPE
	else {
		i = i + 1
		if (array(i) == LETN)
			esc = NEWLINE
		else if (array(i) == LETT)
			esc = TAB
		else
			esc = array(i)
		}
	return
	end
```

Like **xindex**, **esc** conceals complexity in a simple interface, instead of spreading decisions throughout the code.

Most of the code in **filset** is a multi-way branch. If the character under consideration is escaped or not a dash, it is added to the set immediately, as is a dash that occurs as first or last character, or not preceded by a letter or digit. Only if a dash appears between letters or digits that could represent shorthand is it expanded. This is done by **dodash**:

```
# dodash - expand array(i-1)-array(i+1) into set(j)... from valid
      subroutine dodash(valid, array, i, set, j, maxset)
      character esc
      integer addset, index
      integer i, j, junk, k, limit, maxset
      character array(ARB), set(maxset), valid(ARB)

      i = i + 1
      j = j - 1
      limit = index(valid, esc(array, i))
      for (k = index(valid, set(j)); k <= limit; k = k + 1)
            junk = addset(valid(k), set, j, maxset)
      return
      end
```

translit is not a easy program to understand, because it does many things, yet the functions are worth combining because they all address similar problems. You learn the most useful formats, like

```
translit A-Z a-z
```

for case conversion, and study the formation rules only when you encounter a new application. The program itself is not complicated, however, because it was constructed in a modular fashion beginning with the simplest applications. The added complexity is confined to separate new modules and does not clutter up the original structure.

What determines the running time of **translit**? As you might expect for a program that does little computation, it spends most of its CPU time doing processing for I/O — in our case between 70 and 85 percent. Most of this time is *not* in **getc** and **putc**, however, but in the lower-level routines that they call, over which we have no control. Handling characters one at a time with **getc** and **putc** costs a negligible amount. After I/O, the rest of the CPU time goes into **xindex** and **index**, which are called once per input character, and the main routine. For a call like

```
translit a-z A-Z
```

index took 19 percent of the time, the main routine 7 percent, and **xindex** 4 percent. When the **to** set is small, however, as with

```
translit ¬@n @n
```

the times were: **index** 5 percent, **xindex** 6 percent and main 6 percent. So **index** is the routine to speed up (should I/O ever be made sufficiently fast), because the time it consumes varies with both the number of input characters and the size of the **from** set.

Exercise 2-19: Describe the actions performed by the following commands.

```
translit a-b-d abcd
translit a-c xyz
translit -ac xyz
translit @@
```

How would you convert runs of blanks into single occurrences? □

Exercise 2-20: One purpose of the escape mechanism is to let you input characters that are difficult to type or hard to read, or that have special meaning. Extend **esc** to recognize **s** for space, **b** for backspace, and perhaps a string of octal or hexadecimal digits to represent an arbitrary bit pattern. □

Exercise 2-21: When you build the primitive **error**, make use of **esc** so an escaped period can be used to get a literal period into the message. □

2.8 Numbers

translit is used frequently to filter files before counting things in them, as with **charcount** introduced in the previous chapter. Since we were primarily concerned then with introducing Ratfor, we postponed the description of **putdec**, the subroutine that printed the final count. Before going any further, here it is.

putdec(n, w) puts out the number **n** as a string of at least **w** characters, including a sign if **n** is negative. If fewer than **w** characters are needed, blanks are inserted to the left to make up the count; if more than **w** are needed, more are provided. It is this feature that makes **putdec** more useful than conventional output options in most languages.

```
# putdec - put decimal integer n in field width >= w
	subroutine putdec(n, w)
	character chars(MAXCHARS)
	integer itoc
	integer i, n, nd, w

	nd = itoc(n, chars, MAXCHARS)
	for (i = nd + 1; i <= w; i = i + 1)
		call putc(BLANK)
	for (i = 1; i <= nd; i = i + 1)
		call putc(chars(i))
	return
	end
```

putdec in turn calls on **itoc** to do the conversion. **itoc** converts an integer to characters in an array provided by the caller, and returns the number of characters it took, excluding the **EOS**. **itoc** obtains the digits in reverse order because it is easier, then flips them before returning.

```
# itoc - convert integer  int  to char string in  str
      integer function itoc(int, str, size)
      integer abs, mod
      integer d, i, int, intval, j, k, size
      character str(size)
      string digits "0123456789"

      intval = abs(int)
      str(1) = EOS
      i = 1
      repeat {                              # generate digits
            i = i + 1
            d = mod(intval, 10)
            str(i) = digits(d+1)
            intval = intval / 10
            } until (intval == 0 | i >= size)
      if (int < 0 & i < size) {             # then sign
            i = i + 1
            str(i) = MINUS
            }
      itoc = i - 1
      for (j = 1; j < i; j = j + 1) {       # then reverse
            k = str(i)
            str(i) = str(j)
            str(j) = k
            i = i - 1
            }
      return
      end
```

abs is a function that returns the absolute value of its argument. (You can use **iabs** in Fortran.)

The complement of **itoc** is of course **ctoi**, a routine for converting a character string to an integer. A useful design is this: The call

```
n = ctoi(c, i)
```

starts looking at position **i** of **c**. Leading blanks and tabs are ignored; any subsequent digits are converted to the correct numeric value. The first non-digit seen terminates the scan; upon return **i** pointd to this position. **n** is the value of the integer. We will use **ctoi** regularly throughout the book.

```
# ctoi — convert string at in(i) to integer, increment i
        integer function ctoi(in, i)
        character in(ARB)
        integer index
        integer d, i
        string digits "0123456789"

        while (in(i) == BLANK | in(i) == TAB)
                i = i + 1
        for (ctoi = 0; in(i) ¬= EOS; i = i + 1) {
                d = index(digits, in(i))
                if (d == 0)             # non-digit
                        break
                ctoi = 10 * ctoi + d - 1
                }
        return
        end
```

Now for the payoff. We can use **charcount** in series with **translit** to provide all sorts of useful information. Let's invent a bit of job control language: we adopt the notation **|** to indicate a series connection of two programs. (Don't confuse it with the *or* operator in logical conditions. There are only so many characters to go around, so we have to double up on meanings sometimes.)

```
translit ¬@n | charcount
```

means "take the output produced by **translit** and feed it as input to **charcount**." We'll call this construction a *pipeline*. Whether a pipeline is a direct connection between simultaneously executing processes, or just a prescription for what intermediate temporary files to write and read, is not relevant for most applications. Our concern rests with what we can *do* with such pipelines.

The example we just gave, for instance, deletes everything but the newlines in a file, then counts them up. We have a line counting program directly equivalent to **linecount**. Counting words is only a little harder:

```
translit " @t@n" @n | translit ¬@n | charcount
```

First we put one word per line by compressing whitespace, then count lines as before. We can even count all the decimal digit strings in a program:

```
translit 0-9 9 | translit ¬9 | charcount
```

This converts each string of digits into a single **9**, deletes all other characters, then counts the **9**'s.

Writing a program like this latter one is a nuisance; it is not likely that you would want to stockpile such an odd assortment of gadgets against the likelihood of eventually having a need for them. But having a single tool as powerful as **translit** makes sense. You can use it alone or in conjunction with other filters like **charcount** to perform a host of variations. This is what tool building is all about.

Exercise 2-22: Many computers store integers in *two's complement* notation, which has one more negative number than it has positive numbers. Other representations have as many negative numbers as positive numbers but have two representations of zero. Rewrite **putdec** to handle two's complement arithmetic properly. (Do you know where the current version fails?) □

Exercise 2-23: Modify **ctoi** to recognize an optional leading + or −. □

Exercise 2-24: Write **ctof**, which converts a character string to a floating point number; it should recognize an optional sign, an optional decimal point, and scientific notation for an exponent, as in

```
-1.23E-4
```

□

Exercise 2-25: **wordcount** counts words directly, instead of using **translit** and **charcount**. Do you think the greater efficiency you may attain is worth the extra effort? □

Exercise 2-26: Write a pipeline to convert an encrypted file to lower case (assuming you know the key). Should **crypt** be able to translate characters as well as **translit** does? Should **translit** know how to encrypt and decrypt? □

Exercise 2-27: Write a filter **tail** which produces only the last *n* lines of its input as output, where *n* is an optional argument. That is,

```
program | tail 10
```

prints the last ten lines produced by **program**. Of course there is a limit on how large *n* can be in a practical implementation. If no value of *n* is specified, what is a reasonable default? □

Exercise 2-28: Design and implement a filter **calc** to simulate a pocket calculator. **calc** should deal with at least +, − and =, so an expression like

```
1 + 2 - 3 =
```

can be evaluated. Refinements include more operators, parentheses, memory, and the like. How would you modify **calc** to handle numbers too large to fit in one machine word? □

Exercise 2-29: Write a program to take arbitrary bit patterns and interpret them as octal or hexadecimal numbers, as characters, and perhaps as machine instructions, as appropriate for your particular computer. Implement it as a filter. □

2.9 Summary

The filters presented in this chapter are diverse, but most share an important feature. Each encourages, in its own way, a standard representation for text to be passed between programs or to be stored in files for later use. By pushing information about particular devices as far out to the edges of a system as possible, we expand the range of programs that can freely cooperate. And by writing terminal filters to interface these devices to standard format files, we isolate and contain device-dependent information. That way, radical changes can be made in the peripherals attached to a machine without affecting more than a module or two. It also means that you can have considerable assurance that each new device can be put to use with little reprogramming. This is an important consideration in planning for painless growth.

translit is an even more general tool. Having it around, you can ignore many of the little character-set dependencies that so often haunt a computer center and make it difficult to combine software packages. You can use **translit** to take up the slack between two programs that don't quite cooperate, and thus avoid the messy problem of recoding one (or both). And besides, it's useful all by itself.

Once you learn that you can isolate and adapt by introducing filters, you begin to think more freely in terms of combining existing programs instead of writing new ones. You overcome much of the temptation to build a whole new package; instead you adapt pieces that already exist. You become, in short, more of a tool user.

Bibliographic Notes

The idea of pipelines and filters — a uniform mechanism for connecting the input of one program to the output of another — was conceived by M. D. McIlroy. It was anticipated in a somewhat less general way in the "communication files" of the Dartmouth Time-sharing System. Pipelines have an especially clean implementation in the UNIX operating system developed at Bell Labs by K. L. Thompson and D. M. Ritchie. Here the processes in the pipeline run concurrently, with sufficient interlocks to ensure that the receiving process never reads information that isn't there, and that the sending process never creates too much information before the receiver has read some. The vertical bar is the UNIX syntax for a pipeline, and is due to Thompson. See "The UNIX time-sharing system," *CACM,* July, 1974.

The basic design of **translit** is adapted from a program written originally by M. D. McIlroy.

If you're interested in cryptanalysis in any form, read *The Codebreakers,* by David Kahn (MacMillan, 1967).

CHAPTER 3

FILES

Up to this point we have talked about programs which read one input and write one output, without really worrying about how to get the input and output where we want them. Although many useful programs need only one input and one output, this is hardly adequate in general. In this chapter we will discuss programs which have more complicated interactions with their environment — reading or writing more than one file, and creating and deleting files as they run. These programs are mainly intended for an operating system which provides some kind of permanent file system where information can be kept for extended periods on secondary storage and easily accessed by running programs.

Sadly, operations like these are hard even to talk about, let alone program, because:

Each operating system has its own jargon for describing system actions: there is no standard terminology.

Each operating system has its own capabilities and limitations: there are no standard functions.

Some of the things we want to do can't be done easily on some operating systems: there are no perfect systems.

As we did in the previous chapters, we will try to avoid these difficulties by organizing our discussion and programs around *primitive functions* — operations like **getc**, **putc**, and **getarg**, which are conceptually simple, each performing a well-defined task. The mechanics of how a primitive function is accomplished and the way it is expressed will vary from system to system, but the basic functions will be easy to understand, and easy to implement on any system if they do not already exist. Defining and using primitive functions to localize operating system dependencies is a crucial form of modularization. It is the only way to cope with real systems.

3.1 File Comparison

One instance of a more complicated relationship with the operating system is reading multiple input files or data sets. An example of a program that has more than one input is one that compares *two* input sources, and lists the places where they differ. This is a useful tool — for comparing the output of one program with another, for example, or for comparing two versions of a text. It mechanizes a task all too often done manually.

The design of **compare** depends on what is to be compared. We will write a version that compares two text files; variations are left as exercises. For text the natural unit of comparison is the line — if two lines differ in length, we can resynchronize at the next line. Of course a missing line in one of the files will destroy synchronization for the rest of the input, so this is not the best comparison imaginable, but it is a good beginning. In outline the program is

```
repeat {
        get a line from file 1
        get a line from file 2
        if (either input encountered EOF)
                break
        if (line1 ¬= line2)
                print line number, character position,
                        and offending lines
        }
if (only one input is ended)
        print message about which input terminated.
```

First we check the general flow of control by examining some critical boundary cases. As long as the two files are identical, no output will be produced; if they end together all is well, even if both are empty. If one file is a prefix of the other, then a message to that effect is printed. Finally, if the files differ anywhere in some line, the differing lines will be printed.

Now we can begin to fill in details. Comparing two lines is a self-contained task that should be isolated in a separate routine. The function **equal** compares two strings; it returns **YES** if they are identical, **NO** if they differ. Each string must of course be terminated by an **EOS**. We compare strings terminated by **EOS**, not lines terminated by **NEWLINE**, because the more general routine costs nothing extra, yet is much more likely to be useful in other programs.

```
# equal - compare str1 to str2; return YES if equal, NO if not
	integer function equal(str1, str2)
	character str1(ARB), str2(ARB)
	integer i

	for (i = 1; str1(i) == str2(i); i = i + 1)
		if (str1(i) == EOS) {
			equal = YES
			return
			}
	equal = NO
	return
	end
```

The next problem, and the one which is the principal subject of this chapter, is how to connect the program to its sources of input — how to arrange for the operations

```
get a line from file 1
get a line from file 2
```

Up to now, we have assumed that a program has some default standard input and standard output connected to it when it runs, which **getc** and **putc** use implicitly. These are often a card reader and line printer in batch systems, or the user's terminal keyboard and printer in an interactive environment. Almost all operating systems provide some way to change these default assignments, and to add other inputs and outputs. For example, most batch systems have a control card which says (in effect)

```
Connect Fortran logical unit number N to external file F
```

so that the Fortran I/O statements

```
read(N, ...) ...
```

and

```
write(N, ...) ...
```

will operate on F. Interactive systems often provide a command to perform the same function. In PL/I one can connect the internal file name used in

```
get file (name) ...
```

or

```
put file (name) ...
```

with some data source or sink in the external environment. Control card syntax varies wildly from system to system, but the function is always available.

Thus a rudimentary version of **compare** could read from two input streams, with internal names by convention perhaps 1 and 2 in Fortran and **name1** and **name2** in PL/I, and require the *user* to connect the right external files to these internal names by control card or command. This **compare** does not take any explicit action to connect itself to its sources — someone else must do the work.

```
# compare (simple version) — compare file 1 to file 2
	character line1(MAXLINE), line2(MAXLINE)
	integer equal, getlin
	integer lineno, m1, m2

	lineno = 0
	repeat {
		m1 = getlin(line1, INFILE1)
		m2 = getlin(line2, INFILE2)
		if (m1 == EOF | m2 == EOF)
			break
		lineno = lineno + 1
		if (equal(line1, line2) == NO)
			call difmsg(lineno, line1, line2)
		}
	if (m1 == EOF & m2 ¬= EOF)
		call remark("eof on file 1.")
	else if (m2 == EOF & m1 ¬= EOF)
		call remark("eof on file 2.")
	# else they match
	stop
	end
```

remark is a general-purpose message printer, identical to **error** in Chapter 2, except that it returns after printing, instead of stopping. Notice that **compare** produces no message if the files are identical. Generally a program should say nothing unless and until it has something to say.

If there are any discrepancies between the two files, **difmsg** prints the line number and the differing lines; you can fill in the details to suit yourself, using **putc** and **putdec**. Ours is just

```
# difmsg — print line numbers and differing lines
	subroutine difmsg(lineno, line1, line2)
	character line1(ARB), line2(ARB)
	integer lineno

	call putdec(lineno, 5)
	call putc(NEWLINE)
	call putlin(line1, STDOUT)
	call putlin(line2, STDOUT)
	return
	end
```

The function call

```
	getlin(line, infile)
```

copies the next line from the file with the internal name **infile** into the character string **line**. It guarantees that the input line is terminated with a newline and an **EOS**. **getlin** returns **EOF** when it encounters end of file, and otherwise returns the line length (excluding the **EOS**). Like **getc**, **getlin** maps characters into their internal representation. It might even call a form of **getc** to do the work, although more often **getlin** would be the low level primitive, and **getc** would call upon it. (In effect the simple **getc** and **putc** in Chapter 1 work that way.) Since **getlin** returns either the string length or **EOF**, once again **EOF** should probably be a negative value.

putlin is a primitive to output a line onto a given file. It is the complement of **getlin**, performing whatever character translation is needed. We will assume that output produced by interleaved calls to **putc** and **putlin** goes out in the proper order. **STDOUT** is the internal name for the standard output; as you might expect, there is a corresponding **STDIN** for the standard input. The system must arrange that these files are ready to read and write when the program begins to run.

Exercise 3-1: Implement **getlin** and **putlin**. Alter the **getc** and **putc** of Chapter 1 to use **getlin** and **putlin**. Ensure that interleaved calls of **getc** and **getlin** from the same and different files work correctly. Do the same for **putc** and **putlin**. □

Exercise 3-2: In a non-interactive environment, **compare** probably should not print too much output for files that are very different. Add an optional argument so the comparison terminates after a specified number of mismatched lines has occurred. An alternate design is to have **compare** stop after the first mismatch. In that case, the optional argument would allow more than one mismatch. □

Exercise 3-3: Construct a version of **compare** such that two lines are considered to be the same if they are the same after each run of blanks is replaced by a single blank. Can you achieve the same effect by using **translit**? Can you steal any code from **translit**? □

Exercise 3-4: (Hard) Our **compare** is very rudimentary. It is useful for finding out the first place where two files have become different, but it breaks down quickly after that, producing voluminous but uninformative output. Invent a scheme which can cope with missing and transposed lines. How much space and time does your method take, as a function of the file sizes? Can it break down completely? (See the bibliographic notes at the end of this chapter.) □

3.2 Connecting Files by Name

Let us return to the question of how to connect the external name of a file to the name used within the program. Normally the external name will be the name of a file in a file system, or perhaps some temporary file assigned for the duration of the job. Less frequently it will be an I/O device such as a tape drive. As we said, the traditional way to connect the external name and internal name is by a control card; in some environments this is all that is possible. But no one wants to have to say

```
connect file1 to name1
connect file2 to name2
compare
```

just because **compare** can only read the internal streams 1 and 2. It's not even the extra work of preparing the **connect** commands that makes this bad, although that is nuisance enough; it's that you have to remember the internal names the program uses. How much more natural to say

compare file1 file2

and let **compare** worry about accessing the files.

Suppose we pass the actual name of the file to the program and let the program itself arrange the correspondence between external name and internal stream. In effect, the program does during execution what the control cards would have done prior to execution. Let us call the primitive that performs this task **open**. **open** does whatever is necessary to access the file, and assigns it an internal file name or number, which is returned as the function value:

internal-name = **open(***external-name, access-mode***)**

This *internal-name* is now used for subsequent calls to **getlin** and **putlin**.

Depending on the local environment, **open** may need other information in addition to the external name — buffer space, access mode, and so on. We will summarize all this extra material as *access-mode,* which in our programs will always be one of the symbolic constants **READ**, **WRITE**, or **READWRITE**, to indicate how the program intends to use the file. Of course if the system you are using provides file security in some form, **open** has to negotiate for the access you wish.

open signals any kind of error by returning the value **ERR** instead of a legal internal name. A convenient implementation is to have the internal names be small positive integers; **open** simply returns the first unassigned value. In this case **ERR** would best be zero or negative.

Given **open**, **compare** can now be written as

```
# compare — compare two files for equality
        character arg1(MAXLINE), arg2(MAXLINE)
        character line1(MAXLINE), line2(MAXLINE)
        integer equal, getarg, getlin, open
        integer infil1, infil2, lineno, m1, m2

        if (getarg(1, arg1, MAXLINE) == EOF
          | getarg(2, arg2, MAXLINE) == EOF)
                call error("usage: compare file1 file2.")
        infil1 = open(arg1, READ)
        if (infil1 == ERR)
                call cant(arg1)
        infil2 = open(arg2, READ)
        if (infil2 == ERR)
                call cant(arg2)
        lineno = 0
        repeat {
                m1 = getlin(line1, infil1)
                m2 = getlin(line2, infil2)
                if (m1 == EOF | m2 == EOF)
                        break
                lineno = lineno + 1
                if (equal(line1, line2) == NO)
                        call difmsg(lineno, line1, line2)
                }
        if (m1 == EOF & m2 ¬= EOF)
                call remark("eof on file 1.")
        else if (m2 == EOF & m1 ¬= EOF)
                call remark("eof on file 2.")
        stop
        end
```

cant(name) prints

```
name: can't open
```

and exits. Even though this is a trifling task, it occurs often enough to warrant a separate routine.

Most interactive systems provide the connection ability (with varying degrees of grace); it is less common in batch environments. Clearly the function must exist as part of *any* operating system that provides a way to store files by name, for how else could the program that interprets the command language operate? Yet all too often the operation is arbitrarily restricted to "system" programs and forbidden to ordinary users. This is regrettable, for it is important that a program be able to attach input sources dynamically. Programs should be easy to use, as a matter of good human engineering. You should only have to say "compare these files," and let the program do *all* the work. The less setup you have to do before actually using a program, the more likely you are to think of it as a tool.

What can you do if you can't connect files dynamically? One alternative is to specify that the input files are by convention in standard places, like input stream numbers 1, 2, 3, ... The number of inputs can be specified by the user (the less desirable choice) or deduced by the program.

A second variation is to choose your own internal names, which are handed to the program as arguments. Then you say

```
connect file1 2
connect file2 3
compare 2 3
```

You still make the connection, but at least you don't have to remember what names the program uses.

A final possibility, which requires some cooperation from the local operating system, is to specify files by name, then have a program *generate* the appropriate control cards with the proper correspondence between external and internal names, invoking **compare** as the last step. The generated control cards are then run, ideally as part of the same job that generated them.

Exercise 3-5: Does

```
compare f f
```

work on your system? If not, why not? Should it? Why would you want to do such an operation? □

Exercise 3-6: Modify **compare** so that if it is called with a single argument, it assumes the other file is the standard input. Then you can use **compare** in pipelines, like this

```
expand | compare f
```

Is this design of any value when pipelines must be implemented with temporary files? □

Exercise 3-7: (Harder) Extend the syntax and semantics of pipelines so *both* sources for **compare** can be the outputs of programs. □

3.3 File Inclusion

Once **open** exists, we can conveniently build tools that access any number of files. One example is **include**, which just copies its standard input to its standard output, except that any input line that begins

```
include filename
```

is replaced by the entire contents of the file **filename**.

Many of the larger programs in this book use **include**, typically to include a set of **common** declarations. This ensures that all routines which use a **common** block get the same version, and that only one change need be made to affect all routines. Similarly, when we compile a program, all the definitions of the symbolic constants are picked up with an *include* line. Since we tend to use symbolic constants wherever possible, most of our programs **include** a standard set of things like **EOF** and **EOS**, and perhaps another set peculiar to a given set of routines. You might also use **include** to insert canned control card sequences, or, in program testing, a script of tests; the included files would be previously developed test cases. (And the outputs would be compared using **compare**!)

include is a generalization of a facility found in the PL/I preprocessor, where lines of the form

```
% include file;
```

are replaced by the contents of **file**. The mechanism is restricted to PL/I source programs, however, so it is of little use for anything else. Our version can be used for any text files.

The general outline of **include** is

```
while (getlin(line, file) ¬= EOF)
        if (line starts with "include")
                include new file
        else
                output line
```

If the included file can contain further **include**'s, this is obviously a recursive procedure, that is, the operation is defined in terms of itself. If the language you are using does not permit recursion (Fortran, for example), you must either simulate it with a stack of file identifiers or disallow it completely. As it turns out, nested **include**'s are useful and not at all difficult to deal with.

The other question is how to decide if the line contains *include*. This is best broken into two steps — finding the first word on the line, then comparing it with *include*. We write a routine **getwrd** which isolates the next word on the input line, a "word" being a string of non-blank characters delimited by blanks, tabs or newlines. **getwrd** skips any leading blanks and tabs and returns the word and its length (which we don't use here). **getwrd** also sets an index to just past the end of the word, so if the word is *include*, we can use **getwrd** again to find the file name, by starting to look right after the *include*.

```
# getwrd - get non-blank word from in(i) into  out, increment i
      integer function getwrd(in, i, out)
      character in(ARB), out(ARB)
      integer i, j

      while (in(i) == BLANK | in(i) == TAB)
            i = i + 1
      j = 1
      while (in(i) ¬= EOS & in(i) ¬= BLANK
        & in(i) ¬= TAB & in(i) ¬= NEWLINE) {
            out(j) = in(i)
            i = i + 1
            j = j + 1
            }
      out(j) = EOS
      getwrd = j - 1
      return
      end
```

The main routine looks like this:

```
# include - replace  include file  by contents of file
      character line(MAXLINE), str(MAXLINE)
      integer equal, getlin, getwrd, open
      integer infile(NFILES), len, level, loc
      string incl "include"

      infile(1) = STDIN
      for (level = 1; level > 0; level = level - 1) {
            while (getlin(line, infile(level)) ¬= EOF) {
                  loc = 1
                  len = getwrd(line, loc, str)
                  if (equal(str, incl) == NO)
                        call putlin(line, STDOUT)
                  else {
                        level = level + 1
                        if (level > NFILES)
                              call error("includes nested too deeply.")
                        len = getwrd(line, loc, str)
                        infile(level) = open(str, READ)
                        if (infile(level) == ERR)
                              call cant(str)
                        }
                  }
            if (level > 1)
                  call close(infile(level))
            }
      stop
      end
```

equal decides if the word is *include*; we wrote it earlier in this chapter. Notice that it is used to compare two strings, not two lines — generality has paid off already.

We turned the **if-else** around from our pseudo-code version of **include**, because we find it is better to associate shorter segments of code with the **if** and save the longer alternative for the **else**. That way we don't lose track of a tiny trailing **else** clause halfway down the page.

The primitive operation **close** is the opposite of **open**: it breaks the connection between an external name and an internal one, and frees the internal name and any associated resources for some other use. (**close** is *not* the **rewind** operation familiar to Fortran programmers, which repositions without closing.) The reason for using **close** here is that we do not know how many times a particular file will be used nor how many different files there will be. Since most systems have a limit on the number of simultaneously open files, we must explicitly close them to avoid running out of internal names.

Although our programs are careful to close files when finished, it is convenient if the system closes all open files when a program terminates. This simplifies the handling of abnormal terminations.

include also assumes implicitly a property of **open** which we didn't mention earlier — when a file is **open**ed, it must be positioned at its beginning. This behavior is vital for **include**, since most frequently a file is included several times.

> *Exercise 3-8:* Modify **include** for a system where files cannot be opened by name. Describe a systematic way to use it. □

3.4 File Concatenation

The next program we will write is **concat**, which concatenates a set of named input files onto its standard output. A common use for **concat** is to combine multiple files into one, for use by another program which can only read its standard input, like the filters of Chapter 2. It is also the easiest way to print the contents of a file without reformatting or any other interpretation.

In effect, **concat** is a version of **include** that takes all its file names from an argument list instead of from lines saying *include*. This makes it easier to use for many purposes, since it requires no preparation. The code is also easier to write:

```
# concat — concatenate named files onto standard output
	character name(NAMESIZE)
	integer getarg, open
	integer fin, i

	for (i = 1; getarg(i, name, NAMESIZE) ¬= EOF; i = i + 1) {
		fin = open(name, READ)
		if (fin == ERR)
			call cant(name)
		call fcopy(fin, STDOUT)
		call close(fin)
		}
	stop
	end
```

Observe that if there are no input files, **concat** does the right thing — it produces no output whatsoever.

The actual copying is done by **fcopy**. Of course **fcopy** is essentially the example we began with in Chapter 1, packaged as a subroutine. The only difference is that the program reads or writes specified files instead of using the standard input and standard output.

```
# fcopy — copy file  in  to file  out
	subroutine fcopy(in, out)
	character buf(MAXLINE)
	integer getlin
	integer in, out

	while (getlin(buf, in) ¬= EOF)
		call putlin(buf, out)
	return
	end
```

fcopy assumes that its files are all opened, positioned and ready to go; it simply copies. This way we can use it to copy *parts* of files. If **fcopy** carefully opened and closed its files, that would limit its usefulness. Don't put arbitrary restrictions on programs, particularly by making them try do too many things. If you want to open and close files, wrap another layer around **fcopy**, just as we did.

3.5 File Printer

One of the most useful programs that has the form "indeterminate number of inputs, one output" is a file printer or lister. **print** is invoked with one or more files as arguments; it prints the files with top and bottom margins, and, at the top of each page, the file name, page number, and perhaps the date and time. Each new file begins on a new page. **print** is used instead of **concat** when you want a pretty, self-identifying listing of a set of files.

In outline, the program is

```
for each file
        get name
        open(name)
        fprint(name, fin)
        close(fin)

fprint(name, fin)
        initialize
        while (getlin(line, fin) ¬= EOF) {
                if (at top)
                        print page header
                print line
                if (page full)
                        space to bottom
                }
        if (page not full)
                space to bottom
```

This organization puts all of the code for stepping through the argument list at one level, and all the details of counting lines for an individual file at a lower level.

The actual code for **print** is

```
# print — print files with headings
        character name(NAMESIZE)
        integer getarg, open
        integer fin, i

        for (i = 1; getarg(i, name, NAMESIZE) ¬= EOF; i = i + 1) {
                fin = open(name, READ)
                if (fin == ERR)
                        call cant(name)
                call fprint(name, fin)
                call close(fin)
                }
        stop
        end
```

fprint has to be carefully thought out so it doesn't botch its boundary conditions. The most obvious pitfall is that the right number of lines must be printed on each page, or the output will gradually drift up or down successive pages. Less obvious, if a file exactly fills the last page, the next file should begin at the top of the next page, with no intervening blank page (or worse, a page with just a heading on it).

```
# fprint — print file "name" from fin
        subroutine fprint(name, fin)
        character line(MAXLINE), name(NAMESIZE)
        integer getlin, open
        integer fin, lineno, pageno

        pageno = 0
        lineno = 0
        while (getlin(line, fin) ¬= EOF) {
                if (lineno == 0) {
                        call skip(MARGIN1)
                        pageno = pageno + 1
                        call head(name, pageno)
                        call skip(MARGIN2)
                        lineno = MARGIN1 + MARGIN2 + 1
                        }
                call putlin(line, STDOUT)
                lineno = lineno + 1
                if (lineno >= BOTTOM) {
                        call skip(PAGELEN-lineno)
                        lineno = 0
                        }
                }
        if (lineno > 0)
                call skip(PAGELEN-lineno)
        return
        end
```

The symbolic constants **MARGIN1** and **MARGIN2** are the number of lines before and after the heading line. **BOTTOM** is the line number of the last text line on a page; **PAGELEN** is the number of lines on a page. For standard 8½×11 paper with 6 lines per inch, **PAGELEN** is 66. The margins will usually be two or three lines each.

skip produces **n** blank lines; we use a tiny separate routine rather than clutter up **fprint** with four occurrences of the loop.

```
# skip — output n blank lines
        subroutine skip(n)
        integer i, n

        for (i = 1; i <= n; i = i + 1)
                call putc(NEWLINE)
        return
        end
```

Since we want the **print**ed listing to identify the files by name, it is natural and convenient to attach files to the program dynamically by name instead of by some control card mechanism. At the least, subroutine **head** should print a single line with the file name and page number. It might also print the date and time if they are available.

```
# head - print top of page header
        subroutine head(name, pageno)
        character name(NAMESIZE)
        integer pageno
        string page " Page  "

        call putlin(name, STDOUT)
        call putlin(page, STDOUT)
        call putdec(pageno, 1)
        call putc(NEWLINE)
        return
        end
```

Since **putlin** does *not* add a newline at the end of the string it is putting out, you can make several calls to **putlin** to build up one output line, as we did here to get the name and page number on the same line.

Once the basic tool is working, many refinements are possible, and some are very desirable. You might consider adding the capability to

- convert tabs to spaces
- change default paper length, margins, line spacing, tab stops, etc.
- fold long lines
- number lines
- start and stop on specified pages
- print multiple files in parallel
- print multi-column output

All of these are easy except for the last, multi-column printing. That can be done, of course, by accumulating a whole page before printing any of it.

When you write a program, there is a great temptation to add more and more "features" like these, little things that it will do for you. But beware — unless the features work together in a uniform way, the result is going to be a grab-bag of unrelated capabilities, most of which won't get used because nobody can remember them. If you have to look up how to use a program for even the simplest applications, you know you've gone too far. When in doubt, treat "feature" as a pejorative. (Think of a hundred-bladed Swiss army knife.)

We have found the following syntax for optional arguments to be convenient. Optional arguments are usually a single letter, or at least a short string. They are introduced by a character which is unlikely to begin a file name, so arguments can be distinguished from file names. (We use a minus sign.) If **print** provides multi-column output, for example, it might be specified by the argument **−c***n* where *n* is the number of columns.

```
print -c4 file1 file2 ...
```

calls for printing of the files in 4-column format. By processing the arguments strictly left to right, the program permits you to set up parameters for a file, print it, then selectively alter them for the next file.

Once you have optional capabilities, the question arises of what to do when a particular option is left unspecified. This should *never* be considered an error; instead some default value should be chosen. Selecting the right default behavior of a program may seem like a trivial concern, but if you do it wrong, everyone suffers (or your program isn't used). Sometimes the decision is obvious: page lengths are pretty much standardized, for example. But others are less clear: should **print** fold very long lines into several shorter ones by default? If so, where? Keep in mind that you are building tools, and make them as useful and as easy to use as possible. There is a general principle that things that are said often should be concise; therefore the defaults should reflect the most common usage. Furthermore, defaults should be set so the user who doesn't know any options gets reasonable behavior. Try not to surprise your users, and don't limit *their* options.

Exercise 3-9: Implement some of the enhancements of **print**, accessible through optional arguments. Before you do, try to predict which will be heavily used and which not at all. After your new version has been used for a while, determine how accurate your predictions were. What options should **print** choose by default? □

3.6 Multi-stage Processing: Pipelines

This book is about tools, so by now it has probably occurred to you that with a little care you could use **print** as a tool to print the output from any program. If this were easy, then no other program would ever have to contain code for things like multi-column printing — one version of **print** could serve all comers.

Suppose we modify **print** slightly so that if it has no file name arguments, it reverts to taking its input from the standard input. This is an easy task because of the way we organized it in the first place. We need only add a test for no arguments and an empty file name for the standard input.

```
# print (default input STDIN) - print files with headings
	character name(NAMESIZE)
	integer getarg, open
	integer fin, i
	string null ""

	for (i = 1; getarg(i, name, NAMESIZE) ¬= EOF; i = i + 1) {
		fin = open(name, READ)
		if (fin == ERR)
			call cant(name)
		call fprint(name, fin)
		call close(fin)
		}
	if (i == 1)		# no files specified
		call fprint(null, STDIN)
	stop
	end
```

Any program which wants to use **print** as a post-processor need only arrange that its output be directed to the standard input of **print**. **print** itself should not know or care that it is being used by some other program. With the pipeline notation introduced in Chapter 2, for instance, we merely say

```
program ... | print
```

This lets any program have formatted output, within the capabilities of **print**. And since **print** will have wide use, some effort can be lavished on enhancing its capabilities and making it efficient.

Just how to arrange a pipeline varies quite a bit from system to system. Ideally, **program** and **print** should be concurrent processes, connected by the system, neither knowing the other is running. Less desirable, but more likely to be feasible, they can communicate via temporary files. Suppose we adopt the notation

```
prog >file
```

to mean that the standard output of **prog** is to be collected on **file**, which is created if necessary (preferably by the system, automatically and without the program being aware of it.) Then we can simulate the pipeline with

```
prog >tempfile
print <tempfile
remove tempfile
```

where **<file** has the analogous meaning of taking the standard input from **file**, and **remove** causes **tempfile** to be discarded. Temporaries are clumsier than pipes, but you can live with them, especially if your local operating system is gracious about creating files upon demand.

Readers who are sensitive to questions of efficiency may wonder if it is economical to use two programs when one would serve. The answer depends on the true costs involved, which are often not properly estimated. Most people who talk about "efficiency" are concerned primarily with how much machine resources are used in the final run or in hands-off production, not with how much "people" and machine time is consumed in all the compilations, debugging and other false starts that prepare for the final run. Throughout this book we consistently take the view that people cost a great deal more than machines, and that the disparity will increase in the future. Therefore the most important consideration is that people get their jobs done with a minimum of fuss and bother.

One way to help this happen is to provide tools. It is not sufficient, however, to have a large collection of "utilities," if each is hard to use, deals with just one special case (even though it has a lot of "features"), and cannot be connected to other tools in any useful way. Tools must work together. One advantage of the pipeline is that it encourages people who build programs to think in terms of how programs can be connected to other programs. This in turn forces a certain degree of standardization, for a program which will not interface cleanly to other programs cannot share a pipeline with them.

A second consideration in favor of the pipeline is that it encourages the construction of smaller programs to do simpler functions. These smaller programs are much easier to write, debug, document, maintain and improve independently than they would be if combined into a single monster. And of course separate programs can be combined in novel ways, something which is hardly possible if they have already been combined in some "obvious" way.

A final consideration is that many jobs will not get done at all unless they can be done quickly. Efficiency is hardly of importance for a temporary hookup meant to be used only a few times. Should a particular organization of tools prove so useful that it begins to consume significant resources, *then* you can consider replacing it with a more efficient version. And you are way ahead at this point, for you are writing a program that has precise specifications and that has been shown to be useful. This is the best formula known for ensuring the success of a programming effort.

Exercise 3-10: Determine if it is possible in your operating system to construct a program which reads an input line describing a pipeline and arranges the necessary operating system commands to make the operation happen. Build it if possible. If not, what facilities are lacking, and how would you provide them most easily? □

3.7 Creating Files Dynamically

We come now to an area which is of great importance in programs that interact with their environment — the ability to *create* files or information streams dynamically, that is, while the program runs. **makecopy** illustrates the problems.

```
makecopy f g
```

copies file **f** to file **g**. **g** is created if necessary; if it already exists, its contents are overwritten.

How do we create the output file? Since each operating system has a different syntax for this operation, we will assume that the operation of creating a file is done by a primitive function **create**, which you will have to provide in the appropriate form on your machine. Its use is

internal-name = **create**(*external-name, access-mode*)

create and **open** are very similar: the external name is the name that the file is to have in the external world; the internal name is again for use by **getlin** and **putlin**. As with **open**, **create** may well need further information, such as access permissions; we summarize all this in *access-mode.* A **create** of a file that already exists should first remove the old version or truncate it to zero length; this ensures that re-using a file is not a special case. If the file creation fails for any reason, **create** returns **ERR**.

```
# makecopy — copy one file to another
	character iname(NAMESIZE), oname(NAMESIZE)
	integer create, getarg, open
	integer fin, fout

	if (getarg(1, iname, NAMESIZE) == EOF
	  | getarg(2, oname, NAMESIZE) == EOF)
		call error("usage: makecopy input output.")
	fin = open(iname, READ)
	if (fin == ERROR)
		call cant(iname)
	fout = create(oname, WRITE)
	if (fout == ERROR)
		call cant(oname)
	call fcopy(fin, fout)
	call close(fin)
	call close(fout)
	stop
	end
```

Exercise 3-11: Many operating systems offer a "copy" command like **makecopy**. Sometimes if the target file already exists, the command either refuses to proceed, or requests confirmation before destroying the old contents. Is this desirable behavior? What should happen with

```
makecopy f f
```

□

3.8 Putting it All Together: archive

As the final example of this chapter, let us construct a program which requires *all* of the file system primitives we have discussed, and which could profit from a few others not yet mentioned. **archive** is a library maintainer whose purpose is to collect sets of arbitrary files into one big file and to maintain that file as an "archive." This often saves storage space and, more important, gives you a handle by which you can deal with a whole group of related files at once. Files can be extracted from the archive, new ones can be added, old ones can be deleted or replaced by updated versions, and data about the contents can be listed. Thus an archive can provide a library service for other programs like loaders, compilers, and so on.

archive is invoked by the command line

archive *command archname optional filenames*

command is a single-letter command which specifies what operation we want to perform on the archive *archname*. The optional filenames specify individual files that participate in the action. The possible *commands* are

d	delete named members from archive
p	print named members on standard output
t	print table of archive contents
u	update named archive members or add at end
x	extract named files from archive

To make **archive** easy to use, we adopt the rule that if no files are named, the action is done on *all* files in the archive:

```
archive t arch
```

lists the entire table of contents. But if any files are explicitly named, they are the *only* ones that take part in the action. For instance,

```
archive t arch f g
```

lists only information about **f** and **g**. **archive** also provides a warning for each explicitly named file that doesn't exist in the archive. These are services that cost little to implement but add much to the human engineering of the program.

The archive program is a natural for what we like to call "left-corner" construction. The idea is to nibble off a small, manageable corner of the program — a part that does something useful — and make that work. Once it does, more and more pieces are added until the whole thing is done. If care is taken with the original design, later pieces should fit in relatively smoothly. Debugging and testing are easier, for the pieces are only added one at a time. And of course if you decide to scrap the whole thing at some point, you are only scrapping that fraction built so far.

The beauty of left-corner construction is that the program does some part of its job very early in the game. By implementing the most useful functions first, you get an idea of how valuable the program will be before investing any time in the difficult or esoteric services (which often prove to be unnecessary or unwanted anyway). You also ensure that the simpler functions are handled simply, which leads to greater efficiency in the end.

The first function to consider is adding files to an archive. (Creating a new archive can be done by making an empty archive, then adding files to it.) Until we can create and add to an archive, no other operation is very interesting anyway. Thus we come naturally to the question of what the format of an archive file should be. There are at least two possibilities. The first is to have a "dictionary" at the beginning of the archive, which lists the files contained, plus other useful information about them — where they are in the archive, how big they are, when they were archived, and so on. The second method, which we will use, is to distribute this dictionary information throughout the file, one piece per file. Each approach has its advantages and disadvantages; one of the exercises is concerned with making a detailed comparison. Before reading further, you might think about what is likely to be easy and what will be hard for each organization.

As always, the local environment can radically affect the merits of the two organizations, by helping or hindering various operations. Furthermore, any conclusions we draw must take into account how the program is actually used, which often depends on what it does well, which depends in turn on the organization, and so on.

With the centralized dictionary, an operation like listing the table of contents is likely to be faster, because the information is concentrated. This may also allow better error checking, because all the information is available at one time. It also simplifies any task in which the data must be accessed in a different order from the one in which they are stored. On the negative side, however, you really have to be prepared to deal with the dictionary all at once, which can limit the number of members in an archive. With a distributed dictionary, operations on the table of contents will in all probability be slower, unless your system lets you move quickly to any point in a file without reading the intervening data. Even with this facility the time to access a particular file will be longer than with the centralized dictionary, because you have to at least look at dictionary entries until you find the one you want. But this slowdown will be small in comparison to the time required to actually process the file.

After some debate, and having once built a centralized dictionary version, we decided to write **archive** with a distributed dictionary. In retrospect, this seems like a clearer and less complicated organization, with no significant loss of efficiency.

Since we are using a distributed dictionary, each entry in an archive begins with a header, containing as a bare minimum the file name and some reliable way to distinguish a header from the contents of an archive member. The archive looks like this:

```
header for file 1
file 1
header for file 2
file 2
...
```

Given this picture, we can see immediately how to implement some operations. For example, to list the file names, we need merely find the headers and print the relevant parts. Other operations are harder, and depend on what services are provided by the local operating system.

The top level of **archive** is a multi-way branch that calls the routine appropriate for the command. We will show it all, even though at the early stages it need only call those routines currently written.

```
# archive — file maintainer
	character aname(NAMESIZE)
	integer getarg
	integer comand(2)

	if (getarg(1, comand, 2) == EOF
	  | getarg(2, aname, NAMESIZE) == EOF)
		call help
	call getfns
	if (comand(1) == UPD)
		call update(aname)
	else if (comand(1) == TBL)
		call table(aname)
	else if (comand(1) == EXTR | comand(1) == PRINT)
		call extrac(aname, comand(1))
	else if (comand(1) == DEL)
		call delete(aname)
	else
		call help
	stop
	end
```

The extract and print functions are combined in one routine because they will differ only in what file the output is to be sent to. We decided not to use the more readable symbolic constants **UPDATE**, **TABLE**, and so on for the commands, even though they would be more natural, because many computer systems permit letters only in a single case, and there would then be no way to distinguish them from **update** and **table**. We try to avoid these case conflicts in any given program so our programs will move unchanged to such systems.

help is called when **archive** has been used incorrectly. For a program that is easy to describe, the most useful diagnostic is a brief synopsis of how to use it.

```
# help — diagnostic printout
	subroutine help

	call error("usage: archive {dptux} archname [files].")
	return
	end
```

This message is usually enough to remind the user of what to say.

The routine **getfns** fetches the file name arguments from the command line and collects them in an array **fname**; **nfiles** is the number of file arguments. **getfns** also checks the argument list for duplicates and overflow.

```
# getfns — get file names into fname, check for duplicates
        subroutine getfns
        integer equal, getarg
        integer i, j
        include carch

        errcnt = 0
        for (i = 1; i <= MAXFILES; i = i + 1)
                if (getarg(i+2, fname(1, i), NAMESIZE) == EOF)
                        break
        nfiles = i - 1
        if (i > MAXFILES)
                if (getarg(i+2, j, 1) ¬= EOF)
                        call error("too many file names.")
        for (i = 1; i <= nfiles; i = i + 1)
                fstat(i) = NO
        for (i = 1; i < nfiles; i = i + 1)
                for (j = i + 1; j <= nfiles; j = j + 1)
                        if (equal(fname(1, i), fname(1, j)) == YES) {
                                call putlin(fname(1, i), ERROUT)
                                call error(": duplicate file name.")
                                }
        return
        end
```

Since Fortran stores two-dimensional arrays by column instead of by row, we access the ith file name as **fname(1, i)** rather than **fname(i, 1)** so the characters of a name will be contiguous.

A note to PL/I programmers: **fname(1, i)** is a one-dimensional array, in this case a cross-section of the two-dimensional array **fname**. Fortran doesn't know about such matters, so we are obliged to write **fname(1, i)**, which looks like a single element, when in fact we mean the whole ith column. So in PL/I all references in **getfns** of the form **fname(1, i)** must be changed to **fname(*, i)**. This is another of those language difficulties we cannot always avoid (although we try), so we do our best to point them out in advance.

archive is eventually going to print a message about any files which have been named but not seen in the archive. **fstat** is used to record this information: if **fstat(i)** is **NO**, the ith file has not yet been seen in the archive. These variables are needed by several routines, so they are kept in a **common** block **carch**, which is inserted where needed by an **include** statement.

```
common /carch/ fname(NAMESIZE, MAXFILES), fstat(MAXFILES), nfiles, errcnt
   character fname          # file arguments
   integer fstat            # YES if touched, NO otherwise; init = NO
   integer nfiles           # number of file args
   integer errcnt           # error count; init = 0
```

errcnt is used to count errors; it is used by several routines, and is thus best kept in **common** as well.

Notice that the main routine of **archive** does not know about this **common** block, because it doesn't have to. Fortran **common** is a convenient way to deal with a group of related variables, but it is also dangerous since it is less disciplined than passing arguments, and can make it hard to determine what routines are using what variables. In a language with more powerful data structure facilities than Fortran, an alternative is to put a group of related variables in a *structure,* and pass that as a single argument to routines that need access. We don't avoid Fortran **common** or PL/I **external** variables, but we are careful to restrict usage as much as possible to those routines that "need to know." (In some implementations of Fortran, the main routine may need to contain **carch** anyway.)

The line

```
call putlin(fname(1, i), ERROUT)
```

is the first explicit mention of the file **ERROUT**, which is used for diagnostics. We assume it is automatically assigned, like **STDIN** and **STDOUT**, when the program is started. By definition **error** and **remark** write on **ERROUT**. Although **ERROUT** might be synonymous with **STDOUT**, generally it should be distinct; this way informative but not disastrous messages can appear without cluttering up the main output of a program, or disappearing down a pipeline.

Updating an archive breaks cleanly into two stages: replacing existing members with new versions, and adding to the end any files named as arguments but not present in the archive. We assume that the only way to add data to the end of a file is to copy the existing information to a new file, add the new data to the end of that, then copy the whole thing back to the original. Even though some systems allow you to add at the end or rewrite in the middle of a file, it is unwise to do so. It is safer not to alter an existing archive until you're sure that the replacement is complete and correct.

The process of updating can be summarized as

```
open archive (create if new)
create temporary file
update existing archive contents onto temporary
for each new file {
        create header and copy to temporary
        copy file to temporary
        }
if no errors
        move temporary back to archive
```

These operations are controlled by **update**.

```
# update — update existing files, add new ones at end
	subroutine update(aname)
	character aname(NAMESIZE)
	integer create, getarg, open
	integer afd, i, tfd
	include carch
	string tname "archtemp"

	afd = open(aname, READWRITE)
	if (afd == ERR)			# maybe it's a new one
		afd = create(aname, READWRITE)
	if (afd == ERR)
		call cant(aname)
	tfd = create(tname, READWRITE)
	if (tfd == ERR)
		call cant(tname)
	call replac(afd, tfd, UPD, errcnt)		# update existing
	for (i = 1; i <= nfiles; i = i + 1)		# add new ones
		if (fstat(i) == NO) {
			call addfil(fname(1, i), tfd, errcnt)
			fstat(i) = YES
			}
	call close(afd)
	call close(tfd)
	if (errcnt == 0)
		call amove(tname, aname)
	else
		call remark("fatal errors — archive not altered.")
	call remove(tname)
	return
	end
```

update first tries to open the archive; if this fails it tries to create it, under the assumption that it must be a new archive. Only if both operations fail does **update** give up.

archive is designed to identify as many errors as possible per run. **update** processes all the files in the argument list, even though it may have encountered an error trying to open one of them. **errcnt** counts the errors; the archive is updated only if **errcnt** is zero at the end of the run. **replac** copies an archive onto the temporary, updating any files specified. **addfil** adds a single file to the end of the temporary if it can. (We will return to **replac** and **addfil** shortly.) **remove** is the complement of **create**, a primitive for removing a file forever.

amove moves the information from the temporary back onto the archive file if no errors have occurred. In the worst case, this has to be done by physically removing the old archive, creating a new one, then copying the temporary back onto it, like this:

```
# amove - move name1 to name2
      subroutine amove(name1, name2)
      character name1(ARB), name2(ARB)
      integer create, open
      integer fd1, fd2

      fd1 = open(name1, READ)
      if (fd1 == ERR)
            call cant(name1)
      fd2 = create(name2, WRITE)
      if (fd2 == ERR)
            call cant(name2)
      call fcopy(fd1, fd2)
      return
      end
```

In a different environment, you might be able merely to *rename* the temporary to be the new archive. This is a useful primitive to have available, for it is clearly more efficient than physically copying the entire file, and it also minimizes the length of time during which the permanent copy of the archive is in an incomplete state. We use "move" for any file transfer that could be effected by renaming, and "copy" only when we explicitly want the source to remain unaltered.

Let us deal with **addfil** next, since it is relatively self-contained.

```
# addfil - add file "name" to archive
      subroutine addfil(name, fd, errcnt)
      character head(MAXLINE), name(ARB)
      integer open
      integer errcnt, fd, nfd

      nfd = open(name, READ)
      if (nfd == ERR) {
            call putlin(name, ERROUT)
            call remark(": can't add.")
            errcnt = errcnt + 1
            }
      if (errcnt == 0) {
            call makhdr(name, head)
            call putlin(head, fd)
            call fcopy(nfd, fd)
            call close(nfd)
            }
      return
      end
```

makhdr makes the uniquely identifiable header record that precedes each archived file. For testing, any printable string is quite adequate. We use **-h-**, followed by a blank and the filename. For ultimate use, you will probably want to add at least the date and time the file was archived.

Further contents depend on the local system. The main consideration is to eliminate any possibility of confusing a header with the contents of an archive member. If it is easy and fast to find out the size of a file in convenient units, such as the number of characters or the number of records, the header can contain the file size as one of its entries, and there is no difficulty in deciding what is a header and what is text inside an archive. Our version of **makhdr** includes a character count in the header, separated from the file name by a blank.

```
# makhdr — make header line for archive member
      subroutine makhdr(name, head)
      character head(MAXLINE), name(NAMESIZE)
      integer fsize, itoc, length
      integer i
      string hdr "-h-"

      call scopy(hdr, 1, head, 1)
      i = length(hdr) + 1
      head(i) = BLANK
      call scopy(name, 1, head, i+1)
      i = length(head) + 1
      head(i) = BLANK
      i = i + 1 + itoc(fsize(name), head(i+1), MAXCHARS)
      head(i) = NEWLINE
      head(i+1) = EOS
      return
      end
```

makhdr uses **length** and **itoc**, which we wrote in Chapter 2. **scopy** is a basic string copying routine:

```
scopy(from, i, to, j)
```

copies the (sub)string of **from** that starts at **i** to **to(j)**.

```
# scopy — copy string at from(i) to to(j)
      subroutine scopy(from, i, to, j)
      character from(ARB), to(ARB)
      integer i, j, k1, k2

      k2 = j
      for (k1 = i; from(k1) ¬= EOS; k1 = k1 + 1) {
            to(k2) = from(k1)
            k2 = k2 + 1
            }
      to(k2) = EOS
      return
      end
```

The function **fsize** returns the size of a file in characters. Ideally this will be a primitive, a service of the local file system. The less favorable (but common) case is that you can only find out how big a file is by reading through it. Although this is costly, if you extract contents more than you replace them you can endure the extra overhead even with double reading. Remember, **archive** reads and writes the *entire* archive twice to update it; the incremental cost of reading a few of the members one more time is small in comparison.

```
# fsize - size of file in characters
	integer function fsize(name)
	character getch
	character c, name(ARB)
	integer open
	integer fd

	fd = open(name, READ)
	if (fd == ERR)
		fsize = ERR
	else {
		for (fsize = 0; getch(c, fd) ¬= EOF; fsize = fsize + 1)
			;
		call close(fd)
		}
	return
	end
```

fsize reads single characters from the file with **getch**, which is directly analogous to **getc**, except that it uses an explicit file instead of the standard input **STDIN**. Thus **getc(c)** is identical to **getch(c, STDIN)**, and in fact **getc** might well be implemented as a call to **getch**.

Exercise 3-12: How would you test the part of **archive** built so far? What are some critical boundaries? □

Exercise 3-13: **fsize** opens the file anew, even though it has already been opened by **addfil**. Does this work on your system? Should it? If it doesn't, how would you rewrite **fsize** to get around the problem? What primitive operations are needed? □

Exercise 3-14: The subroutine **update** tries to copy a file that has been created but which has never had anything written on it. What is a reasonable behavior in this case? What happens on your system? What primitive should deal with the situation if the system does something unreasonable? □

3.9 More Archive Commands

Now that we can create an archive and put files in it (and presumably have carefully tested that much), can we print the table of contents? That seems to be the next easiest function to add in a left-corner approach. Recall that **archive** is to list the files named as arguments, or all the files if there are no file arguments.

The table of contents operation is basically this:

```
open archive
for each file in archive {
        if (header matches any argument)
                print header information
        skip over archived file
        }
warn about any that couldn't be found
```

This is done by **table**:

```
# table — print table of archive contents
        subroutine table(aname)
        character aname(NAMESIZE), in(MAXLINE), lname(NAMESIZE)
        integer filarg, gethdr, open
        integer afd, size

        afd = open(aname, READ)
        if (afd == ERR)
                call cant(aname)
        while (gethdr(afd, in, lname, size) ¬= EOF) {
                if (filarg(lname) == YES)
                        call tprint(in)
                call fskip(afd, size)
                }
        call notfnd
        return
        end
```

table opens the archive for reading only, so you can read an archive that you might not have permission to alter.

tprint prints the desired information from the header; our dummy version prints the entire header line, which is just what we need for testing the program.

```
# tprint — print table entry for one member
        subroutine tprint(buf)
        character buf(ARB)

        call putlin(buf, STDOUT)
        return
        end
```

gethdr tests whether the next input is a header; if so, it returns the header, the file name and the size. If **gethdr** fails to see an archive header immediately, something has gone awry: either the file in question is not an archive or its contents have been corrupted. In any case, **archive** can proceed no further, so **gethdr** exits with an error message.

```
# gethdr - get header info from fd
      integer function gethdr(fd, buf, name, size)
      character buf(MAXLINE), c, name(NAMESIZE), temp(NAMESIZE)
      integer ctoi, equal, getlin, getwrd
      integer fd, i, len, size
      string hdr "-h-"

      if (getlin(buf, fd) == EOF) {
            gethdr = EOF
            return
            }
      i = 1
      len = getwrd(buf, i, temp)
      if (equal(temp, hdr) == NO)
            call error("archive not in proper format.")
      gethdr = YES
      len = getwrd(buf, i, name)
      size = ctoi(buf, i)
      return
      end
```

gethdr uses **getwrd**, which we wrote for **include**, and **equal**, which we wrote for **compare**, rather than inventing new routines for the same job. And it uses **ctoi** to convert the size as a character string into a number. We are beginning to accumulate a nice library of small utility functions.

makhdr and **gethdr** are independent of the specific header chosen; if you don't care for **-h-**, the literal string is all that need be changed to install a new one.

fskip uses the size returned by **gethdr** to skip over the archived file; if all is consistent, this should leave the file positioned at a new header for the next call of **gethdr**. In a congenial system **fskip** will be a primitive that skips without reading the intervening data. For use in more hostile environments, here is a version that reads the right number of characters:

```
# fskip - skip n characters on file fd
      subroutine fskip(fd, n)
      character getch
      character c
      integer fd, i, n

      for (i = 1; i <= n; i = i + 1)
            if (getch(c, fd) == EOF)
                  break
      return
      end
```

filarg tests whether the file name from the archive matches any of the file names in the argument list, using **equal** to do the string comparison. If there are no file arguments, **filarg** also considers that to be a match.

```
# filarg — check if name matches argument list
      integer function filarg(name)
      character name(ARB)
      integer equal, getarg
      integer i
      include carch

      if (nfiles <= 0) {
            filarg = YES
            return
            }
      for (i = 1; i <= nfiles; i = i + 1)
            if (equal(name, fname(1, i)) == YES) {
                  fstat(i) = YES
                  filarg = YES
                  return
                  }
      filarg = NO
      return
      end
```

fstat(i) records whether the ith named file argument has ever been "found." Initially **NO** for all arguments, the corresponding position is set to **YES** if **filarg** finds a match. This list is used by **notfnd** to print names which were arguments but not in the archive.

```
# notfnd — print "not found" message
      subroutine notfnd
      integer i
      include carch

      for (i = 1; i <= nfiles; i = i + 1)
            if (fstat(i) == NO) {
                  call putlin(fname(1, i), ERROUT)
                  call remark(": not in archive.")
                  errcnt = errcnt + 1
                  }
      return
      end
```

It also sets the error count, but that isn't used by **table**, since it hardly matters when we are not attempting to alter the archive.

The next step in the incremental construction is *extracting* — to get the information back out of the archive once we put it in. The logic is clear enough:

```
open archive
for each file in archive
        if (it's to be extracted) {
                create file
                copy from archive to file
                }
warn about any that couldn't be extracted
```

We also allow archive contents to be collected on the standard output instead of in files. The p command lets you list members, or extract them with different names from those they were stored with. For example,

```
archive p arch file1 >file2
```

extracts file1 into file2. Of course to permit this usage, the program must avoid verbiage like

```
successful extraction
1 files extracted
contents of file1:
```

and so on. This is partly good practice for a tool-using environment, where gratuitous comments interfere with the smooth interconnection of programs, and partly good design for people, who soon get weary of programs that talk too much.

```
# extrac - extract files from archive
      subroutine extrac(aname, cmd)
      character aname(NAMESIZE), ename(NAMESIZE), in(MAXLINE)
      integer create, filarg, gethdr, open
      integer afd, cmd, efd, size
      include carch

      afd = open(aname, READ)
      if (afd == ERR)
            call cant(aname)
      if (cmd == PRINT)
            efd = STDOUT
      else
            efd = ERR
      while (gethdr(afd, in, ename, size) ¬= EOF)
            if (filarg(ename) == NO)
                  call fskip(afd, size)
            else {
                  if (efd ¬= STDOUT)
                        efd = create(ename, WRITE)
                  if (efd == ERR) {
                        call putlin(ename, ERROUT)
                        call remark(": can't create.")
                        errcnt = errcnt + 1
                        call fskip(afd, size)
                        }
                  else {
                        call acopy(afd, efd, size)
                        if (efd ¬= STDOUT)
                              call close(efd)
                        }
                  }
      call notfnd
      return
      end
```

Again, most of the complexity is in error detection and recovery, not in the operation itself.

acopy copies a member of an archive onto a file, using the size information from the header, instead of looking for the next header. (The test for **EOF** is a safety measure.) That way it can be used to copy any kind of information at all — it is completely independent of the content of the archived files.

```
# acopy — copy size characters from fdi to fdo
      subroutine acopy(fdi, fdo, size)
      character getch
      character c
      integer fdi, fdo, i, size

      for (i = 1; i <= size; i = i + 1) {
            if (getch(c, fdi) == EOF)
                  break
            call putch(c, fdo)
            }
      return
      end
```

putch is the complement of **getch**; it puts characters on a given file.

Deleting is identical to updating except that no file replaces a deleted file; we can use **replac** for both the **u** and **d** commands.

```
# delete — delete files from archive
      subroutine delete(aname)
      character aname(NAMESIZE), in(MAXLINE)
      integer create, open
      integer afd, tfd
      include carch
      string tname "archtemp"

      if (nfiles <= 0)      # protect innocents
            call error("delete by name only.")
      afd = open(aname, READWRITE)
      if (afd == ERR)
            call cant(aname)
      tfd = create(tname, READWRITE)
      if (tfd == ERR)
            call cant(tname)
      call replac(afd, tfd, DEL, errcnt)
      call notfnd
      call close(afd)
      call close(tfd)
      if (errcnt == 0)
            call amove(tname, aname)
      else
            call remark("fatal errors — archive not altered.")
      call remove(tname)
      return
      end
```

We have made the command

```
archive d archname
```

illegal — it does *not* delete all the files from the archive. If you really want to do that, you have to remove them explicitly. It is a small refinement, but it makes the program safer.

Finally, here is **replac**.

```
# replac — replace or delete files
      subroutine replac(afd, tfd, cmd, errcnt)
      character in(MAXLINE), uname(NAMESIZE)
      integer filarg, gethdr
      integer afd, cmd, errcnt, size, tfd

      while (gethdr(afd, in, uname, size) ¬= EOF)
            if (filarg(uname) == YES) {
                  if (cmd == UPD)    # add new one
                        call addfil(uname, tfd, errcnt)
                  call fskip(afd, size)  # discard old one
                  }
            else {
                  call putlin(in, tfd)
                  call acopy(afd, tfd, size)
                  }
      return
      end
```

replac uses **addfil** to copy the new version of a file to the temporary, **fskip** to skip over the archived version, and **acopy** to copy members that are unchanged.

By now it may have struck you that about half the code in **archive** is concerned with error-checking. Many programs can afford to be somewhat cavalier about protecting users from the operating system and their own innocence, because even if the program is badly used, the results aren't likely to be calamitous. But error handling is particularly important for a program like **archive**, because it *changes* files rather than simply making new ones. It overwrites existing files with supposedly correct new contents, so it had better be cautious. For example, it may seem paranoid to abort an entire updating operation merely because one of the files couldn't be accessed. But safety first! It's better to have to run it again than to risk destroying an archive.

3.10 Program Structure

At this point you may well be lost, not because **archive** is a complicated program but because there are an awful lot of pieces. Many of the pieces are old friends, however. These include the file maintenance primitives **open**, **create**, **close** and **remove**; the input and output primitives **getlin**, **getarg** and **putlin**; the error printers **cant**, **error**, and **remark**; and utilities like **ctoi**, **itoc**, **length**, **scopy**, **equal** and **getwrd**. You should learn to think of these low level assistants as *language extensions*, facilities that help you express common operations succinctly, and without distracting you from the real task at hand.

The remaining complexity can be grasped by writing out the *hierarchy* of subroutines written specifically for **archive**. This tells you how the program is organized by showing what routines call on what others to do the job. It turns out that the hierarchical structure of a program changes much less from its earliest design than does the code, so a program hierarchy is a useful document to supplement the actual program listing — unlike flowcharts, which merely echo the code and quickly get out of phase with it as changes are made. Some people even draw "structure charts" showing the hierarchy of calls and the arguments passed and returned on each call.

For **archive** we can write the hierarchy as

```
archive
        help
        getfns
        update
                replac
                        gethdr, filarg, fskip, addfil, acopy
                addfil
                        makhdr, fcopy
                amove
        table
                gethdr, filarg, fskip, notfnd, tprint
        extrac
                gethdr, filarg, fskip, notfnd, acopy
        delete
                replac, notfnd, amove
```

This says that **archive** makes calls on **help**, **getfns**, **update**, **table**, **extrac** and **delete** (in addition to various low level routines mentioned above) to do its job. **update** in turn calls **replac**, **addfil**, and **amove**; **replace** and **addfil** call still other routines; and so on. We list some of the sets horizontally, separated by commas, instead of vertically, to save space. We also don't bother to show an expansion more than once (note the instance of **replac** in the last line), for much the same reason that we leave out all the low level routines: it just adds clutter. We will frequently present hierarchies for the larger programs, to help you keep track of the organization.

The hierarchy reveals several things. First, the overall structure of **archive** is clearly just a **case** statement, making a call on one of the four cases **update**, **table**, **extrac** or **delete**. Each case is expanded in terms of a handful of *action* routines. **gethdr**, **filarg**, etc., play a role similar to **open**, **getlin**, and the other primitives — they permit the basic functions that must be performed to be expressed at a more abstract (and readable) level, as well as insulating **archive** from low level implementation decisions. At each level the lower routines are used as building blocks that perform some function, with relatively little dependence on *how* they perform it.

Notice that no one routine must know about more than half a dozen immediate subordinates. It is a good rule of thumb that a person can't properly keep track of more than about seven things at a time, so this hierarchy gives some reassurance that no part of the design will be too difficult to grasp. Finally, it is worth observing that operations as diverse as **update**, **table**, and **delete** make use of essentially the same action routines in different sequences. This is the reward of orderly design, that common operations can be identified and singled out as basic actions. Programs built this way are easier to get right and to maintain, because the strategy for each case (**update**, **table**, etc.) and the details of each action (**gethdr**, **filarg**, etc.)

can all be dealt with separately.

Exercise 3-15: Now that you have seen **archive** with a distributed dictionary, design and implement a version with the dictionary at the beginning. Compare the advantages and disadvantages. Observations about "efficiency" should be supported by empirical studies of the operations people really perform on an archive. □

Exercise 3-16: **archive** could be simpler and faster if the operating system provided certain primitive operations. We mentioned renaming the temporary instead of copying, knowing how big a file is without having to read it, moving to an arbitrary point in a file without reading intervening material, and selectively overwriting parts of a file. Consider these and other primitives that might be useful. Do they exist in your system? Could they? How do these primitives affect the dictionary-at-the-front version? □

Exercise 3-17: In most systems, an archive program saves space because it collects small files into one big one; this eliminates the breakage or fragmentation that normally comes from putting each file into an integral number of blocks or tracks on some secondary storage device. Theoretically, what is this saving? Measure and see if the theoretical prediction is observed in practice. □

Exercise 3-18: **archive** produces no warning about

```
archive u arch
```

Should it? If you could find out the date and time a file was last changed, what would be a useful interpretation for this command? Should there be separate commands for creating a new archive and updating an existing one? Should there be a warning that a new archive is being created? □

Exercise 3-19: If you work in an interactive environment, add a "verbose" option, so **archive** will print out messages about what it is doing as it runs, and offer you the choice on each file of having the command operate or not operate. □

Exercise 3-20: How can you add a file **f** to an archive that already contains an **f**? Should multiple occurrences be allowed in an archive? If you concatenate two archives with **concat**, is the result a valid archive? □

Exercise 3-21: **archive** provides no way to specify the position of a file added to an archive. Does it need one? What syntax would you use? Implement it. □

Exercise 3-22: Our archive files are always made as small as possible, by recreating them when they change. Some systems provide programs rather like our **archive** that don't reclaim space unless explicitly requested. Discuss the merits and demerits of such an organization. □

3.11 Summary

This chapter has discussed how programs interface to their environment, particularly how they access file information. Few systems are regular and systematic in the interface they present, and of course there are great differences between systems. We have tried to write the discussion and the programs in terms of a handful of primitive operations that are likely to exist or at least be implementable on most operating systems. Describing system interactions exclusively with such primitives is the most effective approach we know of for coping with the bewildering complexity of typical operating systems.

The file system primitives we use are:

open Connect the external name of an information stream (a "file") to an internal name which is then usable by the program. Position the file at the beginning. This operation is traditionally available by control card on most systems. Extremely useful but less often available is the ability to open a file by its external name from within a running program. Opening a fresh instance of an already open file should be permissible.

create Create a new file, preferably by name, from within a running program. If the file already exists, the old version should be removed or truncated and overwritten. **create** is a crucial primitive, but the least likely to be available. Even major modern operating systems still do not provide it.

close Break the connection made by **open** or **create**. Mark the end of the file if necessary, so that subsequent reads will find an **EOF**.

remove Remove a file from the file system.

We assume that when a program is started by the operating system it already has the three files **STDIN**, **STDOUT** and **ERROUT** open and ready to go. We presume that when a program terminates for any reason, any open files are closed gracefully. We have also assumed that a file is made the right size by the system — if you write more information on it, it gets bigger automatically. It seems intuitively obvious that a file should be as big as it is, and that it should get bigger as you put more into it, but on all too many systems you have to arrange this yourself, clumsily.

One mark of a good operating system is that all of these operations are available, uniform, easy to use, and applicable without major exception to all files from all programs. You might find it an enlightening experience to read some of the manuals for your operating system and see how well it does by these criteria.

Bibliographic Notes

The problem of file comparison has not been fully solved, but various forms of it are attacked by algorithms conceived by M. L. Fredman and others. These algorithms compute a minimum set of changes necessary to convert one n-line file into another, in time $n^2 \log n$ worst case, but typically *much* better, often linear in the file size. The basic procedure itself is not too difficult, but it requires considerable help from the local operating system in order to handle lines of *a priori* unknown length without wasting great amounts of storage. For more information, see M. D. McIlroy and J. W. Hunt, "An algorithm for differential file comparison," Bell Labs Computing Science Technical Report 40, 1976.

Although there is a substantial literature on the implementation of file systems, relatively little is concerned with the programmer interface. The model for most of our I/O primitives has been the UNIX operating system, which seems to provide an exceptionally clean set. See "The UNIX time-sharing system," by K. L. Thompson and D. M. Ritchie, *CACM,* July, 1974.

Structure charts are described in W. P. Stevens, G. J. Myers and L. L. Constantine, "Structured design," *IBM Systems Journal,* April, 1974.

CHAPTER 4

SORTING

Sorting is an everyday programming task, and often a building block in larger processes. In this chapter we will tackle sorting, but we will be more concerned with the human interface of a sort program than with presenting some "best possible" sorting algorithm. If a sorting program is so poorly packaged that people feel compelled to write their own instead of figuring out how to use it, then the quality of its sorting algorithm is surely irrelevant. But if the packaging is good, if users perceive sorting as a convenient *tool,* then it will be used, the algorithm can be improved as needed; and *all* users will benefit.

4.1 Bubble Sort

Every programmer is familiar with some variant of the interchange sort. For example the *bubble sort* sorts an array into ascending order like this:

```
# bubble — bubble sort v(1) ... v(n) increasing
	subroutine bubble(v, n)
	integer i, j, k, n, v(n)

	for (i = n; i > 1; i = i − 1)
		for (j = 1; j < i; j = j + 1)
			if (v(j) > v(j+1)) {		# compare
				k = v(j)		# exchange
				v(j) = v(j+1)		#
				v(j+1) = k		#
				}
	return
	end
```

The inner loop rearranges out-of-order adjacent elements on each pass; by the end of the pass, the largest element has been "bubbled" to the top, that is, to v(i). The outer loop repeats the process, each time decreasing the current array limit i by one.

The main advantage of the bubble sort is its simplicity. Its drawback, a serious one, is that it gets very slow very fast as the number of elements to be sorted gets large. The *time complexity* of bubble sorting (and similar sorts) is n^2. That is, the time required to sort varies as the square of the number of items to be sorted: twice as big takes about four times as long. How large is too large? That depends on the alternative being considered, and on how often the data is to be sorted, but something between ten and fifty items might be a reasonable limit, above which the bubble sort is better replaced by a more sophisticated algorithm.

In real life, by the way, you would certainly name the routine **sort**, not **bubble**, so you could change the algorithm without upsetting users. We use **bubble** here because we want a unique name for each program.

4.2 Shell Sort

In a sense, the Shell sort is the next step up in complexity from the bubble sort; we present it because it is similar in spirit, compact, but much faster for larger arrays. The time complexity of the Shell sort is approximately $n^{1.5}$.

The basic idea of the Shell sort is that in the early stages far-apart elements are compared, instead of adjacent ones. This tends to eliminate large amounts of disorder quickly, so later stages have less work to do. Gradually the interval between compared elements is decreased, until it reaches one, at which point it effectively becomes an adjacent interchange method.

```
# shell - Shell sort v(1)...v(n) increasing
      subroutine shell(v, n)
      integer gap, i, j, jg, k, n, v(n)

      for (gap = n/2; gap > 0; gap = gap/2)
            for (i = gap + 1; i <= n; i = i + 1)
                  for (j = i - gap; j > 0; j = j - gap) {
                        jg = j + gap
                        if (v(j) <= v(jg))      # compare
                              break
                        k = v(j)                # exchange
                        v(j) = v(jg)            #
                        v(jg) = k               #
                        }
      return
      end
```

The outermost loop controls the gap between compared elements. Initially **n/2**, it shrinks by a factor of two each pass until it becomes zero. The middle loop compares elements separated by **gap**; the innermost loop reverses any that are out of order. Since **gap** is eventually reduced to one, eventually all elements are ordered correctly.

A word on modularity. Many sorting procedures have three distinct parts. A *comparison* operation decides what the order of two elements is. An *exchange* operation interchanges two out-of-order elements. Finally, a *sorting algorithm* decides what comparisons and exchanges must be made. Often the only thing that need change between two sorting procedures is the algorithm, so a program should be carefully organized to take this into account. If the three aspects are clearly separated, each may be individually improved without affecting the others.

Exercise 4-1: How would you test a sorting program? What are the obvious boundary conditions that must be checked to ensure correct operation? What programs would you write to help in your verification? What programs have we already written that help? □

Exercise 4-2: Compare the bubble sort and the Shell sort experimentally. Where is the crossover point at which the Shell sort becomes better on your machine? □

Exercise 4-3: In our version of the Shell sort, when two out-of-order elements are found they are immediately exchanged. If an element is small relative to the other elements at the current gap, however, several unnecessary exchanges may be performed. Redistribute the exchange so the element moving toward the beginning of the array is held in a temporary location until its correct position has been found. Measure this version to decide if the increase in speed outweighs the loss of clarity in the algorithm. □

Exercise 4-4: The Shell sort has been observed to run somewhat faster when the value of **gap** is always odd. Modify **shell** accordingly and experiment to see how large the effect is. □

4.3 Sorting Text

Since many of the tools we discuss in this book are for manipulating text, it is useful to adapt our sorting procedure for this kind of operation too. One especially useful form is a program that sorts a text file line by line into increasing lexicographic order. As we shall soon see, this operation is useful in its own right, and also as a part of other processes.

There are two major considerations in the design — convenience and efficiency. **sort** should be dead easy to use, requiring no setup at all for common sorting tasks. At the same time it should be reasonably effective (i.e., cheap) on both small files and on moderately big ones. **sort** is not intended to replace a carefully tailored sort for a repeated production application, but it should be a tool that is convenient and economical over a wide spectrum of input file sizes — one which will encourage a casual user to select it as a matter of course. The first draft will be a program which sorts a set of lines that fits into memory all at once. Later we will expand it to handle files too big to be stored completely in memory.

We will write the sorting program to read its standard input and write its standard output, so it can be used as a filter. Of course **sort** can't produce any output until all of the input has been read (why?), so calling it a filter may seem to be stretching a point, but that is not important. What is important is that as far as the user is concerned, the program *looks like* a filter, so it can be used in a pipeline. Later on we shall see how this organization makes sorting a flexible tool.

The subroutines presented earlier in this chapter sorted arrays of integers; here we want to treat lines of text. Unfortunately lines are not all of the same length and typically they are much longer than a single integer, so they cannot be moved or compared directly, at least not in Fortran. What data representation will cope efficiently and conveniently with variable length lines?

One solution is to refer to the lines *indirectly,* by pointers. An array **linbuf** holds the lines to be sorted, packed end to end. A second array, **linptr**, contains indices which indicate where the corresponding lines begin in **linbuf**. That is,

linptr(i) is the index in **linbuf** of the beginning of the ith line. When an exchange is called for, the *pointers* are exchanged, not the text lines themselves. This eliminates the twin problems of complicated storage management and high overhead that would be part of moving the lines themselves.

The in-memory **sort** is:

```
# sort — sort text lines in memory
	character linbuf(MAXTEXT)
	integer gtext
	integer linptr(MAXPTR), nlines

	if (gtext(linptr, nlines, linbuf, STDIN) == EOF) {
		call shell(linptr, nlines, linbuf)
		call ptext(linptr, nlines, linbuf, STDOUT)
		}
	else
		call error("too big to sort.")
	stop
	end
```

It calls a modified version of **shell**, which we will show in a moment, that moves the pointers in **linptr**, not the lines themselves. **gtext** reads the lines and sets up the pointers; **ptext** uses the pointers to output the lines in sorted order.

gtext returns **EOF** if end of file was encountered during input; it is used here only to provide some error checking. **linptr(i)** is set to the index of the first character of the ith line. **MAXLINE** is the length of the longest line we are willing to deal with and **MAXPTR** the maximum number of lines.

```
# gtext — get text lines into linbuf
	integer function gtext(linptr, nlines, linbuf, infile)
	character linbuf(MAXTEXT)
	integer getlin
	integer infile, lbp, len, linptr(MAXPTR), nlines

	nlines = 0
	lbp = 1
	repeat {
		len = getlin(linbuf(lbp), infile)
		if (len == EOF)
			break
		nlines = nlines + 1
		linptr(nlines) = lbp
		lbp = lbp + len + 1		# "1" = room for EOS
		} until (lbp >= MAXTEXT-MAXLINE | nlines >= MAXPTR)
	gtext = len
	return
	end
```

```
# ptext — output text lines from linbuf
      subroutine ptext(linptr, nlines, linbuf, outfil)
      character linbuf(ARB)
      integer i, j, linptr(MAXPTR), nlines, outfil

      for (i = 1; i <= nlines; i = i + 1) {
            j = linptr(i)
            call putlin(linbuf(j), outfil)
            }
      return
      end
```

Once again there are problems in translating this code to PL/I or some other languages, because of the way Fortran deals with portions of an array. The subscripted references to **linbuf** are used by the called routines as starting points for subarrays that happen to be imbedded in **linbuf**, not as single array elements. There are more suitable ways of allocating storage and pointers in PL/I, but if you just want to replicate this code, the changes are few. First, declare an array of characters **line**, then change the subscripted **linbuf** references from **linbuf(i)** to **addr(linbuf(i))−>line**. PL/I may be wordier here, but it does avoid the Fortran problem of an array reference that looks like a scalar.

Of course we can write and test **gtext** and **ptext** independently of whatever sorting procedure we use. In fact there need not even be a sort: a dummy **shell** that returns without doing anything is enough for verifying that **gtext** indeed builds arrays that **ptext** can interpret properly. This is a typical example of incremental construction and testing. It's easier to test a program whose pieces implement separate functions and interact only through clear, well-defined interfaces than it is to cope with a single routine of tightly interwoven code.

Our sort must also be modified to treat comparison and exchange as subroutines. Here is the Shell sort.

```
# shell — Shell sort for character lines
      subroutine shell(linptr, nlines, linbuf)
      character linbuf(ARB)
      integer compar
      integer gap, i, ig, j, k, linptr(ARB), nlines

      for (gap = nlines/2; gap > 0; gap = gap/2)
            for (j = gap + 1; j <= nlines; j = j + 1)
                  for (i = j - gap; i > 0; i = i - gap) {
                        ig = i + gap
                        if (compar(linptr(i), linptr(ig), linbuf) <= 0)
                              break
                        call exchan(linptr(i), linptr(ig), linbuf)
                        }
      return
      end
```

The exchange operation is the easier part: **exchan** only needs to exchange the two pointers but it is also passed **linbuf** to avoid having to change the calling sequence for more general applications.

```
# exchan — exchange linbuf(lp1) with linbuf(lp2)
      subroutine exchan(lp1, lp2, linbuf)
      character linbuf(ARB)
      integer k, lp1, lp2

      k = lp1
      lp1 = lp2
      lp2 = k
      return
      end
```

compar returns a negative value if its first argument is less than its second, zero if its arguments are equal, and a positive value if the first is greater than the second. How do we handle comparisons? The main difficulty is the perennial problem of the character set being used. In Fortran, at least, there is typically no guarantee that the letter 'a', as entered with a **read** statement, will compare less than the letter 'z'. (On many machines it won't!) In PL/I, the problem should not arise with letters stored as **character** variables — 'a' *is* less than 'z' — but there may well be punctuation characters *within* the alphabet. (And PL/I **character** variables may not have enough bits to hold extra codes like **EOS**.) The whole topic is a can of worms!

One solution is to provide a two-argument routine **lexord**, which returns the lexical ordering that holds between any pair of characters:

```
lexord(c1, c2)
```

returns **−1** if **c1<c2**, zero if **c1==c2**, and **+1** if **c1>c2**. **compar** could then call **lexord** when it needs to know the relationship between two characters. Of course it typically only has to call **lexord** once per call of **compar** (why?), so this organization is not as expensive as you might think at first.

A second solution is to tune **compar** for a particular environment, as we will do here. Each character is mapped into its correct place in the ordering immediately upon input. All subsequent comparisons may be made directly. The characters are mapped back into external representation before final output. This is a compromise between efficiency and portability. In fact, if the character set is truly disorderly, it's the cheapest organization. It's better to map the characters once on input and once on output rather than every time they must be compared. Here is a version of **compar** which is appropriate if letters and numbers each sort in increasing order.

```
# compar — compare linbuf(lp1) with linbuf(lp2)
	integer function compar(lp1, lp2, linbuf)
	character linbuf(ARB)
	integer i, j, lp1, lp2

	i = lp1
	j = lp2
	while (linbuf(i) == linbuf(j)) {
		if (linbuf(i) == EOS) {
			compar = 0
			return
			}
		i = i + 1
		j = j + 1
		}
	if (linbuf(i) < linbuf(j))
		compar = -1
	else
		compar = +1
	return
	end
```

The subroutine organization in **sort** is such that a knowledgable user could provide private versions of **compar** and **exchan** for special applications, while still deriving the benefit of whatever sophistication has gone into the sorting algorithm. It is even possible to use this code directly for sorting integers: if **compar** ignores **linbuf**, everything works.

Exercise 4-5: The sorting program has a fair amount of overhead in the inner loop. Experiment with moving the comparison and exchange into **shell**. How much improvement does this make? Make some reasonable assumptions about how often **sort** will be used and how big the files will be, then decide if it should be changed. □

Exercise 4-6: Add an option to **sort** to allow the direction of sorting to be reversed:

```
sort -r
```

sorts into decreasing order instead of ascending. Where should the direction-changing code go — in **compar**, in **shell**, in **ptext**, or somewhere else? □

4.4 Quicksort

One of the best sorting methods known is *quicksort*, developed originally by C. A. R. Hoare. Although in the worst case its running time can be proportional to n^2, quicksort can be arranged so the worst case rarely occurs, and its average running time is $n \log n$.

Quicksort is best described as a recursive procedure. The essential idea is to partition the original set to be sorted by rearranging it into two groups — all those elements less than some arbitrary value chosen from the set, and all those greater than or equal to the value. Then the same partitioning process is applied to the two subsets in turn until each subset contains only one element. When all subsets have been partitioned, the original set is sorted.

```
subroutine quick(v, i, j)

if (i >= j)
        return
partition the elements v(i) ... v(j) so that
        v(i), v(i+1) ... v(k-1) ≤ v(k) ≤ v(k+1) ... v(j)
                where i ≤ k ≤ j
call quick(v, i, k-1)
call quick(v, k+1, j)
return
end
```

To sort an array v, you just say

```
call quick(v, 1, n)
```

and stand well back. You should walk through a few small test cases by hand to be sure you understand the basic flow of control, before reading on into the details.

The heart of the algorithm is "partition the elements so that ... ." The recursive algorithm does not make any copies of the original array v; all work is done by passing indices to indicate what range of v is to be rearranged at a particular step. This means that the only extra storage needed by quicksort is space for the stack of array limits describing subsets not yet partitioned. It is easy to show that if at each stage quicksort deals with the *shorter* subset before the longer, the stack never gets deeper than $\log_2 n$. Even for n equal to a million, $\log_2 n$ is only 20, so this extra space requirement is insignificant.

As a practical matter, we don't want to use recursion — not because it's expensive, for it isn't in quicksort (the recursion is not in the innermost loop), but because it's not available in Fortran. To simulate the recursion, we need a stack containing the indices of the as-yet-unpartitioned subsets of the original array. In outline, the non-recursive quicksort is

```
subroutine quick(v, m, n)

lv(1) = m      # lower limit
uv(1) = n      # upper limit
p = 1          # stack pointer for simulated recursion
while (p > 0)
        if (lv(p) >= uv(p))         # subset has only one element
                p = p - 1           # pop stack
        else {
                partition v(lv(p)) ... v(uv(p)) so that for some i
                  v(lv(p)) ... v(i-1) ≤ v(i) ≤ v(i+1) ... v(uv(p))
                if (lower partition longer) { # stack so shorter done first
                        stack lower at p
                        stack upper at p+1
                        }
                else {
                        stack upper at p
                        stack lower at p+1
                        }
                p = p + 1           # push onto stack
                }
return
end
```

Partitioning is the important step. We select a "pivot" element **pivlin** arbitrarily — the last element in the set — and rearrange all lines with respect to the pivot. The elements are rearranged entirely within the subset of **v** between **lv(p)** and **uv(p)**.

```
i = lv(p) - 1
j = uv(p)
pivlin = last line, i.e., line(j)
while (i < j) {
        increase i until line(i) >= pivlin
        decrease j until j <= i | line(j) <= pivlin
        # at this point, either i and j have met
        # or we have an out-of-order pair
        if (i < j)      # exchange out-of-order pair
                exchange line(i) and line(j)
        }
# i and j have met
# move the pivot element pivlin to the "middle"
exchange line(i) and last line
```

Writing the actual code requires real care. We found that the only way we could be confident of the result was to write a series of *assertions* — statements that have to be true at particular points in the code — ending with the assertion that a successful partition has been done. Not all code requires you to write and verify formal assertions, but the method is a valuable technique for understanding what your program really does. And only with understanding can you be truly confident that your code is right.

We begin partitioning by picking the end element **linbuf(linptr(j))** as our pivot. When the partitioning is done we want to have

i set to some value between **lv(p)** and **uv(p)** inclusive;

all lines with indices less than **i** less than or equal to **linbuf(linptr(i))**;

all lines with indices greater than **i** greater than or equal to **linbuf(linptr(i))**.

And of course we must be sure that we don't access outside the limits of the array, or inadvertently destroy any elements. Here is the partitioning code.

```
i = lv(p) - 1
j = uv(p)
pivlin = linptr(j)        # the pivot line
while (i < j) {
        for (i = i + 1; compar(linptr(i), pivlin, linbuf) < 0; i = i + 1)
                ;
          # linptr(lv(p)) ... linptr(i-1) all point to lines ≤ pivot line
          # i ≤ uv(p)  because there is a pivot line to stop it
        for (j = j - 1; j > i; j = j - 1)
                if (compar(linptr(j), pivlin, linbuf) <= 0)
                        break
          # linptr(j+1) ... linptr(uv(p)-1) all point to lines ≥ pivot
          # j ≥ i ≥ lv(p) so we haven't fallen off the end
        if (i < j)
                call exchan(linptr(i), linptr(j), linbuf)
          # i < j; i and j point to out-of-order lines
          # if i < j, linbuf(linptr(i)) ≤ pivot & linbuf(linptr(j)) ≥ pivot
        }
  # i and j have met
  # move pivot element to position i
call exchan(linptr(i), linptr(uv(p)), linbuf)
  # i is a valid pivot point
```

These assertions are not formally complete, but they are enough that we can be reasonably sure of the code.

We can now put the pieces together for the final version of quicksort, subroutine **quick**:

```
# quick — quicksort for character lines
      subroutine quick(linptr, nlines, linbuf)
      character linbuf(ARB)
      integer compar
      integer i, j, linptr(ARB), lv(LOGPTR), nlines, p, pivlin, uv(LOGPTR)

      lv(1) = 1
      uv(1) = nlines
      p = 1
      while (p > 0)
            if (lv(p) >= uv(p))          # only one element in this subset
                  p = p - 1              # pop stack
            else {
                  i = lv(p) - 1
                  j = uv(p)
                  pivlin = linptr(j)     # pivot line
                  while (i < j) {
                        for (i=i+1; compar(linptr(i), pivlin, linbuf) < 0; i=i+1)
                              ;
                        for (j = j - 1; j > i; j = j - 1)
                              if (compar(linptr(j), pivlin, linbuf) <= 0)
                                    break
                        if (i < j)             # out of order pair
                              call exchan(linptr(i), linptr(j), linbuf)
                        }
                  j = uv(p)                    # move pivot to position i
                  call exchan(linptr(i), linptr(j), linbuf)
                  if (i-lv(p) < uv(p)-i) {     # stack so shorter done first
                        lv(p+1) = lv(p)
                        uv(p+1) = i - 1
                        lv(p) = i + 1
                        }
                  else {
                        lv(p+1) = i + 1
                        uv(p+1) = uv(p)
                        uv(p) = i - 1
                        }
                  p = p + 1                    # push onto stack
                  }
      return
      end
```

LOGPTR is the smallest integer at least as big as $\log_2$ MAXPTR, the maximum number of lines that are to be sorted. As we said before, this is only 20 even for files of a million lines.

Like most sorting algorithms, quicksort has many variations. We can only suggest a few here; the bibliography at the end of the chapter indicates others.

As presented, **quick** does not use the fact that there may be several elements all equal to the pivot. If all such elements are brought together at one partitioning, no further partitions need involve them. The "fat pivot" algorithm returns two values **k1** and **k2** from the partitioning, such that

v(lv(p)) ... v(k1−1) < v(k1) = ... = v(k2) < v(k2+1) ... v(uv(p))

and successive partitions are done on the subsets

lv(p) ... k1−1 and k2+1 ... uv(p)

This organization is faster for sorting data like word lists which frequently contain many duplicate entries.

Exercise 4-7: Experiment with a fat pivot algorithm. How much faster is it on files with significant duplication? How much slower is it than a regular quicksort on files with little or no duplication? □

Exercise 4-8: If an array is already sorted in either order, pivoting on the end element is a bad thing to do: it converts the algorithm into an n^2 procedure. (Why?) One solution is to pivot on the middle element of a set instead. More complicated but more effective is to pivot on the median of three or more elements. Investigate these variations. □

Exercise 4-9: Our quicksort may make more comparisons than are absolutely necessary. Find a version that cuts down on the number of comparisons between actual lines, even at the expense of doing more of other bookkeeping operations, and see how much difference this makes. □

4.5 Sorting Big Files

"Big" means more data than will fit in memory all at once; this is where life gets complicated. This kind of sorting is often called *external* sorting, because some of the data has to reside on temporary intermediate files. What we did in the previous section is by contrast *internal* sorting.

As with internal sorting, there is an astonishing variety of external sorting methods to choose from. The essential idea of most is simple: chunks of the input (as big as possible) are sorted internally and copied onto intermediate files; each chunk is called a run. When the entire input has been split into sorted runs, the runs are merged, typically onto further intermediate files. Eventually all the data winds up merged on one file; this final run is the sorted output.

Not all operating systems let you create an arbitrary number of files, which is implied by this approach, so it may be necessary to add the complexity of managing a limited number of intermediates. Even if you can have lots of intermediate files, however, merging from a large number of sources has to be properly organized or it becomes too slow. (Consider the extreme case: if each file contains only one line of the original input, how long would merging take, as a function of the number of lines?)

One of the clearest sorting procedures is to place each run on a separate file, until the input is exhausted. Then the first *m* files are merged onto a new file, and the *m* files removed. (*m* is a parameter, typically between 3 and 7, called the *merge order*). This process is repeated with the next *m* files until there is only one file left, which is the sorted output. This procedure never has to deal with more than *m* merge files plus one output file at a time.

The main routine of **sort** implements this strategy. Most of it is concerned with creating, opening, closing and removing files at the right times.

```
# sort - external sort of text lines
    character linbuf(MAXTEXT), name(NAMESIZE)
    integer gtext, makfil, min, open
    integer infil(MERGEORDER), linptr(MAXPTR), nlines
    integer high, lim, low, outfil, t

    high = 0
    repeat {                          # initial formation of runs
        t = gtext(linptr, nlines, linbuf, STDIN)
        call quick(linptr, nlines, linbuf)
        high = high + 1
        outfil = makfil(high)
        call ptext(linptr, nlines, linbuf, outfil)
        call close(outfil)
        } until (t == EOF)

    for (low = 1; low < high; low = low + MERGEORDER) {    # merge
        lim = min(low+MERGEORDER-1, high)
        call gopen(infil, low, lim)
        high = high + 1
        outfil = makfil(high)
        call merge(infil, lim-low+1, outfil)
        call close(outfil)
        call gremov(infil, low, lim)
        }

    call gname(high, name)     # final cleanup
    outfil = open(name, READ)
    call fcopy(outfil, STDOUT)
    call close(outfil)
    call remove(name)
    stop
    end
```

The merge phase of **sort** uses two indices **low** and **high** to indicate the range of files still active. **high** is incremented by 1, **MERGEORDER** files starting at **low** are merged onto file **high**, then **low** is incremented by **MERGEORDER**. When **low** catches up to **high**, merging is done and the single run on the last file is copied onto the final output.

We have already seen **gtext**, **ptext**, and **quick** earlier in this chapter, and **fcopy**, which copies one file to another, is from Chapter 3. **min** computes the minimum of two numbers; it can be replaced by **min0** in Fortran.

Within the main routine, files are referred to by a number corresponding to their order of creation. **makfil** creates a new temporary file for a given number, using **gname** to convert the number into a unique, systematic name.

```
# makfil — make new file for number n
      integer function makfil(n)
      character name(NAMESIZE)
      integer create
      integer n

      call gname(n, name)
      makfil = create(name, READWRITE)
      if (makfil == ERR)
            call cant(name)
      return
      end
```

gname copies a standard prefix (**stemp**) into **name**, then appends **n** as a character string. Thus the temporary files used by **sort** are called **stemp1**, **stemp2**, and so on.

```
# gname — make unique name for file id n
      subroutine gname(n, name)
      character name(NAMESIZE)
      integer itoc, length
      integer i, junk, n
      string stemp "stemp"

      call scopy(stemp, 1, name, 1)
      i = length(stemp) + 1
      junk = itoc(n, name(i), NAMESIZE-i)
      return
      end
```

Recall that we use **junk** to discard an unwanted function value, as discussed in Chapter 2.

gopen and **gremov** open and remove consecutively numbered sets of files. Notice that they both regenerate the file name, rather than deal with the complexity of carrying the names around.

```
# gopen — open group of files low ... lim
      subroutine gopen(infil, low, lim)
      character name(NAMESIZE)
      integer i, infil(MERGEORDER), lim, low
      integer open

      for (i = 1; i <= lim-low+1; i = i + 1) {
            call gname(low+i-1, name)
            infil(i) = open(name, READ)
            if (infil(i) == ERR)
                  call cant(name)
            }
      return
      end
```

```
# gremov — remove group of files  low ... lim
      subroutine gremov(infil, low, lim)
      character name(NAMESIZE)
      integer i, infil(MERGEORDER), lim, low

      for (i = 1; i <= lim-low+1; i = i + 1) {
            call close(infil(i))
            call gname(low+i-1, name)
            call remove(name)
            }
      return
      end
```

At any given time there are no more than **MERGEORDER** input files and one output file open, although there may be other temporary files created but not open. **sort** assumes that files can be created dynamically and made as large as necessary while the input is being read, although on some systems you may in fact have to specify size limits for these files. In any case, it is critically important that the files come and go without the knowledge of the user. Few things put people off so fast as having to provide a collection of scratch files with mystical parameters for what should be a simple process.

merge is now the only unspecified code. In principle its task is easy. Since the input files are sorted, the first line on each file is the smallest. **merge** selects the smallest of these, which is necessarily the smallest line in the entire group, and copies it to the output. The next line from that file replaces the line that went out, and a fresh smallest one is identified. When **EOF** is encountered on a file, the corresponding run is finished. When the run on each file is finished, **merge** is done.

The main question is how to efficiently select the smallest line each time. The obvious method, linearly searching the **MERGEORDER** lines currently available, is acceptable if **MERGEORDER** is small, but we can do better with a better algorithm and data structure.

One of the best is to arrange the lines as a *heap*. A heap has the desirable properties that its smallest entry can be found immediately, and a new element can be put into the proper position in a heap in a time that grows only logarithmically with the heap size. Pictorially you can imagine a heap as a binary tree (that is, each element has at most two descendants) in which each element is less than or equal to its children. From a programming standpoint, it is easier to represent a heap as an array **h** such that the children of element **k** are stored at positions **2k** and **2k+1**. Then **h(1)** is less than or equal to **h(2)** and **h(3)**; **h(2)** is less than or equal to **h(4)** and **h(5)**, and in general, **h(k)** is less than or equal to **h(2k)** and **h(2k+1)**. **h(1)** is the smallest thing in the heap.

With a heap, the merging process is as follows.

```
read one line from each file
form a heap
while (there's still input) {
        output smallest line [heap(1)]
        get a new line into heap(1)
        reheap: move new line into its proper place in the heap
        }
```

The smallest line is in the first position. That element is output, a new one is read in to take its place, and the new element is moved to its proper place in the heap ("reheaping"). The initial heap can be formed by using **quick** to sort the lines, since a sorted array is a heap (why?) although the converse is not true (why?). True, sorting does a bit more work than necessary, but the difference will be imperceptible. Why write extra code?

```
# merge - merge infil(1) ... infil(nfiles) onto outfil
        subroutine merge(infil, nfiles, outfil)
        character linbuf(MERGETEXT)
        integer getlin
        integer i, inf, lbp, lp1, nf, nfiles, outfil
        integer infil(MERGEORDER), linptr(MERGEORDER)

        lbp = 1
        nf = 0
        for (i = 1; i <= nfiles; i = i + 1)# get one line from each file
                if (getlin(linbuf(lbp), infil(i)) ¬= EOF) {
                        nf = nf + 1
                        linptr(nf) = lbp
                        lbp = lbp + MAXLINE        # room for largest line
                        }
        call quick(linptr, nf, linbuf)             # make initial heap
        while (nf > 0) {
                lp1 = linptr(1)
                call putlin(linbuf(lp1), outfil)
                inf = lp1 / MAXLINE + 1            # compute file index
                if (getlin(linbuf(lp1), infil(inf)) == EOF) {
                        linptr(1) = linptr(nf)
                        nf = nf - 1
                        }
                call reheap(linptr, nf, linbuf)
                }
        return
        end
```

To avoid complicated storage management, **merge** reserves space for the longest possible line in each slot. This makes it easy to decide which file is associated with a particular line by dividing the line origin by the maximum line size.

Reheaping compares the top element to its children. If the element is less than or equal to both, it is in its proper position and the job is done. If not, then the element is exchanged with the smaller of its children, and the process repeated at the next level of the tree, i.e., by comparing the element with its children in its new position. Eventually the element percolates through the tree to the place where it belongs.

It is easy to show that the reheaping time is proportional to the logarithm of **MERGEORDER**, while a linear search of course takes time linearly proportional to **MERGEORDER**. The heap procedure is only a few more lines of code than the linear version and should be faster for typical values of **MERGEORDER**.

```
# reheap — propagate linbuf(linptr(1)) to proper place in heap
	subroutine reheap(linptr, nf, linbuf)
	character linbuf(MAXTEXT)
	integer compar
	integer i, j, nf, linptr(nf)

	for (i = 1; 2 * i <= nf; i = j) {
		j = 2 * i
		if (j < nf)		# find smaller child
			if (compar(linptr(j), linptr(j+1), linbuf) > 0)
				j = j + 1
		if (compar(linptr(i), linptr(j), linbuf) <= 0)
			break		# proper position found
		call exchan(linptr(i), linptr(j), linbuf)	# percolate
		}
	return
	end
```

Notice that **quick**, **merge** and **reheap** all work properly if called with no data items. This is entirely because all of the loops in the code test at the top instead of the bottom. It is a good omen for the overall reliability of a program when its boundaries are reliable without special attention.

You should also glance back over the organization of **sort** and observe the way in which it is broken into functional modules. The sort, the merge, the compare, the input and the output can each be replaced separately without upsetting the rest of the program.

Exercise 4-10: How much intermediate file space is needed all at once to sort input containing *n* characters? □

4.6 Improvements

Once the basic version works, we can make **sort** faster and we can make it do more things. Since this is a book about tools, not algorithms, we are more interested in functional enhancements, but let us first mention some efficiency considerations.

We measured **sort** on two different inputs. The first consisted of 270 lines with 6900 characters, the second 1330 lines and 34800 characters. We allowed 10000 characters in **linbuf**, so the first set of data were processed on a single temporary with no merge phase. The second set produced four initial runs, which were then merged onto a fifth file before being copied to the final output.

Here are the CPU times for the two tests.

total time	6.5 sec.	36.9 sec.
(all I/O)	94.1%	91.6%
compar	4.6	6.1
quick	0.9	1.2
merge	...	0.3
reheap	...	0.3

Everything else is less than 0.15%.

The I/O times are truly remarkable. As we have said before, and will say again, Fortran character I/O pays heavily for its generality. You can certainly improve these times by using specialized routines. But even so, for any likely improvement, I/O will still dominate. Since you can't avoid copying the data in and out, you have to find an algorithm that reduces *intermediate* I/O.

> *Exercise 4-11:* When there are at most **MERGEORDER** intermediate files left, one complete pass over the data can be avoided by merging directly onto the final output file instead of onto an intermediate file. And as a special case, if the original input fits entirely into memory, there is no need for any merging or any intermediate files. Modify **sort** to handle these situations efficiently. According to the measurements above, how much faster will these changes make **sort**? □

The running time of **sort** is strongly affected by the number of passes made over the input data, which in turn depends on the length of the runs created in the initial pass. You can always get longer runs with more memory, but you can't always get more memory.

> *Exercise 4-12:* One possibility is to make better use of the memory you have, for example by placing more than one character into an integer. Modify **sort** to pack several characters into one integer upon input and unpack them upon output. How much code must be changed and in what routines? How much speed improvement is obtained for a given amount of memory? □

A particularly elegant way to create long initial runs is "replacement selection." A memory-load is sorted as before. But then, as **ptext** outputs a line, a fresh line is immediately read in to replace it. If this fresh line is greater than or equal to the line that it replaced it can form part of the run that is currently going out! If it's smaller, it can't go out in this run and must be held until the next one.

The payoff from this organization is significant. For files with random contents, it turns out that the expected run length is twice the memory size, so we can save one full pass over the data. And of course the effect is even stronger on files that are already partly sorted.

Replacement selection needs careful storage management if the lines are not all the same length. More important, it also requires an algorithm for quickly finding the right position for a replacement among the already-sorted elements in memory. It is too slow to search through all the current lines to find the right place. The solution is to use a data structure like a heap, where the right position can be found in logarithmic time instead of linear. We will not go into this here; the topic is discussed in considerable detail in Knuth's *The Art of Computer Programming; Volume 3: Sorting and Searching.*

What can you do if your system won't let you create a lot of files? One method of getting by with few files is the "balanced two-way merge." Suppose you are allowed four intermediates. During the first phase runs are placed alternately on files 1 and 2 until the input is exhausted. Then the runs on files 1 and 2 are merged, with the output runs (half as many, each twice as big) going alternately onto files 3 and 4. Then the runs on 3 and 4 are merged back onto 1 and 2, making runs of length four times the original. The process continues until all the data is merged onto one completely sorted file which can then be copied to the output. Since the length of the runs is doubled on each pass and the number of runs cut by a factor of two, there are $\lceil \log_2 r \rceil$ passes made, where r is the number of runs created in the initial phase.

The balanced two-way merge can be generalized to any number (3 or more) of intermediate files. The available files are divided into two groups as nearly equally as possible and merging is done back and forth between the two groups.

Exercise 4-13: Implement a balanced two-way merge sort. The main complication you will have to worry about is keeping track of the end of each run on each file. Compare the complexity and the running time of the balanced merge program with **sort**. □

Let us turn to functional enhancements. We already said that a particularly useful way to package **sort** is as a filter. But it is also likely to be used in more conventional ways.

Exercise 4-14: By default, **sort** reads from the standard input. Modify **sort** so that if it is called with file-name arguments, it will instead take its input from the named files:

sort *file1 file2 ...*

will sort the data on the files named. Reading either from a set of named files, or from the standard input if none are named, is an exceedingly useful design for many programs; you should always consider it. □

Exercise 4-15: Add an option to let the output file be specified by name, instead of just the standard output. Ensure that the output can be the same as one of the inputs. Do you want the final merge done directly onto it? □

Exercise 4-16: Add an option **−m** to merge already-sorted files:

sort −m *file1 file2 ...*

merges the data (presumed sorted) on the files onto the standard output. The command

sort −m

without file names is silly. Does your version do something intelligent anyway? □

Exercise 4-17: Provide a **sort** option **−r** to reverse the direction of sorting. If you did the earlier exercise on this topic, did you have to change your decision about where to put the direction-changing code? □

Exercise 4-18: Add a **-d** option so **sort** sorts by dictionary order: upper and lower case letters should sort together, so that 'a' and 'A' appear together, not separated by an entire case of the alphabet. Is it sufficient to define a<A<b<B...? Should dictionary order be the default behavior? What should be done about special characters like periods, commas, and so on? What about digits? □

Exercise 4-19: Add the **-n** option: an initial numeric string with optional sign is sorted by arithmetic value while the rest of the line is sorted normally. All-numeric lines are a special case of this kind of input. Does your routine work regardless of the size of the numbers? □

Exercise 4-20: Add options so sorting can be done on fields within lines. You will need a way to specify the beginning and end of each field, and you will probably also want to allow fields to be independently numeric, dictionary order, reversed, etc. The challenge here is not so much the bookkeeping needed to make the program work as it is designing the options so they are easy for users to specify. Remember that specifying a field by character position is hard to do, particularly if the input doesn't come in neat columns. □

By now you are near the complexity provided by some commercial sort packages, but at least you got there in modest increments, and you always had a useful tool at each step. By default, though, **sort** still puts text lines into order, taking its input from the standard input and writing on the standard output. It is still an easy-to-use service for people who just want to sort text. The most frequent and easy operations should be easy to remember and to specify; you shouldn't *always* need a reference manual.

Exercise 4-21: Some systems provide a powerful but complicated *sort generator* that creates efficient sorts for big production jobs. If your system has one of these, design and implement a language that makes it easier for casual users to create the sorting process they want. □

4.7 Separation of Function: unique

One common reason for sorting is to bring together all occurrences of a particular item, so they can be treated as a group. Sometimes we do this just to discard all but one occurrence in a group, as for instance when we make a list of all the words in a document. It's certainly easy to add an option to **sort** which discards multiple occurrences of an input line. (Where should this code be inserted?) But should this code be part of **sort** at all?

This question touches on an area of fundamental importance in designing good tools — proper separation of function. What should be included in a program? What should be a separate program? It happens to be "more efficient" to put this particular function into the sort program — we can save a pass over the data. More important, the decision whether two lines are "the same" depends on the comparison function being used, which is of course determined by the sorting options specified. If sorting and casting out duplicates are combined, we are assured that the comparison is done consistently and efficiently.

Why should there be two separate programs when a single slightly more complicated one will do? One good reason is that someone might want one function without the other. By separating the function of stripping duplicates from that of sorting, we can do things that are not possible when they are combined. You might really like to know which lines are *not* duplicated, or which lines *are* duplicated, or you might like to *count* adjacent duplicates. If sorting, duplicate-stripping and counting are all combined, the sort program is more complicated; and of course it's conceivable that you don't want the input sorted before you strip the duplicates!

Combining functions too early is a mistake. In its early stages, at least, a program should implement a single function. Sure, it may eventually have lots of options, but the things it does should be closely related. Then when users come along with new ways to combine programs, you will not have precluded some useful operation by your assumptions about what they are likely to do. Our own experience is instructive here. For years, sorting and duplicate stripping were separate programs. Finally efficiency began to be a major factor, and they were integrated: an option was added to **sort** which specifies the stripping of adjacent duplicates (although of course the old duplicate-stripper remained available and often used). But no one knew at the start that this was a good combination. The lesson: keep functions separate until you know *how* to combine them.

Here is **unique**, for stripping adjacent duplicates. It is most often used with **sort**, but is sufficiently useful in its own right to be worth a separate program.

```
# unique — strip adjacent duplicate lines
	character buf1(MAXLINE), buf2(MAXLINE)
	integer equal, getlin
	integer t

	t = getlin(buf1, STDIN)
	while (t ¬= EOF) {
		call putlin(buf1, STDOUT)
		for (t = getlin(buf2, STDIN); t ¬= EOF; t = getlin(buf2, STDIN))
			if (equal(buf1, buf2) == NO)
				break
		if (t == EOF)
			break
		call putlin(buf2, STDOUT)
		for (t = getlin(buf1, STDIN); t ¬= EOF; t = getlin(buf1, STDIN))
			if (equal(buf1, buf2) == NO)
				break
		}
	stop
	end
```

What are boundaries that should be tested to be confident that **unique** works correctly. □

Exercise 4-22: Our version of **unique** uses the control structure to distinguish which buffer currently holds the line being compared against. Rewrite it with a single inner loop and a switch to interchange the roles of the two buffers. Rewrite it to simply copy a line from **buf2** to **buf1** whenever a comparison fails. Which of the three versions do you prefer? □

Exercise 4-23: Add the option **−n** to **unique**, to prefix each line with the number of occurrences of the line in the original input. The command

```
unique -n
```

with the input

```
a
a
b
```

produces

```
2   a
1   b
```

Why should the count *precede* the line? □

Exercise 4-24: Combine **translit**, **sort**, and **unique** (with the **−n** option) into a pipeline that produces a word frequency list for a document, sorted into order of decreasing frequency. □

Exercise 4-25: Combine **translit**, **sort** (with the **−d** option) and **unique** into a pipeline that checks a program for occurrences of names in both upper and lower case, like **SIZE** and **size**. □

Exercise 4-26: Write the program **common**, for comparing lines in two sorted text files.

common *file1 file2*

produces a three-column output: lines which appear only in *file1*, lines only in *file2*, and lines in both files. **common** allows the optional arguments **−1**, **−2** and **−3**, which specify the printing of only the corresponding column. Thus

common −3 *file1 file2*

prints only the lines common to both files, and

common −1 *file1 file2*

prints lines which are in the first file but not in the second. If there is only one file argument, *file2* refers to the standard input. □

What good is **common**? Suppose we have available a dictionary of English. Then consider this pipeline:

```
concat file1 file2 file3 ... |
 translit A-Z a-z |
  translit ¬a-z @n |
   sort |
    unique |
     common -2 dictionary
```

This collects a set of files together (**concat**), converts them to a single case (**translit**), discards punctuation and spaces and puts each word on a line by itself (**translit**), sorts them (**sort**), casts out duplicates (**unique**), and then selects those words which appear in the original files but not in the dictionary (**common**).

What's a word that appears in a document but not in a dictionary? Right — it's a plausible contender for being a spelling mistake. This pipeline is a first draft of a program for finding spelling mistakes. It won't do a perfect job by any means, but on the other hand it can be made out of spare parts in a few minutes, and it forms an excellent base for a more sophisticated process. That is what tools are all about.

Exercise 4-27: What improvements would you make to the spelling-mistake finder? What experiments would you perform before undertaking "improvements"? □

Exercise 4-28: The output from the spelling mistake finder often consists mostly of technical jargon, words like **byte** and **translit**. Once you have eliminated the true errors from this output, you now have a *glossary* of special words for a document. How would you modify the pipeline to eliminate glossary words from subsequent checks for spelling errors? □

4.8 Permuted Index

Once a flexible sorting program is available, other programs can use it as a component. In this section we will describe one such application, a program for creating a *permuted index* (often called a *keyword-in-context* or "KWIC" index). A permuted index lists each word (or some similar useful *token*) in its original context, but sorted by word and rearranged so the keywords line up. For example, this sentence would produce this output:

```
output:                        For  example, this sentence would produce this
                 this output:       For example, this sentence would produce
  sentence would produce this       output:                   For example, this
  example, this sentence would      produce this output:                    For
             For example, this      sentence would produce this output:
  this sentence would produce       this output:               For example,
                  For example,      this sentence would produce this output:
    For example, this sentence      would produce this output:
```

One program organization is like this.

```
for each input line
        for each token in the line {
                rotate line so token is at front
                output onto temporary file
                }
sort temporary file
for each line in temporary file {
        re-rotate to center first token
        print line
        }
```

This process can be viewed as a pipeline of three independent programs:

```
create rotations | sort | unrotate and print
```

but how it should be implemented on any particular system depends on what mechanisms are available. The advantage of a pipeline is that we already have **sort** nicely packaged, and the other two pieces are easy.

A second way to write **kwic** is to invoke **sort** as a self-contained program *from within* a program that does the rotating and unrotating as normal subroutines. This method assumes that the operating system provides a way to *run any program* from within a running program, and regain control when it is done. We can indicate the structure as

```
do rotations onto temp1
run("sort <temp1 >temp2")
unrotate from temp2
```

sort remains a black box, yet the overall process is effectively confined to one program.

However the program is eventually organized, it is important to observe that the original *design* should always be like this. We want to keep the pieces of the solution as uncoupled as possible, no matter what, so we pretend from the start that the most restrictive implementation possible (such as a pipeline) will be the one chosen. That way, we are less likely to let our guard down and admit sneak paths for communication between modules. Decisions about actual *packaging* should be postponed as late as possible, to maximize alternatives.

We leave the particular organization up to you, and show the routines for rotating and unrotating, written for use in a pipeline. Here is the rotation part.

```
# kwic - make keyword in context index
      character buf(MAXLINE)
      integer getlin

      while (getlin(buf, STDIN) ¬= EOF)
            call putrot(buf, STDOUT)
      stop
      end
```

The work is done in **putrot**, which finds the keywords in each line. A keyword is a string of letters or digits, but excludes punctuation like parentheses, commas and so on. These must be excluded so that words which appear adjacent to them will be properly lined up in columns when the output is printed. **putrot** finds the beginning of each token, that is, the first alphanumeric character, and calls **rotate** to output a line with that character rotated to the front.

```
# putrot — create lines with keyword at front
      subroutine putrot(buf, outfil)
      character type
      character buf(ARB), t
      integer i, outfil

      for (i = 1; buf(i) ¬= NEWLINE; i = i + 1) {
            t = type(buf(i))
            if (t == LETTER | t == DIGIT) {        # alpha
                  call rotate(buf, i, outfil)      # token starts at "i"
                  t = type(buf(i+1))
                  for ( ; t == LETTER | t == DIGIT; t = type(buf(i+1)))
                        i = i + 1
                  }
            }
      return
      end

   # rotate — output rotated line
      subroutine rotate(buf, n, outfil)
      character buf(ARB)
      integer i, n, outfil

      for (i = n; buf(i) ¬= NEWLINE; i = i + 1)
            call putch(buf(i), outfil)
      call putch(FOLD, outfil)
      for (i = 1; i < n; i = i + 1)
            call putch(buf(i), outfil)
      call putch(NEWLINE, outfil)
      return
      end
```

rotate marks the end of the original line (the place where the line has been folded) by adding a **FOLD** character — some character unlikely to occur in normal text. **FOLD** will be used by the unrotating program to position the permuted lines correctly. Thus if we use **$** as the fold character, the input line

```
now is the time
```

will yield the four output lines

```
now is the time$
is the time$now
the time$now is
time$now is the
```

The function **type** determines whether a particular character is a letter, a digit, or something else; it returns **LETTER**, **DIGIT** or the character itself.

```
# type - determine type of character
      character function type(c)
      character c
      integer index
      string digits "0123456789"
      string lowalf "abcdefghijklmnopqrstuvwxyz"
      string upalf "ABCDEFGHIJKLMNOPQRSTUVWXYZ"

      if (index(lowalf, c) > 0)
            type = LETTER
      else if (index(upalf, c) > 0)
            type = LETTER
      else if (index(digits, c) > 0)
            type = DIGIT
      else
            type = c
      return
      end
```

Recall that **index** finds the position of a character in a string, returning zero if it doesn't find it.

Although you can write **type** more efficiently than we have if you take advantage of the numeric properties of a particular character set, the version here has the merit of being independent of character set, and thus it can be transported between machines without change.

The other end of the pipeline is **unrot**, which unrotates and prints the rotated lines, lined up on column **MIDDLE**. It copies the first half of the line, beginning at position **MIDDLE+1** and wraps around at the end if necessary. It then copies the second half of the line, working backwards from **MIDDLE−1**. Finally it deletes trailing blanks.

```
# unrot — unrotate lines rotated by kwic
      character inbuf(MAXLINE), outbuf(MAXOUT)
      integer getlin, index
      integer i, j

      while (getlin(inbuf, STDIN) ¬= EOF) {
            for (i = 1; i < MAXOUT; i = i + 1)       # blank line
                  outbuf(i) = BLANK
            j = MIDDLE
            for (i = 1; inbuf(i) ¬= FOLD & inbuf(i) ¬= NEWLINE; i = i + 1) {
                  j = j + 1                       # copy up to FOLD
                  if (j >= MAXOUT - 1)
                        j = 1
                  outbuf(j) = inbuf(i)
                  }
            if (inbuf(i) == FOLD) {               # copy second half,
                  j = MIDDLE                      # working backwards
                  for (i = index(inbuf, NEWLINE) - 1; i > 0; i = i - 1) {
                        if (inbuf(i) == FOLD)
                              break
                        j = j - 1
                        if (j <= 0)
                              j = MAXOUT - 2
                        outbuf(j) = inbuf(i)
                        }
                  }
            for (i = MAXOUT - 2; i > 0; i = i - 1)
                  if (outbuf(i) ¬= BLANK)         # delete trailing blanks
                        break
            outbuf(i+1) = NEWLINE                 # terminate line properly
            outbuf(i+2) = EOS
            call putlin(outbuf, STDOUT)
            }
      stop
      end
```

You should verify that **unrot** stays sane even on input that has no **FOLD** character, because it tests for both **NEWLINE** and **FOLD**. This is an another example of defensive programming — writing the program so it can cope with small disasters. Of course disasters come in many sizes, and you should avoid paranoia, but in this specific instance the insurance is cheap.

Exercise 4-29: Why did we write

```
for (i = index(inbuf, NEWLINE) - 1; i > 0; i = i - 1) {
      if (inbuf(i) == FOLD)
            break
      ...
```

instead of

```
for (i = index(inbuf, NEWLINE) - 1; i > 0 & inbuf(i) ¬= FOLD; i = i - 1) {
    ...
```

(Hint: see **compress** in Chapter 2.) □

Exercise 4-30: **kwic** and **unrot** don't properly handle text containing tab characters or backspaces. They also ignore the possibility that the text contains **FOLD** characters. Fix them. □

Exercise 4-31: Modify **kwic** so it will not split a word on output. □

Exercise 4-32: You will quickly find that you don't want words like *a, the, and, of,* and so on in your index. Conversely you might want lists that contain *only* certain words. Add the capability to specify either or both of an "omit" file — words that are not to be indexed — or an "include" file — words that must be indexed. (Chapter 8 discusses some rudimentary table handling procedures.) □

Exercise 4-33: Modify **kwic** to handle multiple files as an alternative to the standard input, just as **print** does. In a large document consisting of several input files, it is useful to know precisely where in the input a particular line was found. Add an option **-t** to tag output lines with some identification of their source position, like file name and line number. Should this be the default mode? □

One use we have made of our **kwic** program is as a quick (and dirty) way to check that all variables in our programs were declared. (An undeclared variable is usually a spelling mistake.) This still requires manual effort, however, and so is not as good a solution as it could be.

Exercise 4-34: If your compiler doesn't do it for you, build a program that checks your programs to see that *all* variables are declared. □

Exercise 4-35: Build a program that forms a cross-reference listing of a document (the document often, though not always, being a program). That is, for each token, list the numbers of all lines that contain a reference to that token. □

Bibliographic Notes

The standard reference on internal and external sorting is D. E. Knuth's *The Art of Computer Programming; Volume 3: Sorting and Searching* (Addison-Wesley, 1973). This contains precise descriptions and detailed analyses of a wide variety of sorting methods. Another source for internal sorting methods is R. P. Rich, *Internal Sorting Methods Illustrated With PL/I Programs* (Prentice-Hall, 1972), which contains actual PL/I programs, and extensive run time and space measurements.

Our quicksort is adapted from one presented by Knuth in "Structured programming with goto statements," *Computing Surveys,* December, 1974; he attributes it to R. Sedgewick. Other variants of quicksort are discussed in an article by R. Loeser, "Some performance tests of quicksort and descendants," *CACM,* March, 1974. This article contains Fortran programs for all of the procedures; you might find it rewarding to compare the Fortran with Ratfor.

An article by D. L. Parnas, "On the criteria to be used in decomposing systems into modules" (*CACM,* December, 1972), discusses how to modularize a permuted index program. Compare his organization with ours.

The pipeline for catching spelling mistakes was conceived by S. C. Johnson. For a method of finding spelling mistakes that does not need a dictionary, see "Computer detection of typographical errors," by R. Morris and L. L. Cherry, *IEEE Transactions on Professional Communication,* March, 1975.

CHAPTER 5

TEXT PATTERNS

Remember the **format** finder we discussed in the Introduction? That job needed a program to look for the word **format** anywhere in an input line and to print all such lines found.

But no one wants a program that will only find a particular Fortran statement, nor one limited to looking at Fortran programs, nor even one restricted to looking at programs. **format** is a specific *text pattern;* we want a program **find** that accepts the pattern to be looked for as an argument, so we can say

find *pattern*

to print each input line that contains an occurrence of the specified pattern. For instance, to find **format** statements, we just say

find format

Some people might argue that what is really needed here is a text editor that can search for text patterns. Indeed we do want such an editor, and in the next chapter we will build one. But we still want **find** besides. The reason is that an editor is *too* general for some purposes. We have to invoke the editor, tell it one at a time which files we wish to process, then repeat the search command for each file. There is simply too much setup. **find**, on the other hand, does exactly what is wanted, and it does so with a minimum of fuss.

Hardly a working day goes by that we do not make extensive use of **find**. The most obvious application is to answer questions such as, "When did we first mention the **break** statement?" or, "Where are all the references to that variable?" But it is also a filter to *select* from more voluminous output, as in a pipeline like

program | find error

to print only messages containing the word "error." (This is much harder with a text editor.)

We even use **find** to improve our writing style. You may have noticed that the word "simple" and its derivatives occur frequently in the book. This is understandable, for simplicity in programs is a virtue. But overuse robs the word of force, so periodically we scanned through the text with

```
find simpl
```

(which also catches "simply" and "simplicity"), then replaced some occurrences by appropriate synonyms. We even counted them once, with

```
find simpl | linecount
```

5.1 Text Patterns

There is no point to making **find** capable of recognizing all conceivable text patterns. We could be perverse, for instance, and insist on a program that could look for *all* legal ways of writing a **format** statement in Fortran — with imbedded blanks in the keyword, multiple continuation lines, and so forth. We could further insist that *only* **format** statements be printed — omitting lines with character strings that contain the string **format**, and lines that use **format** as a variable name. But by the time we are able to handle an assignment statement as tricky as

```
10     format(x5h)=b(i)
```

we have written most of the recognizer for a Fortran compiler!

Our **find** program will not handle all these pathological cases, to be sure, but how often do they occur? When was the last time you wrote **format** as **for mat**? When did you last use it as an identifier? So long as *all* the lines you want to see are printed, it doesn't hurt much if a few extra also appear. And if you don't plan to be perfectly precise, you may as well draw the line at a reasonable place. We accept a few shortcomings in any one application in trade for a much broader spectrum of uses. Most users of a tool are willing to meet you halfway; if you do ninety percent of the job, they will be ecstatic.

We will confine ourselves to a simple notation that has been used in a number of conversational text editors and other pattern matching programs. For all its economy, the notation is surprisingly versatile. We will suggest some useful extensions as exercises.

A text pattern can be a simple thing, like the letter **a**, or a more elaborate construct built up from simple things, like the string **format**. To build arbitrary text patterns, you need remember only a handful of rules.

Any literal character, like **a**, is a text pattern that matches that same character in the text being scanned. A sequence of literal characters, like **123** or **format**, is a pattern that matches any occurrence of that sequence of characters in a line of the input.

A pattern is said to *match* part of a text line if the text line contains an occurrence of the pattern. For example, the pattern **aa** matches the line **aabc** once at position 1, the line **aabcaabc** in two places, and the line **aaaaaa** in five (overlapping) places. Matching is done on a line-by-line basis: no pattern can match across a line boundary. Text patterns may be *concatenated:* a text pattern followed by another text pattern forms a new text pattern that matches anything matched by the first, followed immediately by anything matched by the second. A sequence of literal characters is an example of concatenated patterns.

Although it is an easy task to write a program that looks only for literal strings of characters (and it is a useful first step), you will soon find it restrictive.

Accordingly, we will add some more capabilities to **find** — the ability to search for patterns that match classes of characters, that match patterns only at particular positions on a line, or that match text of indefinite length.

To be able to express these more general patterns, we need to preempt some characters to represent other types of text patterns, or to delimit them. For example, we will use the character **?** as a text pattern that matches *any* single character except a newline. The pattern **x?y** matches **x+y**, **xay**, **x?y** and similar strings.

The **?** and other reserved characters are often called *metacharacters.* We try to choose characters which will not appear with high frequency in normal text, but still there are occasions when we want to look for a literal occurrence of a metacharacter. Thus the special meaning of any metacharacter can be turned off by preceding it with the *escape character* **@**, as in the character translator **translit** of Chapter 2. Thus **@?** matches a literal question mark, and **@@** matches a literal at-sign.

The metacharacter **[** signals that the characters following, up to the next **]**, form a *character class,* that is, a text pattern that matches any single character from the bracketed list. Character classes use the same notation that was used to specify **from** strings in **translit**: **[aA]** matches **a** or **A**, **[a−z]** matches any lower case letter, **[¬a]** matches any character *except* an **a**, and so forth. The one difference is that, for convenience, we will say that negated character classes, such as the last example, will never match a newline. The escape convention can also be used inside character classes if the character class is to contain **¬** or **−** or **@** or **]**.

Two other metacharacters do not match literal characters but rather match positions on the input line. **%** matches the *beginning* of a line: **%abc** is a pattern that matches **abc** *only* if it occurs as the first three characters of an input line. Analogously, **$** matches the newline at the *end* of a line: **abc$** matches **abc** only if it is the last thing on a line, before the newline. Of course these can work together: **%abc$** matches a line that contains *only* **abc**; and **%$** matches only empty lines (lines containing only a newline).

Any of the text patterns above that match a single character (everything but **%** and **$**) can be followed by the character ***** to make a text pattern which matches *zero or more* successive occurrences of the single character pattern. The resulting pattern is called a *closure.* For example, **a*** matches zero or more **a**'s; **aa*** matches *one* or more **a**'s; **[a−z]*** matches any string of zero or more lower case letters.

Since a closure matches zero or more instances of the pattern, which do we pick if there's a choice? **find** itself only needs to know whether at least one match occurs in a line, but later we will want to use the matched substring. It turns out to be most convenient if **find** matches the *longest* possible string even when a null-string match would be equally valid. Thus **[a−zA−Z]*** matches an entire word (which may be a null string), **[a−zA−Z][a−zA−Z]*** matches an entire word (one or more letters but not a null string), and **?*** matches a whole line (which may be a null string). Any ambiguity in deciding which part of a line matches a pattern will be resolved by choosing the match beginning with the *leftmost* character, then choosing the *longest* possible match at that point. So **[a−z][a−z0−9]*** matches the leftmost Fortran identifier on a line, **(?*)** matches anything between parentheses, and **??*** matches an entire line of one or more characters (but not a line containing only a newline).

Finally, no pattern will match across a line boundary. This is often most natural and useful, and it prevents an unwise **?*** from eating up an entire input.

Technically, our text patterns are a subclass of the class of patterns called *regular expressions,* which have been extensively studied. General regular expressions typically include a way to specify alternates and the ability to parenthesize patterns, so for example **x(a|bc)y** matches either **xay** or **xbcy**. (The parentheses and bar become metacharacters.) These more general patterns add power at the price of complexity. For our purposes the complexity outweighs the power, but we will discuss some of the issues involved as we proceed.

Exercise 5-1: Write a text pattern that matches only those words that contain the six vowels **aeiouy** in order, like **abstemiously** or **facetiously**. Write a text pattern that matches the words that can be made with the letters you can create by holding a pocket calculator upside down. (The letters are usually **BEhILOS**, from the digits **8341705**.) □

Exercise 5-2: Write text patterns that match PL/I identifiers, Cobol identifiers, identifiers accepted by your local assembly language. How would you use **translit**, **sort**, **unique**, and **find** to list all identifiers and keywords used in a program? Is there any easy way to eliminate the keywords? (Hint: look at the programs for checking spelling mistakes, in Chapter 4.) Is it worth it? □

Exercise 5-3: Most languages actually insist that identifiers have some maximum length; Fortran, for instance, permits at most six characters. Given text patterns as defined above, can you write one that matches Fortran identifiers of at most six characters? □

Exercise 5-4: Can you use **find** to remove all the blank lines from text? To remove all comment cards from a Fortran program? To count them? To remove all comments from a PL/I program? Can you use it to remove all lines after an **end** statement? □

Exercise 5-5: Do any of the following patterns make sense, according to the definitions given above? If not, why not? If so, what do they mean?

```
a**
aa*
a%b$c
%*a
[¬ @t]*[ @t]
%$
%
*
@@t
```

□

5.2 Implementation

Now that we know the sort of patterns we want to look for, we can start laying out the program. Without going into any detail, we can foresee the need for an array **pat** to hold the pattern, and a top-level organization like:

```
# find — find patterns in text
	character arg(MAXARG), lin(MAXLINE), pat(MAXPAT)
	integer getarg, getlin, getpat, match

	if (getarg(1, arg, MAXARG) == EOF)
		call error("usage: find pattern.")
	if (getpat(arg, pat) == ERR)
		call error("illegal pattern.")
	while (getlin(lin, STDIN) ¬= EOF)
		if (match(lin, pat) == YES)
			call putlin(lin, STDOUT)
	stop
	end
```

getpat uses the argument to put the scan pattern into **pat**. **match** looks for an occurrence of the pattern anywhere in the input line **lin** and returns a **YES/NO** answer.

Often it is possible not only to write code without knowing entirely where you're going, but also to test it. That's what we did with **find**. By using dummy versions of **getpat** and **match**, we were able to verify that lines of text are properly read and written — which means that **EOF** is detected at the correct time and that the internal representation in **lin** is consistently treated, at least by **getlin** and **putlin**. A minor variation of **getpat** exercised the error message. And an idiot **match**, which could detect only a leading **a**, verified that lines could be printed selectively.

All this may seem pretty elementary, but it's surprising how many bugs are caught early this way. It is often true in large software projects that the majority of bugs arise because the pieces of the system do not go together as they were expected to, despite detailed interface specifications known to everyone from the start. And many other bugs survive elaborate checks on individual routines, surfacing only when the routine first interacts with the rest of the code.

It seems only natural, then, to test at the highest, most integrated level first — since that's where most bugs are detected anyway — and to start testing *as soon as possible,* even before most of the actual working code is written. This approach is referred to as *top-down testing,* a natural extension of *top-down design* and *top-down coding.* The dummy programs are referred to as program *stubs.* We built and tested **find** that way, a piece at a time, and it paid off. Despite a number of stupid mistakes (some of which we will admit), the program was written and debugged in short order.

Since a match can occur anywhere on a line, it seems easiest to factor the matching into two pieces. **match** looks for a match anywhere on a line, by repeatedly calling **amatch** to look for a match that begins at position **i** — an *anchored* match. This separates checking for a match from deciding what match to try next.

```
# match — find match anywhere on line
        integer function match(lin, pat)
        character lin(MAXLINE), pat(MAXPAT)
        integer amatch
        integer i

        for (i = 1; lin(i) ¬= EOS; i = i + 1)
                if (amatch(lin, i, pat) > 0) {
                        match = YES
                        return
                        }
        match = NO
        return
        end
```

amatch will return some indication of where the matched string is, or zero if there was no match. Although later programs will eventually need to know what part of the text matched the pattern, all **find** cares about is whether or not there was a match.

Leaving aside all metacharacters for the moment, **amatch** has to compare the pattern with the input, character by character, until it either finds a mismatch (in which case it returns zero), or until it gets to the end of the pattern successfully (in which case it can return the next position of the input, which is guaranteed not to be zero). Then the most basic version of **amatch** might be

```
# amatch with no metacharacters
        integer function amatch(lin, from, pat)
        character lin(MAXLINE), pat(MAXPAT)
        integer from, i, j

        i = from
        for (j = 1; pat(j) ¬= EOS; j = j + 1) {
                if (lin(i) ¬= pat(j)) {
                        amatch = 0
                        return          # with no match
                        }
                i = i + 1
                }
        amatch = i
        return                          # successfully
        end
```

Here the pattern characters are stored in successive elements of **pat**.

The metacharacters **?**, **%** and **$** add only minor complications. Character classes, however, bring up a question of representation. Clearly we don't want to have to interpret shorthand like **[a−z]** for every character position within every line of input. It looks as if text patterns are sufficiently complicated to warrant encoding. That way, we can go over the pattern once, carefully check it for illegal specifications, expand shorthand, and rewrite it in a more convenient form. We anticipate looking through rather large files with **find**, so we would like to detect a match or mismatch reasonably quickly. Encoding the pattern is a specific example of a rather general principle — the more time you're willing to spend preprocessing your data, the faster you can use it later.

In our patterns, each text pattern type is represented in **pat** by a special code. Literal characters are represented by two entries — the indicator **CHAR** in position j and the character itself in position j+1. The metacharacters %, $ and ? are represented by the single entries **BOL**, **EOL** and **ANY** respectively. Character classes are represented as either **CCL** (for [...]) or **NCCL** (for [¬...]), followed by a count of the number of characters in the class and the characters themselves, after any shorthand has been expanded. We will ignore closures for a while yet, until the easier part is under control. Thus the pattern

```
%[¬x]?[0-9]x$
```

is encoded as

```
BOL  NCCL 1 x  ANY  CCL 10 0 1 2 3 4 5 6 7 8 9  CHAR x  EOL
```

(The first 1 and the 10 are numbers in the encoding, not characters.) Conversion of an input pattern to this encoded form is done by **getpat** and its subordinates, to which we shall return.

Given this much complexity in the representation of a pattern, it's also worthwhile to put the testing and matching of single characters into a separate routine, to keep **amatch** down to manageable size. **omatch** will test whether a single input character matches the current pattern position, and advance the input position by the right amount if it does. **amatch** can then concentrate on walking through the pattern in proper synchronization with the text to be matched. Now we can write another version of **amatch**:

```
# amatch with some metacharacters
	integer function amatch(lin, from, pat)
	character lin(MAXLINE), pat(MAXPAT)
	integer omatch, patsiz
	integer from, i, j

	i = from
	for (j = 1; pat(j) ¬= EOS; j = j + patsiz(pat, j))
		if (omatch(lin, i, pat, j) == NO) {
			amatch = 0
			return		# with no match
			}
	amatch = i
	return				# successfully
	end
```

omatch handles everything but closures. **patsiz** returns the length of an entry in **pat**, so that it can be skipped over. We will get back to both of these routines once we deal with closures.

Closures cause all of the difficulty. In the text changing program near the end of this chapter and in the editor of Chapter 6, we are going to write code that replaces the matched text by something else. For that purpose, the most useful behavior is to match the longest possible pattern if there is a choice, so encountering a * should cause a loop on the pattern to be replicated, eating up as many occurrences as possible, until the match fails. Scanning then resumes from the point of failure by trying to match the rest of the pattern against the rest of the input line.

But what if the rest of the pattern fails? It does *not* necessarily mean that there is no match. The pattern **b*b**, for instance, does match the line **bb**, but only if the **b*** part is confined to the first **b** (or to the null string before the first **b**). What this means is, every time a match fails, we have to go back to the last closure, shorten it by one and try matching the rest of the pattern once more. Only when the pattern fails with the closure matching a null string can we give up.

And we're *still* not done, for there may be more than one closure in a pattern. (Remember, we said go back to the *last* closure.) So to handle patterns correctly, we must backtrack systematically through *all possible* closure matches, until we either find a match or fail utterly.

One way to manage the backtracking is by a recursive procedure. The advantage of recursion is that the compiler generates code to handle many of the bookkeeping details that complicate a non-recursive program. For example, we could write **amatch** like this:

```
# amatch — a recursive version to handle closures (pseudo-code)
      integer function amatch(lin, from, pat)

      offset = from                          # next unexamined input character
      for (j = 1; pat(j) ¬= EOS; j = j + patsiz(pat, j))
            if (pat(j) == CLOSURE) {  # a closure entry
                  j = [index of pattern to be repeated]
                  for (i = offset; lin(i) ¬= EOS; i = i + 1) # match as many
                        if (omatch(lin, i, pat, j) == NO)    # as possible
                              break
                   # i now points to character that made us fail
                   # try to match rest of pattern against rest of input
                   # shrink the closure by 1 after each failure
                  for (j=[pattern to repeat]; i >= offset; i = i - 1) {
                        k = amatch(lin, i, pat(j))
                        if (k > 0)       # successful match of rest of pattern
                              break
                        }
                  offset = k             # if k==0, failure; if k>0, success
                  break
                  }
            else if (omatch(lin, offset, pat, j) == NO) { # non-closure
                  amatch = 0
                  return                 # failure on non-closure
                  }
            # else omatch succeeded
      amatch = offset
      return
```

The recursion occurs in the line

```
k = amatch(lin, i, pat(j))
```

We can implement this version in PL/I by giving the procedure **amatch** the attribute **recursive**, but in Fortran the recursion must be handled explicitly. That means **amatch** needs a stack to keep track of where it is on each level.

In this particular case, the stack need only be as deep as the number of closures in an expression, so it is reasonable to leave room in each closure entry in **pat** to hold all of the information about this closure. The stack is implemented as a linked list, with each entry pointing back to the previous one; the necessary links are constructed as the pattern is being built by **getpat** and its subordinates. This is the structure of a closure entry in **pat**:

pat(i + 0)	[type]	holds **CLOSURE** for closure
pat(i + 1)	COUNT	repeat count for matches
pat(i + 2)	PREVCL	index of previous closure in pattern
pat(i + 3)	START	index in input line where match starts

The symbolic constants **COUNT**, **PREVCL**, and **START** represent the offsets, and **CLOSIZE** is the size of a closure entry, which happens to be 4.

Whenever a closure pattern is encountered, its entry in **pat** is made the current stack frame. The pattern to be repeated is assumed to *follow* the closure entry in **pat**, so that when **pat** is scanned the closure indicator will be encountered before the pattern itself; we will have to arrange this order when we build the pattern array. The pattern is matched as many times as possible, then the repeat count and starting text index are saved in the current frame and we go on to try the next pattern entry.

If a pattern entry fails, and if the last closure match can still be made shorter, **amatch** shortens it by one match and retries from there. Otherwise, it goes back to the previous closure and tries to shorten that one. Only when it exhausts all alternatives does it report failure. And of course if it fails before the first closure, there are no alternatives.

The final, non-recursive **amatch** becomes

```
# amatch  (non-recursive) — look for match starting at lin(from)
      integer function amatch(lin, from, pat)
      character lin(MAXLINE), pat(MAXPAT)
      integer omatch, patsiz
      integer from, i, j, offset, stack

      stack = 0
      offset = from                  # next unexamined input character
      for (j = 1; pat(j) ¬= EOS; j = j + patsiz(pat, j))
            if (pat(j) == CLOSURE) {           # a closure entry
                  stack = j
                  j = j + CLOSIZE              # step over CLOSURE
                  for (i = offset; lin(i) ¬= EOS; )   # match as many as
                        if (omatch(lin, i, pat, j) == NO)   # possible
                              break
                  pat(stack+COUNT) = i - offset
                  pat(stack+START) = offset
                  offset = i             # character that made us fail
                  }
            else if (omatch(lin, offset, pat, j) == NO) {      # non-closure
                  for ( ; stack > 0; stack = pat(stack+PREVCL))
                        if (pat(stack+COUNT) > 0)
                              break
                  if (stack <= 0) {            # stack is empty
                        amatch = 0             # return failure
                        return
                        }
                  pat(stack+COUNT) = pat(stack+COUNT) - 1
                  j = stack + CLOSIZE
                  offset = pat(stack+START) + pat(stack+COUNT)
                  }
            # else omatch succeeded
      amatch = offset
      return            # success
      end
```

The accompanying routines **patsiz** and **omatch** can now be spelled out:

```
# patsiz — returns size of pattern entry at pat(n)
	integer function patsiz(pat, n)
	character pat(MAXPAT)
	integer n

	if (pat(n) == CHAR)
		patsiz = 2
	else if (pat(n) == BOL | pat(n) == EOL | pat(n) == ANY)
		patsiz = 1
	else if (pat(n) == CCL | pat(n) == NCCL)
		patsiz = pat(n + 1) + 2
	else if (pat(n) == CLOSURE)		# optional
		patsiz = CLOSIZE
	else
		call error("in patsiz: can't happen.")
	return
	end
```

The entry in **patsiz** that checks for closures is labeled "optional" because **patsiz** is never called to report the length of such a pattern. It was originally put in during the early design stages as insurance, in case we changed our minds, then was left in to appease a gnawing sense of insecurity. A function should do what its name *says,* even if it doesn't have to, because some day a programmer modifying **find** may make a change that calls on the function in a new way. Programmers have the right to be ignorant of many details of your code and still make reasonable changes.

```
# omatch — try to match a single pattern at pat(j)
	integer function omatch(lin, i, pat, j)
	character lin(MAXLINE), pat(MAXPAT)
	integer locate
	integer bump, i, j

	omatch = NO
	if (lin(i) == EOS)
		return
	bump = -1
	if (pat(j) == CHAR) {
		if (lin(i) == pat(j + 1))
			bump = 1
		}
	else if (pat(j) == BOL) {
		if (i == 1)
			bump = 0
		}
	else if (pat(j) == ANY) {
		if (lin(i) ¬= NEWLINE)
			bump = 1
		}
	else if (pat(j) == EOL) {
		if (lin(i) == NEWLINE)
			bump = 0
		}
	else if (pat(j) == CCL) {
		if (locate(lin(i), pat, j + 1) == YES)
			bump = 1
		}
	else if (pat(j) == NCCL) {
		if (lin(i) ¬= NEWLINE & locate(lin(i), pat, j + 1) == NO)
			bump = 1
		}
	else
		call error("in omatch: can't happen.")
	if (bump >= 0) {
		i = i + bump
		omatch = YES
		}
	return
	end
```

bump is the amount to advance the input position if **omatch** finds a match. This is zero for patterns that match null strings and one otherwise.

locate looks for a character in a character class.

```
# locate — look for c in char class at pat(offset)
	integer function locate(c, pat, offset)
	character c, pat(MAXPAT)
	integer i, offset
	# size of class is at pat(offset), characters follow

	for (i = offset + pat(offset); i > offset; i = i - 1)
		if (c == pat(i)) {
			locate = YES
			return
			}
	locate = NO
	return
	end
```

The last alternatives in **patsiz** and in **omatch** are interesting. Since the program builds its own patterns, we know precisely what sorts of entries can be encountered. Once we have eliminated all but one possibility (with the **else if** chain) there is no need to verify that the pattern is indeed the last possibility. Or is there?

pat is a hodgepodge. What we really want is a linear list whose elements are a variety of structures:

BOL, EOL, ANY	identifying code
CHAR	identifying code, character to match
CLOSURE	identifying code, repeat count, pointer to previous closure, pointer to first matched character
CCL, NCCL	identifying code, size of class, list of characters in class

Each structure also contains, in principle, a pointer to the next list element. But since we cannot describe arbitrary structures in Fortran, since we cannot allocate storage from a language-maintained pool, since we cannot even talk about pointers, we have to cheat. We represent diverse data types all as integers, we do our own storage allocation from an integer array, we use indexes as pointers, and we sidestep the use of pointers as much as possible by knowing where things are in the array. Such trickery permits us to do many things in Fortran that were not originally intended, but at the cost of readability and some validity checks.

We can expect problems, therefore, and should prepare for them. There are many common coding and design errors that will botch what gets put into **pat**. If we blindly assume that all is well, **patsiz** and **omatch** will treat garbage as a valid pattern and act on it. In a sequence of tests, we tend to save the more elaborate alternatives for last, and in **omatch** negated character classes (**NCCL**) are at the end of the line. Garbage is bad enough, but garbage which is expected to contain a count to tell you how long it is can be much worse. So we test explicitly for the last possible condition and print "can't happen" when the impossible occurs.

The first time we ran this code, it said "can't happen." We got that message perhaps a hundred times in the process of adding the rest of the code and shaking it down. This experience speaks for itself: if you're going to walk a high-wire, use a net. You might meditate upon how much harder it would have been to debug a program that merely goes crazy whenever it's run.

Even after the initial development period, various pieces of **find** were modified, sometimes quite dramatically. Whenever a change was made with more enthusiasm than caution, "can't happen" brought us back on the track again. We finally decided to leave the messages in for all time instead of pretending to be perfect. Removing the error messages "now that the program is working" is like wearing a parachute on the ground, but taking it off once you're in the air.

We can test the new code extensively by writing **getpat** stubs that make predetermined patterns. First we try an **a** as before, only this time with a full working **match**. Then we turn on one new feature at a time, until we eventually have arbitrary mixes of patterns working with multiple closures.

Exercise 5-6: Estimate or measure how much execution time is added by leaving the debugging tests in **patsiz** and **omatch**. What fraction of the total time spent by the program does this constitute? How is it affected by the frequency with which different patterns occur in everyday use? How many extra storage locations are added by the extra code? What fraction of the total size of the program is it? □

Exercise 5-7: Write and debug **match** and its sub-modules, using various stubs to introduce patterns via **getpat**. List, in order of increasing difficulty, ten text patterns you should try. (Hint: What kinds of patterns do you have to write to visit *every* part of the code?) Try them. □

5.3 Building Patterns

Now that we have most of a working pattern finder, let's concentrate on reading and encoding the pattern. Although **find** is always concerned with a pattern that begins at position one and terminates with an **EOS**, we would still prefer a more general pattern builder — one which terminates on an arbitrary delimiter and which tells you where to continue scanning if you want. (We prefer it partly on general principles and partly because we know where we are going in this chapter and the next.) So **getpat** is a trivial routine that interfaces between **find** and **makpat**, which does the real work.

```
# getpat — convert argument into pattern
      integer function getpat(arg, pat)
      character arg(MAXARG), pat(MAXPAT)
      integer makpat

      getpat = makpat(arg, 1, EOS, pat)
      return
      end
```

As we were writing **makpat**, it became clear that we could modify it to make **find** easier to use. If a % is not at the beginning of a pattern, it loses its special meaning, as does a **$** not at the end, or a * at the very beginning. In many cases this eliminates the need to escape these characters when we are looking for literal occurrences of them. (It also eliminates the need for an error message, which is nice.) A * which does not occur at the beginning of the line is checked to make sure it never calls for repetition of anything that can match a null string, since the rest of the program is not prepared to handle that situation. In this case, however, the * is not taken literally; instead the pattern is abandoned and a diagnostic results. This seems to be the safer course in practice.

We emphasize that these "features" are *ad hoc* decisions made as we implemented the pattern builder. A number of curious situations turned out to be unspecified, as is often the case, and had to be resolved during coding. We chose to complete the specification in what appeared to be the most convenient way for the user.

There is no question, however, that too much of this sort of thing is bad. Our goal is always to write to clear, unambiguous functional specifications that are easy to remember, as opposed to writing routines any old way and trying to live with them. Too many exceptions, too much *ad hoc*-ery can lead to programs that are hard to get right and hard to use. As always, it is necessary to strike a careful balance.

Here is **makpat**, which converts the pattern argument into its encoded form in the array **pat**. **makpat** does the easy cases itself, and leaves the complicated ones to subroutines.

```
# makpat — make pattern from arg(from), terminate at delim
      integer function makpat(arg, from, delim, pat)
      character esc
      character arg(MAXARG), delim, pat(MAXPAT)
      integer addset, getccl, stclos
      integer from, i, j, junk, lastcl, lastj, lj

      j = 1          # pat index
      lastj = 1
      lastcl = 0
      for (i = from; arg(i) ¬= delim & arg(i) ¬= EOS; i = i + 1) {
            lj = j
            if (arg(i) == ANY)
                  junk = addset(ANY, pat, j, MAXPAT)
            else if (arg(i) == BOL & i == from)
                  junk = addset(BOL, pat, j, MAXPAT)
            else if (arg(i) == EOL & arg(i + 1) == delim)
                  junk = addset(EOL, pat, j, MAXPAT)
            else if (arg(i) == CCL) {
                  if (getccl(arg, i, pat, j) == ERR)
                        break
                  }
            else if (arg(i) == CLOSURE & i > from) {
                  lj = lastj
                  if (pat(lj)==BOL | pat(lj)==EOL | pat(lj)==CLOSURE)
                        break
                  lastcl = stclos(pat, j, lastj, lastcl)
                  }
            else {
                  junk = addset(CHAR, pat, j, MAXPAT)
                  junk = addset(esc(arg, i), pat, j, MAXPAT)
                  }
            lastj = lj
            }
      if (arg(i) ¬= delim)  # terminated early
            makpat = ERR
      else if (addset(EOS, pat, j, MAXPAT) == NO)  # no room
            makpat = ERR
      else
            makpat = i
      return
      end
```

All entries into the **pat** array are made via calls to **addset**. This is the same routine used in **translit** to check for overwrites, store an entry, and update the store index. (**esc** is also from **translit**; it handles an escape character if one should be present.)

Rather than test each call to **addset** to see if there was room for the new character, we ignore the status return (by assigning it to **junk**, as in Chapter 2), since **addset** will never write beyond the specified limit. If there is room for the **EOS** that terminates the pattern, all is well; if not, something went wrong and **makpat** returns **ERR**.

Character classes are encoded by **getccl**. We have organized **getccl** so that it uses **filset** (and all its sub-modules) to build character class entries as in **translit**. That way, we avoid writing a lot of new code, we have some assurance that the code is correct, and we *know* **find** and **translit** apply the same rules for specifying character classes.

```
# getccl — expand char class at arg(i) into pat(j)
	integer function getccl(arg, i, pat, j)
	character arg(MAXARG), pat(MAXPAT)
	integer addset
	integer i, j, jstart, junk

	i = i + 1		# skip over [
	if (arg(i) == NOT) {
		junk = addset(NCCL, pat, j, MAXPAT)
		i = i + 1
		}
	else
		junk = addset(CCL, pat, j, MAXPAT)
	jstart = j
	junk = addset(0, pat, j, MAXPAT)		# leave room for count
	call filset(CCLEND, arg, i, pat, j, MAXPAT)
	pat(jstart) = j - jstart - 1
	if (arg(i) == CCLEND)
		getccl = OK
	else
		getccl = ERR
	return
	end
```

CCLEND is, of course, a].

Since closure entries are moderately involved, **makpat** uses a separate routine **stclos** to build each such entry and link it to previous entries (making the stack). The value it returns is saved in **lastcl** for later linking. When a * is encountered, we have to move the previous pattern over far enough that we can stick in a closure entry, since it has to be seen *first* when **amatch** scans. **stclos** also does this, being careful not to move anything off the end of **pat** inadvertently.

```
# stclos — insert closure entry at pat(j)
      integer function stclos(pat, j, lastj, lastcl)
      character pat(MAXPAT)
      integer addset
      integer j, jp, jt, junk, lastcl, lastj

      for (jp = j - 1; jp >= lastj; jp = jp - 1) {     # make a hole
            jt = jp + CLOSIZE
            junk = addset(pat(jp), pat, jt, MAXPAT)
            }
      j = j + CLOSIZE
      stclos = lastj
      junk = addset(CLOSURE, pat, lastj, MAXPAT)  # put closure in it
      junk = addset(0, pat, lastj, MAXPAT)        # COUNT
      junk = addset(lastcl, pat, lastj, MAXPAT)   # PREVCL
      junk = addset(0, pat, lastj, MAXPAT)        # START
      return
      end
```

When we built **find**, the identifying codes stored in **pat** were the actual characters from the argument, wherever possible. (This may not have been entirely obvious because we use symbolic constants like **EOL** and **CLOSURE** instead of **DOLLAR** and **STAR**, in case you want to replace them with characters of your own choosing.) We always try to use printable internal codes, so we can insert debugging lines like

```
call putlin(pat, ERROUT)
```

and get out something more or less readable. As a matter of fact, we defined **CHAR** to be the letter **a** and **NCCL** to be **n**. Counts and indexes come out funny, but most patterns tend to be readable.

We only mentioned three testing plateaus in the process of building **find**, but actually there were many more. As we designed the mechanism for handling each type of pattern, we stuck it in and tried it out with the existing skeleton. Since we are presenting you with a finished design, however, it would have been artificial to go through the several false starts we discarded. When you build your own designs top-down, plan on more than three tests!

Getting closures right was the hardest part, for the logic involved in handling them constitutes about half the code. Most of the errors were made, as expected, in the **pat** array. Either an entry was built wrong or it was not read as it should have been. In either event the program responded by saying "can't happen" when we tried a new feature. That made it easy to locate and correct mistakes.

It is interesting to note that nearly all the design difficulties arose in our attempt to simulate structures, dynamic storage allocation, and recursion. The fact that Fortran and many other languages lack these features is a legitimate complaint. When we have to spend time doing things that the language does not do for us, it dilutes our efforts and takes time away from our original goal. The lesson once again is clear — it should not just be *possible* to do commonplace things, it must also be convenient.

find is not a big program, only about 225 lines, excluding the contribution of **translit**, but it is big enough to warrant a diagram of the relationship among the subroutines and functions, just as we did with **archive** in Chapter 3.

```
find
        getpat
                makpat
                        getccl
                                filset
                        stclos
        match
                amatch
                        omatch
                                locate
                        patsiz
```

This picture excludes utility routines like **getlin**, **putlin** and **addset**, and of course **filset** calls several routines developed for **translit** in Chapter 2.

Notice how both major branches on the hierarchy, **getpat** and **match**, progress from the abstract to the specific as you get further from the root of the tree. This is a natural result of the way we wrote **find**. We took an abstract problem, to find all the occurrences of a pattern in the input, and refined it into two steps:

get the pattern
match input lines against the pattern

Each of these was refined in turn (although we attacked the second one first), until all of the details were filled in at the lowest levels. At each stage, if the operation to be performed was simple enough, it was coded directly. If not, part of it was coded in terms of calls on lower routines, which were expanded later on.

Starting at the top and working towards the bottom by filling in details is often called "successive refinement." It is a valuable approach for programs of even modest size. At no point does the design bog down in details, for they are deferred to later stages of refinement. Testing can begin early, because the "unrefined" parts of the design can be replaced by temporary stubs that implement very limited functions. (We did that in **find**.) And revisions are easier because different aspects of the implementation tend to appear at separate levels. The important thing is to recognize the appropriate level of abstraction at each stage and to avoid mixing in lower-level details.

Exercise 5-8: Write the rest of the routines for **find** and debug them. Use the same series of tests you used before. Can you think of any others that will better test **makpat**? (Once again: Have you visited *all* parts of the code?) □

Exercise 5-9: Now that you have a working **find**, add multiple file capabilities, so that

find *pattern file1 file2 ...*

will read the specified files in order or, if no file arguments are given, read the standard input. You should print the file name before each matched line if there is more than one file argument. Would you ever want to turn this extra printout off? □

Exercise 5-10: Modify **find** so

find ¬*pattern*

will print *all* those lines that do *not* match the pattern. To what routine should the test be added? How do you specify a pattern beginning with a literal ¬? □

Exercise 5-11: Add to **find** the metacharacter +, which stands for "one or more occurrences" of a pattern in the same way that * stands for zero or more. □

Exercise 5-12: Invent a syntax for specifying an arbitrary bit string in a pattern; modify **find** to scan for such patterns. (See the discussion of **esc** in Chapter 2.) □

5.4 Some Measurements

We ran **find** with a number of patterns on a input of 225 lines and 3540 characters (a Ratfor program). Here are some CPU times as measured on a Honeywell 6070.

pattern:	% (start of line)	1 character (not present)	3-letter word	?*x x not present
total time	2.3 sec	2.4 sec.	2.4 sec.	15.0 sec.
getlin	78.4%	76.5%	76.8%	12.0%
putlin	19.5	0.1	2.0	0.0
match	0.3	5.2	4.5	0.8
amatch	0.6	10.0	9.2	38.1
omatch	0.5	7.3	6.6	33.6
patsiz	0.3	0.0	0.1	15.4

As is often the case, the CPU time for simple patterns is dominated by I/O processing. (Our **getlin** merely invokes a Fortran **read** statement for character input; **putlin** uses a **write**. Thus we have no control over their CPU time.) The pattern **?*x**, where **x** is a character not present in the input, is a bad case, since **find** must backtrack through each character position on each line before deciding that the character doesn't occur. Of course a pattern like **?*?*x** would be even worse.

To decide whether **find** is efficient enough, you have to weight its performance on different patterns by the frequency with which they occur and by the size of the inputs being searched. If the workload consists entirely of nasty patterns and large texts, then clearly **find** needs a better algorithm. As written, **find** can not be readily improved because it would require a complete backtrack through all matches to guarantee finding the leftmost and longest one. It is possible, however, to recognize any regular expression with no backtracking whatsoever. The most efficient methods convert the regular expression into a "machine" that looks for all possible matches in parallel as it reads the input, and signals whenever one is found. The construction of such a machine is of course a more time-consuming encoding than the one we used, but has a correspondingly greater payoff in running time. For more details, see Chapter 9 of *The Design and Analysis of Computer Algorithms,* referenced at the end of this chapter.

Fortunately the combination of difficult pattern and large input seems to be infrequent in practice. Much more common is a search for a particular word, for which **find** is acceptably efficient.

5.5 Changing Text

Now that we know how to identify patterns in text, let's consider a useful tool for making selective changes. Change usually implies one of three different operations. When we discard what we found, we call it a *deletion;* when we put something new in its place, we call it a *replacement;* and when we leave what we found intact and stick something before or after, we call it an *insertion.* Many "update" utilities make quite a thing out of preserving these distinctions, but the differences are irrelevant.

There is a simple notation that lets us express all these operations plus a few additional interesting alternatives. The program **change** lets us say

change *from to*

to look for all occurrences of text patterns that match *from* and replace each with the substitution string *to.* The substitution string can be just a string of replacement characters:

```
change mispell misspell
```

Or it can be null, to effect a deletion:

```
change "very, "
change " *$"
```

Or it can include the special "ditto" character **&** to put back the matched stuff and thus effect an insertion:

```
change active in&
```

The last example changes all instances of **active** to **inactive**.

The ditto character can appear at either end:

```
change able &-bodied
```

in the middle:

```
change a+b (&)
```

or more than once:

```
change very "&, &"
```

It can also be used literally with the help of an escape:

```
change and @&
```

For **change**, it is important to know not only what line matches a pattern but also what *substring* of the line caused the match to succeed. The task is to make the specified changes in that substring, then look for additional matches on the remainder of the line. **find** finds the leftmost longest match; once that match is located, we can resume scanning the input at the first character after the matched substring and so pick up all disjoint instances of a given pattern in a text file. We never rescan replacement text; this avoids any possibility of looping.

Very little code need be added to what was written for **find** in order to implement **change**. From the start we were careful to specify exactly how text patterns match pattern strings, so the size of the match string is well defined; and we wrote **amatch** so that it returns the index of the first character past the end of the match. Here is the top level.

```
# change — change "from" into "to"
        character lin(MAXLINE), new(MAXLINE), pat(MAXPAT), sub(MAXPAT)
        character arg(MAXARG)
        integer addset, amatch, getarg, getlin, getpat, getsub
        integer i, junk, k, lastm, m

        if (getarg(1, arg, MAXARG) == EOF)
                call error("usage: change from to.")
        if (getpat(arg, pat) == ERR)
                call error("illegal from pattern.")
        if (getarg(2, arg, MAXARG) == EOF)
                arg(1) = EOS
        if (getsub(arg, sub) == ERR)
                call error("illegal to.")
        while (getlin(lin, STDIN) ¬= EOF) {
                k = 1
                lastm = 0
                for ( i =1; lin(i) ¬= EOS; ) {
                        m = amatch(lin, i, pat)
                        if (m > 0 & lastm ¬= m) {  # replace matched text
                                call catsub(lin, i, m, sub, new, k, MAXLINE)
                                lastm = m
                                }
                        if (m == 0 | m == i) {      # no match or null match
                                junk = addset(lin(i), new, k, MAXLINE)
                                i = i + 1
                                }
                        else                        # skip matched text
                                i = m
                }
                if (addset(EOS, new, k, MAXLINE) == NO) {
                        k = MAXLINE
                        junk = addset(EOS, new, k, MAXLINE)
                        call remark("line truncated:.")
                        call putlin(new, ERROUT)
                        call putch(NEWLINE, ERROUT)
                        }
                call putlin(new, STDOUT)
                }
        stop
        end
```

Arguments are analyzed and converted into the appropriate forms by **getpat**, which we wrote for **find**, and **getsub**, to which we will return shortly.

amatch is attempted for every starting position on each line. If there is a match (**m > 0**) and if it is not the same match as the last time (**lastm ¬= m**), **catsub** concatenates the expanded substitution pattern onto the **new** line being built, at position **k**, and the entire matched string is skipped over. If there is no match (**m==0**) or the match was to a null string (**m==i**), one character is copied to the output and skipped over on input.

The main problem is what to do with null string matches, because unless one is careful, there can be unexpected null strings. We have arranged **change** so there are never two adjacent null strings. This ensures that the pattern **a*** matches the line **xy** at three points — before **x**, between **x** and **y**, and after **y**. We are also careful that **a*** matches **xay** at only three places as well; this is the least astonishing behavior.

A second complication is error checking, which adds a lot of code. Although we could avoid the problem of output line overflow by calling **putc** directly from **catsub**, this would destroy the generality of a module that we plan to use later. The warning message seems a better organization.

getsub, like **getpat**, divides the work of building the substitution pattern into two pieces, one specific and one more general.

```
# getsub — get substitution pattern into sub
      integer function getsub(arg, sub)
      character arg(MAXARG), sub(MAXPAT)
      integer maksub

      getsub = maksub(arg, 1, EOS, sub)
      return
      end
```

maksub copies the substitution pattern into **sub** until it finds an occurrence of the delimiter, in this case an **EOS**. Any instances of the ditto character **&** are replaced by a special code.

```
# maksub — make substitution string in sub
      integer function maksub(arg, from, delim, sub)
      character esc
      character arg(MAXARG), delim, sub(MAXPAT)
      integer addset
      integer from, i, j, junk

      j = 1
      for (i = from; arg(i) ¬= delim & arg(i) ¬= EOS; i = i + 1)
            if (arg(i) == AND)
                  junk = addset(DITTO, sub, j, MAXPAT)
            else
                  junk = addset(esc(arg, i), sub, j, MAXPAT)
      if (arg(i) ¬= delim)   # missing delimiter
            maksub = ERR
      else if (addset(EOS, sub, j, MAXPAT) == NO) # no room
            maksub = ERR
      else
            maksub = i
      return
      end
```

DITTO is a code distinguishable from all representable characters; like EOF and EOS, it is best given a small negative value.

All that remains is catsub, which is straightforward:

```
# catsub — add replacement text to end of  new
      subroutine catsub(lin, from, to, sub, new, k, maxnew)
      integer addset
      integer from, i, j, junk, k, maxnew, to
      character lin(MAXLINE), new(maxnew), sub(MAXPAT)

      for (i = 1; sub(i) ¬= EOS; i = i + 1)
            if (sub(i) == DITTO)
                  for (j = from; j < to; j = j + 1)
                        junk = addset(lin(j), new, k, maxnew)
            else
                  junk = addset(sub(i), new, k, maxnew)
      return
      end
```

Exercise 5-13: What does

```
change  active  in&
```

do to **inactive**, **attractive**, and **radioactive**? What procedures would you establish for verifying that "small" changes to a document actually have the desired effect? □

Exercise 5-14: What happens if you try to change something into a newline? What happens if you try to remove the newline at the end of a line? □

Exercise 5-15: Is there anything you can do with **translit** that you can't do with **change**? □

Exercise 5-16: Extend **change** to perform multiple changes; for example,

```
change a b c d
```

changes all **a**'s to **b**'s, then changes all **c**'s to **d**'s on the resulting line. Is this equivalent to

```
change a b | change c d
```

for all possible patterns and substitution strings? □

Exercise 5-17: Consider a file, each line of which consists of two fields separated by a tab. Write a pipeline to produce a new file with the fields interchanged on each line, i.e.,

```
1234 5678
```

becomes

```
5678 1234
```

(Hint: Try duplicating the contents of each line, with a separator between the two instances.) □

Often useful is the ability to *tag* parts of a text pattern so that the pieces of a matched string can be put back selectively or rearranged. Suppose we invent two metacharacters { and } in a text pattern to "remember" the substring matched by that part of the pattern. For example in the pattern

```
%{???}{?*}
```

the first pair of braces will remember the three characters at the beginning of the line, whatever they are; the second braces remember the rest of the line. Now we need a notation to recall the saved substrings. Suppose that @*n* refers to the string remembered by the *n*th pair of braces, where *n* is a single digit. Then we can move a three-character sequence number from the beginning of a line to the end like this:

```
change %{???}{?*} @2@1
```

As a harder-to-read example,

```
change {[¬@t]*}@t{?*} @2@t@1
```

reverses two tab-separated fields, as you did by brute force in the previous exercise.

Exercise 5-18: Rewrite the pattern-finding code to remember tagged patterns as cleanly as possible, then alter **change** to insert them on demand in the substitution string. Does your code handle nested braces? You might consider using @(and @) in place of { and }, particularly if your machine has a restricted character set. Why is this a better convention than making ordinary parentheses into metacharacters? □

Exercise 5-19: Given pattern tagging, how would you specify that only the leftmost integer in a line of integers is to be changed to zero? Only the rightmost? The second one from the left? □

Exercise 5-20: Add an option **−n** to **find**, to print the line number, followed by a space, before each line that matches. This is useful for subsequently identifying the matched lines. What is the effect of

```
find −n % | sort −n −r | change "%[0−9]* "
```

(Recall that **sort −n −r** calls for a *reverse* sort with a *numeric* field at the start of a line.) How hard would it be to write a special program to do this particular job for all file sizes? Would it be worth it? □

Exercise 5-21: A problem suggested by D. E. Knuth is to find the largest set of eight-letter words that have the same *middle* four letters. Assuming you have a machine-readable dictionary (with one word per line), how would you solve this problem with **find**, **change**, **sort** and **unique**? Do you need anything else? □

5.6 Summary

We have introduced a lot of machinery to handle text patterns, and a lot of notation to go with it. Here is a brief summary of the things you can specify.

A text pattern consists of the following elements:

c	literal character
?	any character except newline
%	beginning of line
$	end of line (null string before newline)
[...]	character class (any one of these characters)
[¬...]	negated character class (all but these characters)
*	closure (zero or more occurrences of previous pattern)
@*c*	escaped character (e.g., @%, @[, @*)

Any special meaning of characters in a text pattern is lost when escaped, inside [...], or for:

%	not at beginning
$	not at end
*	at beginning

A character class consists of zero or more of the following elements, surrounded by [and]:

c	literal character, including [
a−*c*	range of characters (digits, lower or upper case)
¬	negated character class if at beginning
@*c*	escaped character (@¬ @− @@ @])

Special meaning of characters in a character class is lost when escaped or for

¬	not at beginning
−	at beginning or end

A substitution pattern consists of zero or more of the following elements:

c	literal character
&	ditto, i.e., whatever was matched
@*c*	escaped character (@&)

An escape sequence consists of the character @ followed by a single character:

@n	newline
@t	tab
@*c*	*c* (including @@)

Bibliographic Notes

For a comprehensive discussion of how to recognize the broader class of text patterns called regular expressions, see Chapter 9 of A. V. Aho, J. E. Hopcroft and J. D. Ullman, *The Design and Analysis of Computer Algorithms* (Addison-Wesley, 1974). You might also read J. F. Gimpel's "A theory of discrete patterns and their implementation in Snobol4," *CACM,* February, 1973). Snobol is of course a widely used pattern-matching language. A fast algorithm for searching for keywords in parallel is described in "Efficient string matching: an aid to bibliographic search," A. V. Aho and M. J. Corasick, *CACM,* June, 1975.

An excellent treatise on recursion, when to use it, and how to avoid it, is D. W. Barron's *Recursive Techniques in Programming* (American-Elsevier, 1968).

find is modelled after the UNIX utility grep (globally look for regular expressions and print) by K. L. Thompson.

CHAPTER 6

EDITING

Now that we have some pattern matching and changing code handy, we are ready to tackle the more general problem of text editing — creating and modifying textual information like programs, data, documents, what have you. All interactive computing systems (and some batch systems) have some form of editing facility, but it is often primitive. The reason most users don't complain is that they don't know what they're missing. The ability to do context searches with text patterns, make global changes, or do arbitrary file I/O is often left out of even the more "advanced" editors. Those that include these features often have a command syntax so cumbersome that it is largely unused.

The editor we present here is modeled closely after the latest in a long family of conversational text editors that have achieved wide acceptance. Concern for human engineering dominates the design — **edit** tries to be concise, regular and powerful. Because **edit** is primarily intended for interactive use, it is streamlined and terse, but easy to use. This is especially important for a text editor: for most users it is the primary interface to the system. (On our UNIX system, the editor accounts for fifteen percent of all commands executed, more than three times the nearest competitor.) **edit** is *not* confined to conversational editing, however. It can be driven from prepared scripts and from other programs. It is frequently used to select results from programs or to prepare input to still other programs. It is a tool.

Error recovery is a second major influence on the design of the editor. Like the **archive** program of Chapter 3, **edit** maintains precious files, so it must be cautious. Not only that, but when it is used interactively it cannot just throw up its hands and quit when a user enters an erroneous command. It must recover gracefully, for otherwise some trifling mistake could cause the loss of valuable information.

Finally, since the editor is inherently a big program, it must be well organized, or it will get utterly out of hand (and thus probably fail to achieve its goals of good human engineering and reliability). Accordingly we will design the editor top-down, and push to the lowest possible level any information about how files are handled or how text is represented. As much as possible, details of implementation will be hidden from routines that don't need to know about them, so they can be changed or improved without upsetting the bulk of the program.

6.1 What the User Sees

Although it is generally wise to start small and evolve, an editor, like a programming language, is so heavily used that it should be really good, so that you don't spend all your time fighting its deficiencies. Accordingly, **edit** provides a relatively rich set of facilities, much more than the bare minimum.

This section contains a synopsis of **edit**, enough to give you a feeling for what design decisions were made and why, and for what commands are available. We will expand upon individual commands as we come to them during implementation.

To get started, you type

```
edit
```

or

edit *file*

In the latter case, if *file* already exists, it's assumed you want to access its contents, so they are copied into an internal *buffer,* whose implementation is left unspecified for now. In any case, text is modified in the buffer and perhaps eventually written back to some external file. Files are never modified except by explicit command. This proves to be a safer procedure than working on a file in place, for if you botch an edit you can always read in a fresh copy and start anew.

edit is basically "line oriented," in that most editing commands operate on groups of one or more lines in the buffer. This is a natural organization, since text intrinsically comes in lines. Other units might be selected — characters, words, sentences, or arbitrary strings — but lines seem to be most suitable for a wide variety of applications. It is certainly possible to access parts of lines as well; we'll get to that in a moment.

We should emphasize that the editor imposes no structure on lines. It doesn't know that columns 6 and 73 are especially significant in a Fortran program, for instance, nor does it know about any other special format. In our experience, editors that presume to know too much about what you're doing are more hindrance than help.

As we said, **edit** tries to be concise and regular. *All* editing commands consist of a single letter, which may be optionally preceded by one or two "line numbers," which specify the inclusive range of lines in the buffer over which the command is to act. Thus the command

```
1p
```

calls for the printing of the first line, and

```
1,3p
```

prints lines 1, 2, and 3. Only one command per line is permitted, since this reduces the possibility that erroneous input will cause serious damage.

The *delete* command **d** is analogous to **p**; it deletes the lines in the specified range:

```
1,3d
```

deletes the first three lines from the buffer. It is always an error to refer to a line that doesn't exist; **edit** complains when you do.

Line numbers are *relative* to the beginning of the buffer. After the first three lines have been deleted, the first remaining line (the old line 4) becomes the new line 1, and all other lines are renumbered correspondingly. This behavior may be unfamiliar if you're used to an editor where "line numbers" have a physical existence as part of text lines themselves. Our line numbers are not part of the file, and indeed have no physical representation anywhere; they are just the relative positions of the lines in the buffer. As you will see shortly, this organization gives invaluable flexibility in specifying and rearranging lines.

Although it is possible to edit entirely in terms of line numbers, be they relative or absolute, it's often an unwieldy nuisance, so **edit** lets you specify the lines in which you're interested in several other ways. For instance, the editor always keeps track of the *current line,* typically the most recent line affected by the previous command. The current line is specified by the character **.** (period or "dot"), which you can use anywhere you would have used an integer line number. The *last line* in the buffer is also known; it is called **$**. So

```
.,$p
```

would print the current line and any subsequent lines through to the end of the buffer;

```
1,$p
```

prints everything; and

```
1,$d
```

deletes everything.

Dot is altered by many commands. In particular, it is set to the last line printed after a **p** command and to the next undeleted line after **d**, except that it never moves past **$**. Thus a single

```
d
```

deletes the current line, and leaves dot pointing to the next line, while

```
.,$d
p
```

deletes all lines from here to the end, and prints the new last line.

The purpose of **.** and **$** is to reduce the need for specific line numbers. This is further helped by the ability to do line number arithmetic. To print the last few lines of the file (perhaps to see how far you got in a previous editing session), say

```
$-10,$p
```

Or you can say

```
.-5,.+5p
```

to print a group of lines around where you're working.

Even when augmented by **.**, **$** and arithmetic, line number editing is still clumsy. When you're editing, you want to be able to say, "Find me an occurrence of this string," so you can work on it without having to know precisely where it occurs. In **edit** you can do a *context search* to find a line, simply by writing a pattern between slashes.

```
/abc/
```

means: Starting with the next line after the current line, scan forward until you find a line which matches the pattern **abc**. The pattern is of course anything of the sort that we described in Chapter 5; we will use the same pattern matching code to ensure this. The search wraps around from line **$** to line 1 if necessary. Thus

```
/abc/,$p
```

would locate the next line (after the current line) that matches **abc**, and print from there to the end of the buffer. (If a context search proceeds forward around the ring back to the current line without finding a match, an error is signalled.)

Similarly, you can scan backwards by writing a pattern between backslashes. **\def** means: Starting with the line right before the current line, scan backward until you find a line which matches the specified pattern (**def**). Again, the search wraps around from line 1 to line **$**, and if no line satisfies the search, an error is signalled. Editing a Ratfor program, for instance, you might say

```
\subroutine\,/end/p
```

to print the subroutine in which the current line is imbedded.

A line number standing by itself (i.e., followed only by a newline) is taken as a request to print that line, so

```
$
```

prints the last line, and the common case of "Find me the next line with an **abc**" is

```
/abc/
```

It finds the line, prints it, and sets dot to that line so you can begin to work there. As a special case, a newline all by itself is a request to print the next line, to make it easy to step through the buffer a line at a time.

It is hard to overstate the importance of context searching. Most of the time you use context searches to get to the next place where you want to do some editing. Even when you know the source line numbers, it's often better to scan. If you've used an identifier two different ways, for instance, you might overlook an instance or two while correcting the listing. A context search, however, will lead you in turn to every place in the source where the offending identifier is referenced.

Placing line numbers before the command instead of after may seem unnatural at first, but one adapts rapidly. This choice lets individual commands use different syntaxes for optional information *after* the command letter without destroying the regularity with which a range of lines is specified.

The most important of the commands which take further information is the *substitute* command **s**, used for changing characters *within* a line.

```
s/ofrmat/format/
```

changes the *first* occurrence of **ofrmat** to **format** on the current line. If there should be more than one on that line (we hope not), you can say

```
s/ofrmat/format/g
```

to do it *globally* (i.e., everywhere) on the line. Of course the left side of an **s** command can be any legal pattern, since the same pattern-matching code is used for context searches and substitutions. The right hand side can include the ditto character **&** as shorthand for whatever was matched by the left hand side, as in the **change** program of Chapter 5.

An **s** command, with or without **g**, can be followed by a **p** to print the last affected line, to verify that the desired substitution was made. Printout is not automatic for any of the commands, so **edit** is only as chatty as you want to make it. (You can also follow a delete command by a **p**; the first undeleted line is printed.) An **s** command can be preceded by one or two line numbers, to indicate that the substitution is to be done on a range of lines:

```
.+1 s/ofrmat/format/
```

fixes the mistake on the next line, and

```
1,$ s/ofrmat/format/g
```

does it everywhere on all lines. (This is handy for consistent misspellers.) Dot is left pointing to the last line which was changed.

s is probably the most useful command in the editor, since it permits you to specify changes in a line or lines succinctly. It is frequently used to add text to the end of a line

```
s/$/ new end/
```

or the beginning

```
s/%/new beginning /
```

or the middle

```
s/and/& furthermore/p
```

The character that delimits the pieces of a substitute command need not be a slash; any character will do, so

```
s:/::g
```

deletes all slashes in a line. Of course you could achieve the same effect by "escaping" the slash, as in

```
s/@///g
```

but this can be confusing.

The last pattern used in a context search or substitute is remembered, and can be specified by a null pattern like // or \\. If you say **/format/** to find a **format** statement, and it's not the one you want, you can say // to get to the next one, or \\ to go back to the previous one. The remembered pattern eliminates a lot of tedious and error-prone re-typing. A typical use of remembered patterns while substituting is

```
/ofrmat/s//format/p
//s//format/p
//s//format/p
...
```

to walk (slowly) through a document, picking up the misspellings one by one. You know you have them all when a search fails. You can change them all at once with

```
1,$s/ofrmat/format/gp
```

but this form prints only the last one for verification.

We return now to operations that affect whole lines of text. Most important is the *append* command **a**, to add new lines of text to the buffer. It is the basic mechanism for adding text to a file, or for making a file to begin with. This entire book and all the programs that go with it were at one time or another appended to the buffer of a text editor very similar to the one we are presenting here.

Since it is used so much, the append mechanism tries to be as unobtrusive as possible. Once it encounters the command **a**, the editor enters a special *append mode* where everything following is tucked away in the appropriate part of the buffer. Escapes and all other characters lose their special meaning, until a line is encountered that contains only a period at the beginning. This signal, which is easy to type and pretty unlikely to appear in ordinary text, marks the end of append mode and is not itself copied into the buffer. Subsequent lines are interpreted as commands once again.

So to add text to the buffer, you specify where you want to put it and do an append. To tack stuff on to the end, for instance,

$a
anything you want to type
except a line containing only a .
as in the following line
.

This adds three lines to the buffer, then resumes looking for commands. It was not necessary to escape the period at the end of the second line, since that character is magic only when it stands alone at the beginning of a line. To add something at the beginning of the buffer, you can use the line number zero, as in **0a**. If no line number is specified, the text is appended after the current line (dot).

The *insert* command **i** is identical to **a**, except that it inserts lines before the line named, instead of after it. The *change* command **c** replaces one or more lines with a fresh group of zero or more lines:

line1, line2 **c**
stuff
.

replaces *line1* through *line2* with whatever lines follow the **c**. If no line numbers are given, dot is used by both **i** and **c**.

Clearly if you have **a** and **d**, you don't need either **c** or **i**. The extra flexibility appears to be worthwhile, however, and the amount of additional code turns out to be insignificant.

Dot is left at the last line of text appended, changed or inserted, so you can correct errors as you go, as in this sequence. (The annotations in italics are to clarify what is going on.)

```
a                        append some text
10    ofrmat(...)        oops!
.                        stop appending
s/ofr/for/               fix it
a                        resume appending right after corrected line
... more text ...
botched line             oops again
.                        stop appending
c                        just replace it entirely
... corrected stuff ...  and continue typing
```

The behavior of dot and the default line numbers may seem like a minor concern, but in fact proper choices are crucial for smooth editing. The example above works naturally, without any explicit line numbers, because dot and the default line numbers are "right" each time. We have tried to take similar care with other commands.

The *move* command **m** lets you move a block of one or more lines to any place in the buffer, and thus provides for "cut and paste" editing. The command

line1, line2 **m** *line3*

moves *line1* through *line2* inclusive to after *line3*. Thus

```
.,.+1m$
```

moves the current line and the one following to the end of the buffer, and

```
$m0
```

moves the last line to the beginning ("after line zero"). If no *line1* or *line2* is present, line dot is moved. Dot is left pointing to the last line moved.

You can add the contents of any file to the buffer with the *read* command **r**:

```
r file
```

reads **file**, places its contents right after line dot, and sets dot to the last line read in. Lines already in the buffer are not altered. If a line is specified with the **r** command, the text is read in after that line.

Any part of the buffer can be written onto any file with the *write* command **w**;

```
\subroutine\, /end/w test
```

writes the current subroutine on **test**. If no lines are given, a **w** command writes out the entire contents of the buffer, and if you leave out the file name (a bare **w** command), it writes on the file name used in the original **edit** *file* command. **w** does not change dot, nor does it alter the buffer.

Finally, the *quit* command **q** lets you leave the editor gracefully. The file you were working on is *not* saved automatically — if you want it saved, you have to issue an appropriate **w** command before the **q**.

Any editor command except **a**, **c**, **i** and **q** can be preceded by a *global prefix:*

g/*pattern*/ *command*

specifies that *command* is to be performed for each line in the buffer that contains an instance of *pattern*. **g**, like **w**, has a default range of all lines, but a smaller range can be given. A common use of the global prefix is to print all lines containing an interesting pattern:

```
g/interesting/p
```

(which is what the program **find** does), or to delete all lines with an undesirable pattern:

```
g/undesirable/d
```

For example,

```
g/% *$/d
```

deletes empty lines and lines that contain *only* blanks. You could use

```
g/ofrmat/s//format/gp
```

to find all **ofrmat**'s, fix them, and print *each* corrected line as a check. Since the command that follows a global prefix can have a range of lines, we can even print all lines near ones that contain an interesting pattern:

```
g/interesting/.-1,.+1p
```

The **g** prefix is definitely an advanced feature, not the concern of a first-time user, but it's worth learning.

There is also a **x** command which is identical to **g** except that it operates only on those lines that *do not* contain the pattern (**x** is for "exclude"):

```
x/% *$/p
```

prints *only* non-blank lines.

That pretty much covers the commands, but before we get into the code, here are a few more notes on line numbers, since much of editing is concerned with specifying the lines you want to do things to.

A semicolon may be used to separate line numbers just as a comma does, but it has the additional effect of setting dot to the latest line number before evaluating the next argument.

```
/abc/; .+1p
```

scans forward to the next line containing **abc**, then prints that line and the one following it (**.+1**).

A line number expression may be arbitrarily complex, so long as its value lies between 0 and **$**, inclusive. And there can be any number of expressions, so long as the last one or two are legal for the particular command. Thus

```
\function\; \\
```

finds the second previous **function** declaration, and

```
/#/; //; //; //p
```

prints from the third succeeding line containing # to the fourth, inclusive.

You can do a lot of editing without global prefixes, semicolons and multiple context searches, and indeed there is seldom call for anything as elaborate as the last example. But as you gain familiarity with the editor, more and more of these things become natural. And when you write scripts to perform complex editing sequences on a series of files, these facilities are invaluable.

Exercise 6-1: Compare the external characteristics of **edit** with the editing facilities available on your system. □

6.2 Implementation

A warning: **edit** is a big program; at 900 lines (excluding contributions from **translit**, **find** and **change**), it is fifty percent bigger than anything else in this book. Although we have done our best to write it well and to present it well, it will take study to assimilate fully. Bear with us as you read and be willing to take a couple of passes over difficult parts.

Input to the editor is a series of command lines, each of which looks like

line1, line2 command stuff

where *line1*, *line2* and *stuff* are all typically optional. Thus the main loop of the editor is

```
while (getlin(lin, STDIN) ¬= EOF) {
        get list of line numbers from lin
        if (status is OK)
                do command
        }
```

We observed earlier that **edit** is among those programs that *must* be absolutely reliable and robust. It can't just exit, even when the most ghastly errors happen, because giving up might cost the user whatever work has been accomplished so far. An editor that dies without a struggle will not be much used.

Accordingly, nearly all parts of **edit** pass back status, sometimes as both the value of the function and in the argument **status**. There are three status values: **OK** if all is well, **ERR** if not, and **EOF** if any sub-module has consumed the last of the input (or if the result was neither **OK** nor **ERR**).

"Doing the command" is a multi-way decision with one entry for each command. Most commands validate line numbers, set up defaults if appropriate, then act, usually by calling further subroutines. Underpinning all of this are routines that maintain the text in the buffer.

Let us begin with the code for obtaining line numbers for a command. This is a clearly isolated piece which we can understand and get working before doing much else. That way, when the time comes to start checking editing functions, we can use it to poke around in the lines of text at will.

The command line is held in the array **lin**, with **lin(i)** the next character to be examined. The top level for handling line numbers is **getlst**, which gets whatever line numbers there are on the input line, updates **i** so it points one position beyond the last number, and returns status (**OK** or **ERR**) both as the value of the function and in **status**.

getlst reads a whole list of line numbers by repeatedly calling on **getone**, and remembers the last two in **line1** and **line2**. It ensures that if no lines were specified, **line1** and **line2** are both set to **curln**, the current line (dot). If one line is given, **line1** and **line2** are both set to it. **getlst** also records in **nlines** the number of actual line numbers (zero, one, or two) and updates **curln** whenever a semicolon is encountered.

There are too many control variables to pass around on each call (although that is often the preferred way of making data known to sub-modules), so we define **common** blocks to hold related groups. As we mentioned before, this is the nearest we can come in Fortran to specifying a *structure,* i.e., an aggregate of related variables, perhaps of different types, which can be referenced by one name. All the declarations for each group are held in a file which is **included** as need be in each routine. We have consistently given the files the same names as the **common** blocks. Line number control, for instance, is in **clines**:

```
common /clines/ line1, line2, nlines, curln, lastln
  integer line1       # first line number
  integer line2       # second line number
  integer nlines      # number of line numbers specified
  integer curln       # current line: value of dot
  integer lastln      # last line: value of $
```

Here is **getlst**, which obtains the line numbers that precede a command.

```
# getlst — collect line numbers (if any) at lin(i), increment i
      integer function getlst(lin, i, status)
      character lin(MAXLINE)
      integer getone, min
      integer i, num, status
      include clines

      line2 = 0
      for (nlines = 0; getone(lin, i, num, status) == OK; ) {
            line1 = line2
            line2 = num
            nlines = nlines + 1
            if (lin(i) ¬= COMMA & lin(i) ¬= SEMICOL)
                  break
            if (lin(i) == SEMICOL)
                  curln = num
            i = i + 1
            }
      nlines = min(nlines, 2)
      if (nlines == 0)
            line2 = curln
      if (nlines <= 1)
            line1 = line2
      if (status ¬= ERR)
            status = OK
      getlst = status
      return
      end
```

All the arithmetic and general validity checking for line numbers occurs in **getone**, which returns **OK** for a valid number, **ERR** for error conditions, and eventually **EOF** when it sees something that is not a line number.

Why do we divide up the code this way? For much the same reason we separated out the functions of **match** in Chapter 5 — each level is preoccupied with a rather different aspect of control; mixing different aspects in one module only serves to confuse. Here, **getlst** has quite enough to do keeping track of how many line numbers have been seen and whether a semicolon has been encountered. Reading the code at this level, we couldn't care less how an individual line number is obtained, so we defer that to **getone**.

And it is clear that obtaining a line number is not all that easy either, for **getone** in turn passes on some of the work to a subordinate **getnum**, which collects a single term of a line number expression. First, here is **getone**.

```
# getone - evaluate one line number expression
      integer function getone(lin, i, num, status)
      character lin(MAXLINE)
      integer getnum
      integer i, istart, mul, num, pnum, status
      include clines

      istart = i
      num = 0
      call skipbl(lin, i)
      if (getnum(lin, i, num, status) == OK)   # first term
            repeat {                              # + or - terms
                  call skipbl(lin, i)
                  if (lin(i) ¬= PLUS & lin(i) ¬= MINUS) {
                        status = EOF
                        break
                        }
                  if (lin(i) == PLUS)
                        mul = +1
                  else
                        mul = -1
                  i = i + 1
                  call skipbl(lin, i)
                  if (getnum(lin, i, pnum, status) == OK)
                        num = num + mul * pnum
                  if (status == EOF)
                        status = ERR
                  } until (status ¬= OK)
      if (num < 0 | num > lastln)
            status = ERR

      if (status == ERR)
            getone = ERR
      else if (i <= istart)
            getone = EOF
      else
            getone = OK

      status = getone
      return
      end
```

skipbl merely skips blanks and tabs; it is used in **getone** to permit spaces between terms of a line number expression. We could have used it in **ctoi** (Chapter 2) and **getwrd** (Chapter 3), for it performs a common operation. It will be used regularly from now on.

```
# skipbl — skip blanks and tabs at lin(i)...
      subroutine skipbl(lin, i)
      character lin(ARB)
      integer i

      while (lin(i) == BLANK | lin(i) == TAB)
            i = i + 1
      return
      end
```

getnum evaluates one term of a line number expression, where a term is either an integer, **.** (dot), **$**, or a context search.

```
# getnum — convert one term to line number
      integer function getnum(lin, i, pnum, status)
      character lin(MAXLINE)
      integer ctoi, index, optpat, ptscan
      integer i, pnum, status
      include clines
      include cpat
      string digits "0123456789"

      getnum = OK
      if (index(digits, lin(i)) > 0) {
            pnum = ctoi(lin, i)
            i = i - 1      # move back; to be advanced at the end
            }
      else if (lin(i) == CURLINE)
            pnum = curln
      else if (lin(i) == LASTLINE)
            pnum = lastln
      else if (lin(i) == SCAN | lin(i) == BACKSCAN) {
            if (optpat(lin, i) == ERR)   # build the pattern
                  getnum = ERR
            else if (lin(i) == SCAN)
                  getnum = ptscan(FORWARD, pnum)
            else
                  getnum = ptscan(BACKWARD, pnum)
            }
      else
            getnum = EOF
      if (getnum == OK)
            i = i + 1      # point at next character to be examined
      status = getnum
      return
      end
```

ctoi, which we wrote in Chapter 2, converts a character string into an integer. **index**, also from Chapter 2, returns the position of a character in a string, or zero if it doesn't occur.

optpat builds a scan pattern; if the pattern in **lin** is empty, the previous pattern will be used. **ptscan** performs the actual context search.

```
# optpat - make pattern if specified at lin(i)
      integer function optpat(lin, i)
      character lin(MAXLINE)
      integer makpat
      integer i
      include cpat

      if (lin(i) == EOS)
            i = ERR
      else if (lin(i + 1) == EOS)
            i = ERR
      else if (lin(i + 1) == lin(i))          # repeated delimiter
            i = i + 1                         # leave existing pattern alone
      else
            i = makpat(lin, i + 1, lin(i), pat)
      if (pat(1) == EOS)
            i = ERR
      if (i == ERR) {
            pat(1) = EOS
            optpat = ERR
            }
      else
            optpat = OK
      return
      end
```

The chain of **else if**'s ensures that the tests are performed in exactly the right order. (We don't want to look at **lin(i+1)** if **lin(i)** is **EOS**.) The chain of tests is superior, in this regard, to the **case** statement in some languages, because the tests can be much more general and the order of evaluation controlled.

makpat and its supporting routines were defined in Chapter 5. At that time we wrote **makpat** to use an arbitrary delimiter to stop the scan. **optpat** is the first place which uses the facility; here the delimiter is the character at **lin(i)**, which is either \ or / for context searches.

ptscan starts at **.+1** or **.-1**, depending on direction, and scans around the buffer until it either finds a match or gets back to **curln**. Searching begins one line away from the current line because presumably we just did something to the current line and we'd like to get on with the next one. Testing for a pattern match is done by **match** and its subordinates, which we also wrote in Chapter 5.

```
# ptscan — scan for next occurrence of pattern
     integer function ptscan(way, num)
     integer gettxt, match, nextln, prevln
     integer k, num, way
     include clines
     include cpat
     include ctxt

     num = curln
     repeat {
          if (way == FORWARD)
               num = nextln(num)
          else
               num = prevln(num)
          k = gettxt(num)
          if (match(txt, pat) == YES) {
               ptscan = OK
               return
               }
          } until (num == curln)
     ptscan = ERR
     return
     end
```

optpat and **ptscan** must know about the pattern array **pat**, contained in the **common** block **cpat**:

```
common /cpat/ pat(MAXPAT)
  character pat              # pattern
```

In addition, **ptscan** must be able to obtain actual lines of text for **match**. It does so by invoking **gettxt**, which returns the line in the **common** block **ctxt**:

```
common /ctxt/ txt(MAXLINE)
  character txt              # text line for matching and output
```

It also maps the line number into an index for use by routines that rearrange lines. Since **ptscan** does not use this information, we will discuss implementation at this level later.

prevln and **nextln** are functions for walking around the buffer, one line at a time. It turns out to be convenient to have in the buffer at all times a "line zero" that contains nothing, so nothing will match it, which can serve as a legal line number for commands like **a**, **m** and **r**, which must be able to put things before the first line. Line zero is an instance of a useful technique — simplifying a program by adding a dummy element to a data structure, to make the boundary conditions easier to work with.

```
# nextln — get line after "line"
      integer function nextln(line)
      integer line
      include clines

      nextln = line + 1
      if (nextln > lastln)
            nextln = 0
      return
      end

# prevln — get line before "line"
      integer function prevln(line)
      integer line
      include clines

      prevln = line - 1
      if (prevln < 0)
            prevln = lastln
      return
      end
```

To summarize the line number code, here is the tree of calls for the major subroutines and functions so far.

```
edit
      getlst
            getone
                  getnum
                        optpat
                              makpat
                        ptscan
                              gettxt, match, nextln, prevln
```

Once again the progression is from the general (**getlst**) to the specific (**optpat**, **ptscan**) in several stages. Each level of the hierarchy handles a progressively smaller part of the whole problem, eliminating the need to know many details at any level.

makpat and **match** in turn call upon additional routines that we wrote in Chapters 2 and 5. Of course this saves us a fair amount of coding, but much more important is consistency. **translit**, **find**, **change** and **edit** all use the same rules and conventions for patterns; there is no need to learn and remember separate rules for each. This reduces the burden on users and encourages those who know one program to try the others.

Exercise 6-2: Write a main routine to read command lines and call **getlst**. Write a dummy **gettxt** and define **buf** so you can gain access to two or three predefined text lines. Exercise **getlst** and its subordinates with this minimum test harness. □

6.3 Control Program

Let's go back to the top now, and specify command handling in detail. Basically, the editor is a loop, reading command lines, decoding them and carrying them out. We will want to ensure that as much as possible each command line is completely sensible before carrying out any irreversible action, for otherwise a small slip could cause us to destroy a whole file of text. This means that, like **expand** in Chapter 2, the control structure of **edit** will mostly reflect error checking.

edit will accept only one command per line, although that command may optionally be preceded by a global prefix. We will fill in the details of global processing later, after learning more about what can be done with the basic commands. For now, we can write the main processing loop of **edit** as

```
while (getlin(lin, STDIN) ¬= EOF) {
        i = 1
        cursav = curln
        if (getlst(lin, i, status) == OK) {
                if (ckglob(lin, i, status) == OK)
                        status = doglob(lin, i, cursav, status)
                else if (status ¬= ERR)
                        status = docmd(lin, i, NO, status)
                # else error, do nothing
                }
        if (status == ERR) {
                call remark("?.")
                curln = cursav
                }
        else if (status == EOF)
                break
        # else OK, loop
        }
stop
```

ckglob looks for **g/.../** or **x/.../**; if either is found, **ckglob** marks the lines for processing by **doglob**, which does the desired command on each marked line. We will get back to these later; for now we can assume a dummy **ckglob** that returns **EOF** (no global command seen). If no global prefix is found, and if there was no error, **docmd** executes the command for the range of lines found by **getlst**. The **NO** argument to **docmd** says that it is not being called from within a global prefix.

The main routine must restore **curln** on an error, since it is changed with each semicolon found by **getlst** and may be altered by commands done by **doglob** and **docmd**.

Because the editor is streamlined for conversational use, its response to all errors is a terse ?. This brevity is appropriate because the error is almost always obvious, usually a slip in typing or a search that failed. In such cases an error message impedes getting on with the job. However, **edit** is structured so that wordier error messages could readily be inserted; one of the exercises is concerned with filling in the details.

Most of the code in **docmd** is in a long **if** ... **else if** ... **else if** to identify which command is to be performed; each case is followed by a few lines to perform the task, most often by subroutine call.

The entry for *print* (**p**), for example, is

```
else if (lin(i) == PRINT) {
	if (lin(i + 1) == NEWLINE)
	  andif (defalt(curln, curln, status) == OK)
		status = doprnt(line1, line2)
	}
```

This checks for a valid command format, verifies that the line numbers are reasonable, then performs the appropriate routine. **andif** is a synonym for **if**, used here to emphasize that a sequence of tests must be performed *in the given order.* As we discussed in Chapter 2, Fortran, like many languages, does not guarantee any particular order for evaluation of logical expressions (or any other expressions, for that matter), nor does it guarantee that evaluation of a logical expression will terminate as soon as the truth value is known. We cannot use

```
if (lin(i + 1) == NEWLINE & defalt(curln, curln, status) == OK)
```

because we do not want a call to **defalt** to set **status** to **OK** after we have established that **lin(i+1)** is not a **NEWLINE**. There is never a balancing **else** for an **andif**; consequently we must be careful always to surround an **if...andif** sequence with braces.

The **p** command expects two line numbers. If only one is given, it is used for both line numbers (i.e., print only one line). If none are given, the current line is used for both line numbers. Our notation for this is **(.,.)p**, the parentheses indicating that line numbers are optional, and the two dots showing the default values. **defalt** sets defaulted line numbers to the specified values.

```
# defalt - set defaulted line numbers
	integer function defalt(def1, def2, status)
	integer def1, def2, status
	include clines

	if (nlines == 0) {
		line1 = def1
		line2 = def2
		}
	if (line1 > line2 | line1 <= 0)
		status = ERR
	else
		status = OK
	defalt = status
	return
	end
```

In no case is it permissible to print line zero or wrap around the end of the buffer, so **defalt** flags this as an error. Notice also that **defalt** tests whether **line1<=0**, even though **getone** ensures that it can't be negative. This is again defensive programming — guarding against an error from somewhere else in the program.

The actual printing is straightforward:

```
# doprnt — print lines from through to
	integer function doprnt(from, to)
	integer gettxt
	integer from, i, j, to
	include clines
	include ctxt

	if (from <= 0)
		doprnt = ERR
	else {
		for (i = from; i <= to; i = i + 1) {
			j = gettxt(i)
			call putlin(txt, STDOUT)
			}
		curln = to
		doprnt = OK
		}
	return
	end
```

doprnt is called from several places in **docmd**, so it is necessary to check for line zero here as well as in **defalt**. We use the same mechanism as in **ptscan** to locate actual text, by calling on **gettxt** to get the line we want to print. Once again the index returned by **gettxt** is not needed.

Note that there is no printing of gratuitous noise like "end of file" when line **$** is printed. Indeed **edit** is quiet in most ways. Just because a program is used interactively, it does not mean that you should be forced to listen to it babble. One trouble with chatty programs is that you can't turn them off when you want to use them with other programs. Thus printing occurs only when you specify it, so that commands can work silently. But it is called for often enough to warrant some extra notation and shorthand. **s**, **m** and **d** commands can be followed by a **p**, to print the (last) line affected. And a command line containing only line numbers (no command) causes the last line specified to be printed. Most commonly, this will be a single line, as in **1** or **$** or **/abc/−2**, but it also could be many:

```
/abc/; //; //; //
```

will print only the fourth occurrence of **abc**, not the third through the fourth as when the trailing **p** is present. And finally, a completely empty command line (newline only) is taken as **.+1p**, so you can walk through the buffer by typing newlines.

docmd is the first routine in this book which is longer than one page. Although it is foolish to set arbitrary limits, it does seem wise to keep individual routines shorter than a page, for the shorter a program is, the easier it is to grasp. (And once a page boundary is crossed, it's hard to keep track of indentation.) The median size of our routines is 20 lines; the mean is 15 lines. Even our bigger-than-a-page subroutines are carefully designed to be easy to understand — each is just a chain of **else if**'s that chooses among a large set of alternatives; each alternative is readily comprehended. **docmd** is shown in its entirety later in this chapter; for now, the part that controls printing is

```
# docmd — handle all commands except globals (incomplete)
     integer function docmd(lin, i, glob, status)

     pflag = NO            # may be set by d, m, s
     status = ERR
     if (lin(i) == APPENDCOM) {
          do append command
          }
     # and so on for other commands
     else if (lin(i) == PRINT) {
          if (lin(i + 1) == NEWLINE)
            andif (defalt(curln, curln, status) == OK)
               status = doprnt(line1, line2)
          }
     else if (lin(i) == NEWLINE) {
          if (nlines == 0)
               line2 = nextln(curln)
          status = doprnt(line2, line2)
          }
     else if (lin(i) == QUIT) {
          if (lin(i + 1) == NEWLINE & nlines == 0 & glob == NO)
               status = EOF
          }
     # else status is ERR
     if (status == OK & pflag == YES)
          status = doprnt(curln, curln)
     docmd = status
     return
     end
```

This also shows the code for the *quit* command **q**, which is called for by a command line containing only **q**. It causes the editor to exit, just as if it had encountered an **EOF** while reading commands. Nothing is printed, for the same reasons that most commands are silent.

Furthermore, nothing is written onto any file after a **q** command. You might ask whether it would be better to write out the editing buffer automatically, or at least to ask the user for confirmation before exiting. It is hard to decide how much to protect users from their own behavior, but in our experience, it is generally wisest to keep out of people's way: assume they know what they are doing and let them do it with as few prohibitions and warnings as you can manage. For instance, one common use of **edit** is to examine and perhaps alter a file in the buffer without any intention of rewriting it. An editor that rewrites anyway is a poor design, because it severely constrains this sort of editing. Even a request for verification is intrusive, and it may well interfere with a pre-defined script.

You may recall that the **archive** program of Chapter 3 refused to delete all the files in an archive when that was implicitly requested. Are we being inconsistent? The difference is that **archive** is a rather specialized tool for long-term storage of precious information, and probably not used daily by the average person. Thus it is cautious in everything it does. **edit**, on the other hand, is the primary interface to a system, used constantly, and a general purpose tool. It can more confidently take users' commands at face value.

6.4 Buffer Representations

The other command we hinted at in **docmd** is *append*, which adds text to the buffer. The lines to be appended are placed in the buffer right *after* the line specified, or right after the current line if no line number is provided. Our shorthand for this discipline is **(.)a**. It should be clear why we want to be particular about what is acceptable as a command. If you forget to enter append mode before typing text, you don't want arbitrary letters in a word to cause changes in the text. Instead a **?** will bring you up short after just one line of nonsense.

The actual code in **docmd** that calls **append** is

```
if (lin(i) == APPENDCOM) {
        if (lin(i + 1) == NEWLINE)
                status = append(line2, global)
        }
```

and **append** itself is

```
# append - append lines after "line"
        integer function append(line, glob)
        character lin(MAXLINE)
        integer getlin, inject
        integer line, glob
        include clines

        if (glob == YES)
                append = ERR
        else {
                curln = line
                for (append = NOSTATUS; append == NOSTATUS; )
                        if (getlin(lin, STDIN) == EOF)
                                append = EOF
                        else if (lin(1) == PERIOD & lin(2) == NEWLINE)
                                append = OK
                        else if (inject(lin) == ERR)
                                append = ERR
                }
        return
        end
```

NOSTATUS must have a value different from **OK**, **ERR**, and **EOF**. Appending text under control of a global prefix can lead to difficulties, which we choose to avoid for now, since you can achieve the same effect with an **r** command. This version of

append outlaws global appends, but the possibility of special treatment for them later is left open.

The actual work of inserting each new line (and updating **curln** to point at it) is done by the routine **inject**. To see how it works, we must learn a little more about how the buffer is organized.

We want to be able to rearrange lines freely, and to scan in either direction efficiently. We could have a single array of pointers to text lines and rearrange the pointers as lines are deleted or moved, as we did for **sort** in Chapter 4. But since appending, deleting, and reading all change the number of lines, some bookkeeping will be needed to keep the pointers in a compact set. So the next thing to consider is a *two-way linked list* of text lines where each line entry contains pointers to the previous line and to the next line. (We use links in both directions so operations like scanning backwards do not pay a time penalty.) That way, we can rewrite pointer information to move lines around as needed. Appending and deleting entire sections are also easy.

Where should the lines be stored? The easiest thing is to hold everything in memory, but that can put a severe limit on the size of file we can deal with. We could compromise and put the text out on some working file, keeping the links in memory along with enough information to locate each text line in the file. That limits the total number of lines we can handle, but allows for many more characters of text. Or we could keep the entire linked list on a file, and access only what we need through a fixed size "window."

However we choose to do it, the important thing is to isolate the actual implementation as much as possible from the program as a whole. That way we can optimize a given implementation, even change the entire strategy, just by altering a handful of low-level buffer management routines.

In this particular case, we can implement *any* of the possibilities mentioned above by writing six functions:

> **setbuf** initializes the buffer to contain only a valid line zero, and creates a scratch file if necessary.
>
> **clrbuf** discards a scratch file, if one is used.
>
> **inject(lin)** copies the text in **lin** into the buffer immediately after the current line, beginning a new line as necessary after each newline, and sets **curln** to the last line injected.
>
> **getind(n)** maps line number **n** into a unique index that can be used to access all the information about that line.
>
> **gettxt(n)** does the same mapping as **getind**, but also copies the contents of the line into the array **txt** in **common** block **ctxt**.
>
> **relink(k1, k2, k3, k4)** does a re-linking, by making the **k2** entry point back to **k1** and **k3** point forward to **k4**, where the **k***i* are obtained from calls on **getind** or **gettxt**.

The **k** indices are needed, in addition to line numbers, to keep track of actual lines of text during rearrangements, when the meaning of a line number can change several times.

It is not necessary to know (and there is no way of knowing) whether the text resides in memory, or the links do, or anything. So long as one line of text and the last four links located with **getind** and **gettxt** calls are available, we can do everything we have to in the way of editing. That means that the buffer in memory can contain all the data, or it can be a fixed size window on a much larger world. The point is, we can do many things once we have a working text editor because the interface to the buffer manager is well specified and the code for it is isolated.

We should stress that we didn't start with these six routines right at the beginning. Instead we "discovered" them as we wrote the editor from top to bottom. By seeing at each stage what operations we wanted to perform on the text, we were able to abstract this handful of basic functions. It also helped that we wanted to put off deciding the actual implementation as long as possible — that goal steered us away from a number of more restrictive designs. Given this set of basic operations, and measurements showing where the editor spends its time, we can improve **edit**'s efficiency as it becomes necessary, without touching the bulk of the code.

But the first order of business is to get a working editor. So we pick the easiest form of buffer management to implement, keeping everything in memory in the array **buf**. The structure of a list element is

buf(k + 0)	**PREV**	index of previous line
buf(k + 1)	**NEXT**	index of next line
buf(k + 2)	**MARK**	used by global modifier
buf(k + 3)	**TEXT**	first character of text string
buf(k + 4)	...	second character, etc.

Each text string is terminated by an **EOS**. The **common** block **cbuf** contains:

```
common /cbuf/ buf(MAXBUF), lastbf
  character buf             # buffer for pointers plus text
  integer lastbf            # last element used in buf
```

Lines of text are copied as needed into the buffer **txt**, kept in the **common** block **ctxt**. We showed you **ctxt** in conjunction with **ptscan**, and it was also used with **doprnt**. Here it is again for completeness:

```
common /ctxt/ txt(MAXLINE)
  character txt             # text line for matching and output
```

We can now write in-memory versions of the buffer management routines. **clrbuf** is easiest, when there is no scratch file.

```
# clrbuf (in memory) — initialize for new file
      subroutine clrbuf

      return        # nothing to do
      end
```

getind and **gettxt** find the specified line by following the linked list from the beginning. **getind** finds the index only; **gettxt** uses **getind** to locate the line, then returns the text as well. They are separate functions because many editor commands can operate quite nicely on line indexes, without looking at the line contents.

When we later use a scratch file to hold text, this separation will keep us from accessing the file unless we need to.

```
# getind — locate line index in buffer
      integer function getind(line)
      integer j, k, line
      include cbuf

      k = LINE0
      for (j = 0; j < line; j = j + 1)
            k = buf(k + NEXT)
      getind = k
      return
      end
```

LINE0 is, of course, 1 in this implementation.

```
# gettxt (in memory) — locate text for line and make available
      integer function gettxt(line)
      integer getind
      integer line
      include cbuf
      include ctxt

      gettxt = getind(line)
      call scopy(buf, gettxt + TEXT, txt, 1)
      return
      end
```

gettxt uses **scopy**, which we wrote in Chapter 3, to copy the line into **txt**.

relink only modifies two links; for many tasks it must be called more than once, but there are situations where the limited function is necessary.

```
# relink — rewrite two half links
      subroutine relink(a, x, y, b)
      integer a, b, x, y
      include cbuf

      buf(x + PREV) = a
      buf(y + NEXT) = b
      return
      end
```

setbuf sets up the buffer initially, by creating line zero and linking it to itself. Line zero contains only an **EOS**, so nothing will match it, but its presence regularizes the code — so that appending after line zero is not a special case, for instance.

```
# setbuf (in memory) — initialize line storage buffer
      subroutine setbuf
      integer addset
      integer junk
      include cbuf
      include clines

      call relink(LINE0, LINE0, LINE0, LINE0)
      lastbf = LINE0 + TEXT
      junk = addset(EOS, buf, lastbf, MAXBUF)
      curln = 0
      lastln = 0
      return
      end
```

inject is complicated mainly by its ability to handle a line containing imbedded newlines. We haven't yet mentioned these, but if you think back to the code for **change** in Chapter 5, you will realize that there is no reason why you can't change something in the middle of a line into a newline. To preserve this useful property for the **s** command, **inject** must split a "line" with imbedded newlines into separate lines and add them to the buffer one at a time. **inject** also updates **curln** and **lastln** appropriately.

```
# inject (in memory) — put text from lin after curln
      integer function inject(lin)
      character lin(MAXLINE)
      integer addset, getind, nextln
      integer i, junk, k1, k2, k3
      include cbuf
      include clines

      for (i = 1; lin(i) ¬= EOS; ) {
            k3 = lastbf
            lastbf = lastbf + TEXT
            while (lin(i) ¬= EOS) {
                  junk = addset(lin(i), buf, lastbf, MAXBUF)
                  i = i + 1
                  if (lin(i - 1) == NEWLINE)
                        break
                  }
            if (addset(EOS, buf, lastbf, MAXBUF) == NO) {
                  inject = ERR
                  break
                  }
            k1 = getind(curln)
            k2 = getind(nextln(curln))
            call relink(k1, k3, k3, k2)
            call relink(k3, k2, k1, k3)
            curln = curln + 1
            lastln = lastln + 1
            inject = OK
            }
      return
      end
```

We can now show some more of the subroutine hierarchy, to help you keep track of who calls whom.

```
edit
      setbuf
            relink
      getlst
      docmd
            append
                  getlin
                  inject
                        getind, nextln, relink
            defalt
            doprnt
                  gettxt, putlin
      clrbuf
```

Most of the growth will be in **docmd** as we add more cases.

Exercise 6-3: Implement the text editor with these buffer management routines and the piece of **edit** we have shown so far and test it. You will need stubs for **ckglob** and **doglob**. What should they do? You should be able to append text, print various lines, do context searches, and quit. Make sure you visit all the crannies of the code. □

Exercise 6-4: How would you get a line containing only a dot into the buffer? □

Exercise 6-5: What happens to the current line when you append nothing, that is, when you write the command sequence

```
a
.
```

Is this a reasonable thing to happen? □

Exercise 6-6: Is there any circumstance under which a context search could match line zero? □

6.5 More Commands: Delete, Insert, Change, Print line number, Move

Another important capability besides appending is making unwanted text go away. This is done with the *delete* command **(.,.)d**. In **docmd** we add:

```
else if (lin(i) == DELCOM) {
        if (ckp(lin, i + 1, pflag, status) == OK)
          andif (defalt(curln, curln, status) == OK)
          andif (delete(line1, line2, status) == OK)
          andif (nextln(curln) ¬= 0)
                curln = nextln(curln)
        }
```

The *delete* command removes the line or lines specified and leaves **curln** pointing at the next line after the stuff removed, unless that would be off the end of the buffer, in which case **curln** is set to **lastln**. The optional **p**, to print this line as a check, is checked and recorded in **pflag** by **ckp**:

```
# ckp — check for "p" after command
      integer function ckp(lin, i, pflag, status)
      character lin(MAXLINE)
      integer i, j, pflag, status

      j = i
      if (lin(j) == PRINT) {
            j = j + 1
            pflag = YES
            }
      else
            pflag = NO
      if (lin(j) == NEWLINE)
            status = OK
      else
            status = ERR
      ckp = status
      return
      end
```

The actual work is done in the function **delete**, which leaves **curln** pointing to the line just *before* the lines removed, and resets **lastln** to the new last line.

```
# delete — delete lines from through to
      integer function delete(from, to, status)
      integer getind, nextln, prevln
      integer from, k1, k2, status, to
      include clines

      if (from <= 0)
            status = ERR
      else {
            k1 = getind(prevln(from))
            k2 = getind(nextln(to))
            lastln = lastln - (to - from + 1)
            curln = prevln(from)
            call relink(k1, k2, k1, k2)
            status = OK
            }
      delete = status
      return
      end
```

Three other commands are easily implemented using existing routines. *Insert* or (.)i injects text immediately *before* the specified line number.

```
else if (lin(i) == INSERT) {
        if (lin(i + 1) == NEWLINE)
                status = append(prevln(line2), global)
        }
```

Change or **(.,.)c** deletes the lines in the specified range, then injects text in their place.

```
else if (lin(i) == CHANGE) {
        if (lin(i + 1) == NEWLINE)
          andif (defalt(curln, curln, status) == OK)
          andif (delete(line1, line2, status) == OK)
                status = append(prevln(line1), glob)
        }
```

And **(.)=** is used to print the value of a line number expression (or of the current line number), so you can see where some line is. It is most often used as **$=** to tell how many lines are in the buffer.

```
else if (lin(i) == PRINTCUR) {
        if (ckp(lin, i + 1, pflag, status) == OK) {
                call putdec(line2, 1)
                call putc(NEWLINE)
                }
        }
```

The *move* command **m** rearranges lines of text:

(.,.)m *line3*

causes the specified line or lines to be taken from wherever they currently reside and placed immediately after *line3*. Since **getone** is used to obtain *line3*, any valid expression can be used, such as

```
/format/m/end/-1p
```

which moves the next line containing **format** to immediately before the next line containing **end**. **curln** is left pointing at the last line moved, which would contain **format** in this case. The optional trailing **p** prints this line. The code in **docmd** is

```
else if (lin(i) == MOVECOM) {
        i = i + 1
        if (getone(lin, i, line3, status) == EOF)
                status = ERR
        if (status == OK)
          andif (ckp(lin, i, pflag, status) == OK)
          andif (defalt(curln, curln, status) == OK)
                status = move(line3)
        }
```

and the work is done in **move**:

```
# move — move line1 through line2 after line3
      integer function move(line3)
      integer getind, nextln, prevln
      integer k0, k1, k2, k3, k4, k5, line3
      include clines

      if (line1 <= 0 | (line1 <= line3 & line3 <= line2))
            move = ERR
      else {
            k0 = getind(prevln(line1))
            k3 = getind(nextln(line2))
            k1 = getind(line1)
            k2 = getind(line2)
            call relink(k0, k3, k0, k3)
            if (line3 > line1) {
                  curln = line3
                  line3 = line3 - (line2 - line1 + 1)
                  }
            else
                  curln = line3 + (line2 - line1 + 1)
            k4 = getind(line3)
            k5 = getind(nextln(line3))
            call relink(k4, k1, k2, k5)
            call relink(k2, k5, k4, k1)
            move = OK
            }
      return
      end
```

Exercise 6-7: Why are the calls to **getind** and **relink** made in such a curious order in **move**? What can happen if you do all the **getind** calls first, then all the **relink** calls? What can happen if **k3** is computed *after* **k1** and **k2**? Why didn't we make the first **relink** call immediately after obtaining **k3**? □

Exercise 6-8: Add the code for these commands to your skeleton editor and test them. Pay particular attention to behavior at the "boundaries," such as **0i**, **.m.−1**, and **1,$d**. □

Exercise 6-9: No attempt is made to reclaim storage used by deleted lines. What problems can this cause? How would you implement a *garbage collection* scheme, modifying **delete** as little as possible? (**delete** is the only subroutine where space is thrown away; it is called for **c**, **d** and **s** commands.) Is it better to recycle collected garbage as soon as possible or only when necessary? What measurements would you make to justify your prejudice? □

Exercise 6-10: Implement a *copy* command **k**

(.,.)k *line3* **p**

which makes a copy of a block of lines after *line3*, instead of moving them. (The mnemonic **k** for "copy" is strained but we're running out of letters, and it seems worthwhile to retain the single-letter convention for command names.) □

6.6 The Substitute Command

So far we have dealt with entire lines of text, which is all that many editors will let you talk about. But we have the **change** program of Chapter 5 to draw upon, so we can easily add a *substitute* command **s** that selectively replaces text matched by a text pattern. This proves to be superior, from a human engineering standpoint, to always replacing entire lines, or to specifying character positions by column number. It also seems to be easier to work in terms of lines most of the time (using context to identify them, of course) and descend to the character level only for substitutions.

The format of a *substitute* command is

(.,.) s/*pattern*/*new*/g

where the delimiter / can actually be any character other than newline. The **g** suffix is used when you want to alter *all* matching substrings, as in **change**; if the **g** is absent only the leftmost match is altered.

The code in **docmd** that checks for *substitute* is

```
else if (lin(i) == SUBSTITUTE) {
        i = i + 1
        if (optpat(lin, i) == OK)
          andif (getrhs(lin, i, sub, gflag) == OK)
          andif (ckp(lin, i + 1, pflag, status) == OK)
          andif (defalt(curln, curln, status) == OK)
                status = subst(sub, gflag)
        }
```

It uses **optpat**, as does **getnum**, to encode the pattern, then calls on **getrhs** to encode the replacement string and look for a **g**. **getrhs** in turn relies on **maksub**, which we wrote for **change**, to do most of the work. Both **makpat** and **maksub** were written so the delimiter can be any character. This permits substitute commands to be delimited by any convenient character, not necessarily the slashes we have used in most of our examples. (This is handy when you want to substitute instances of / and don't feel like escaping it every time.) **ckp** again checks for the optional trailing **p** that prints the resulting line, and **defalt** sets the default line numbers if necessary.

```
# getrhs — get substitution string for "s" command
      integer function getrhs(lin, i, sub, gflag)
      character lin(MAXLINE), sub(MAXPAT)
      integer maksub
      integer gflag, i

      getrhs = ERR
      if (lin(i) == EOS)
            return
      if (lin(i + 1) == EOS)
            return
      i = maksub(lin, i + 1, lin(i), sub)
      if (i == ERR)
            return
      if (lin(i + 1) == GLOBAL) {
            i = i + 1
            gflag = YES
            }
      else
            gflag = NO
      getrhs = OK
      return
      end
```

All that remains is the code for **subst**, which is modeled after the main routine of **change** in Chapter 5.

```
# subst - substitute "sub" for occurrences of pattern
      integer function subst(sub, gflag)
      character new(MAXLINE), sub(MAXPAT)
      integer addset, amatch, gettxt, inject
      integer gflag, j, junk, k, lastm, line, m, status, subbed
      include clines
      include cpat
      include ctxt

      subst = ERR
      if (line1 <= 0)
            return
      for (line = line1; line <= line2; line = line + 1) {
            j = 1
            subbed = NO
            junk = gettxt(line)
            lastm = 0
            for (k = 1; txt(k) ¬= EOS; ) {
                  if (gflag == YES | subbed == NO)
                        m = amatch(txt, k, pat)
                  else
                        m = 0
                  if (m > 0 & lastm ¬= m) { # replace matched text
                        subbed = YES
                        call catsub(txt, k, m, sub, new, j, MAXLINE)
                        lastm = m
                        }
                  if (m == 0 | m == k) {    # no match or null match
                        junk = addset(txt(k), new, j, MAXLINE)
                        k = k + 1
                        }
                  else                      # skip matched text
                        k = m
                  }
            if (subbed == YES) {
                  if (addset(EOS, new, j, MAXLINE) == NO) {
                        subst = ERR
                        break
                        }
                  call delete(line, line, status)      # remembers dot
                  subst = inject(new)
                  if (subst == ERR)
                        break
                  subst = OK
                  }
            }
      return
      end
```

It is considered an error for a substitute command to make no substitutions at all, since that often indicates that you didn't type the right pattern, or that you applied it to the wrong line.

Exercise 6-11: What is the meaning of each occurrence of // in

/abc/; //; //s///

What does the command do? □

Exercise 6-12: What happens when you delete all the characters on a line, as in

s/?*//

What if you then delete the newline, as in

s/@n//

What happens if you delete the newline at the end of a non-empty line? What happens if you substitute additional newlines into existence? Express this behavior in one or two concise rules. □

Exercise 6-13: Implement the *transliterate* command **(.,.)t**, which maps one character set into another, as in the **translit** program of Chapter 2. That is

1,$t/a−z/A−Z/

would convert lower case letters to upper case on all lines. Why would you want this facility in addition to **translit**? Why would you want **translit** in addition to this facility? □

Exercise 6-14: How would you implement an *undo* command **u**, which would undo the effect of the last substitute command (that is, replace the new line by the old one)? Can you extend it to other commands? □

6.7 Input/Output

We could quit right about now and have a pretty comprehensive text editor. By adding a little more code, we could have a program we could invoke as

edit *file*

which reads *file* into its internal buffer for processing and, just before exiting, writes it back.

Instead, we are going to add a few more commands that will let us read and write files explicitly, so we can selectively merge and split files or make multiple copies without going outside the editor. These extra commands greatly increase the ease with which you can do "cut and paste" editing. For example, we used all of them extensively while editing the manuscript of this book, to isolate programs for testing, then to reinstall the revised versions.

The *enter* command **e** *file* clears the internal buffer and copies *file* into it. There is also a *read* command **(.)r** *file* which *appends* the contents of *file* right after the specified line, as if they had been typed after an **a** command, without altering text already in the buffer. Files are created or rewritten with the *write* command **(1,$)w** *file*, which copies the specified range of lines onto *file*, replacing its previous contents. The default for this command is to write the entire buffer, if there are no line numbers, or to write one line if there is but one line number. Dot is set to the last line read on **e** and **r** commands. The **w** command does not change dot or the buffer contents, so you can write intermediate versions of the file without interfering with editing.

A filename is remembered from the argument in **edit** *file*, or from the first **r** or **w** command that specifies one, or from the most recent **e** command. An I/O command with no *file* uses the remembered name, so an unadorned **e**, **r** or **w** command refers to the file you began with. The *filename* command **f** does nothing but print the remembered name for inspection, or optionally set it if a name is given, as in the command **f** *file*. We introduce another **common** block **cfile**, to hold the remembered file name.

```
common /cfile/ savfil(MAXLINE)
  character savfil    # remembered file name
```

The remaining code for **docmd** is

```
else if (lin(i) == ENTER) {
        if (nlines == 0)
          andif (getfn(lin, i, file) == OK) {
                call scopy(file, 1, savfil, 1)
                call clrbuf
                call setbuf
                status = doread(0, file)
                }
        }
else if (lin(i) == PRINTFIL) {
        if (nlines == 0)
          andif (getfn(lin, i, file) == OK) {
                call scopy(file, 1, savfil, 1)
                call putlin(savfil, STDOUT)
                call putc(NEWLINE)
                status = OK
                }
        }
else if (lin(i) == READCOM) {
        if (getfn(lin, i, file) == OK)
                status = doread(line2, file)
        }
else if (lin(i) == WRITECOM) {
        if (getfn(lin, i, file) == OK)
          andif (defalt(1, lastln, status) == OK)
                status = dowrit(line1, line2, file)
        }
```

The **(1,$)** line number discipline for the **w** command is enforced by **defalt**, described earlier.

Filenames are obtained and checked by **getfn**, which insists on at least one space and a filename, or nothing at all.

```
# getfn - get file name from lin(i)...
      integer function getfn(lin, i, file)
      character lin(MAXLINE), file(MAXLINE)
      integer i, j, k
      include cfile

      getfn = ERR
      if (lin(i + 1) == BLANK) {
            j = i + 2                  # get new file name
            call skipbl(lin, j)
            for (k = 1; lin(j) ¬= NEWLINE; k = k + 1) {
                  file(k) = lin(j)
                  j = j + 1
                  }
            file(k) = EOS
            if (k > 1)
                  getfn = OK
            }
      else if (lin(i + 1) == NEWLINE & savfil(1) ¬= EOS) {
            call scopy(savfil, 1, file, 1) # or old name
            getfn = OK
            }
      # else error
      if (getfn == OK & savfil(1) == EOS)
            call scopy(file, 1, savfil, 1) # save if no old one
      return
      end
```

doread and **dowrit** both print the number of lines transmitted, as a check and to signal completion of the operation. This design is inconsistent with our earlier lecture about programs that talk too much, but it has been our experience that users prefer some feedback for operations like **r** and **w** which involve a significant change in the status of either local or external file copy. The line count provides a rough confirmation that you transmitted what you really wanted to. A design principle like "avoid excessive chatter" is a guideline to be applied intelligently, not an absolute rule to be followed blindly.

```
# doread — read "file" after "line"
      integer function doread(line, file)
      character file(MAXLINE), lin(MAXLINE)
      integer getlin, inject, open
      integer count, fd, line
      include clines

      fd = open(file, READ)
      if (fd == ERR)
            doread = ERR
      else {
            curln = line
            doread = OK
            for (count = 0; getlin(lin, fd) ¬= EOF; count = count + 1) {
                  doread = inject(lin)
                  if (doread == ERR)
                        break
                  }
            call close(fd)
            call putdec(count, 1)
            call putc(NEWLINE)
            }
      return
      end

# dowrit — write "from" through "to" into file
      integer function dowrit(from, to, file)
      character file(MAXLINE)
      integer create, gettxt
      integer fd, from, k, line, to
      include ctxt

      fd = create(file, WRITE)
      if (fd == ERR)
            dowrit = ERR
      else {
            for (line = from; line <= to; line = line + 1) {
                  k = gettxt(line)
                  call putlin(txt, fd)
                  }
            call close(fd)
            call putdec(to-from+1, 1)
            call putc(NEWLINE)
            dowrit = OK
            }
      return
      end
```

Exercise 6-15: Add the I/O commands to your editor and test them. If you cannot specify files by name in your system, see Chapter 3 for a discussion of alternatives. □

Exercise 6-16: Modify the **r** and **w** commands so they produce no confirming line count. Experiment with both versions. Which do you prefer? □

Exercise 6-17: The sequence

```
1,$d
r file
```

differs from

```
e file
```

in at least two important respects. What are they? Is it worth modifying the **d** command to gain some of the advantages of **e**? □

6.8 Global Commands

We have now specified everything in the editor except the details of the global prefix **g**, which we recall has the format

(1,$) g/*pattern*/ *command*

Default line numbers are the same as for the **w** command: if none are given the entire buffer is examined. For every line that matches *pattern* the *command* will be obeyed. But sometimes it is more convenient to specify a pattern that matches those lines we want to leave alone, so we define the complement of **g** to be **x**:

(1,$) x/*pattern*/ *command*

does *command* on every line that *does not* contain *pattern*. (The mnemonic significance of **x** is "exclude." The code is written entirely in terms of symbolic constants, however, only one of which needs to be changed to alter our selection if you prefer something else.)

command can be any **edit** command except **a**, **c** or **i**, whose operation in global commands we have left as an exercise. Furthermore, it may be preceded by line numbers with context searches and so on. For example,

```
g/%#/p
```

prints lines that begin with a #, such as the comment lines that introduce our subroutines. Then

```
g/%#/.,.+1p
```

prints both the comment line and the next line, which is usually the **subroutine** or **function** declaration.

Since we allow **d**, **m** and **r** after a global prefix, executing a command can cause all sorts of rearrangements of the lines in the buffer, so we must be precise in defining the order in which lines are examined and acted upon. We must also take care that the editor does not get into infinite loops, yet still does more or less what we want and expect.

The scheme we settled on may not be perfect, but it works and is simple. First we go through the entire range *marking* lines that match (**g**) or do not match (**x**) the **pattern**. We also *erase* any leftover marks on all other lines. All this is done in **ckglob**, the routine that picks off the global prefix if it exists.

```
# ckglob - if global prefix, mark lines to be affected
      integer function ckglob(lin, i, status)
      character lin(MAXLINE)
      integer defalt, getind, gettxt, match, nextln, optpat
      integer gflag, i, k, line, status
      include cbuf
      include clines
      include cpat
      include ctxt

      if (lin(i) ¬= GLOBAL & lin(i) ¬= EXCLUDE)
            status = EOF
      else {
            if (lin(i) == GLOBAL)
                  gflag = YES
            else
                  gflag = NO
            i = i + 1
            if (optpat(lin, i) == ERR | defalt(1, lastln, status) == ERR)
                  status = ERR
            else {
                  i = i + 1
                  for (line = line1; line <= line2; line = line + 1) {
                        k = gettxt(line)
                        if (match(txt, pat) == gflag)
                              buf(k+MARK) = YES
                        else
                              buf(k+MARK) = NO
                        }
                  for (line = nextln(line2); line ¬= line1; line = nextln(line)) {
                        k = getind(line)
                        buf(k+MARK) = NO
                        }
                  status = OK
                  }
            }
      ckglob = status
      return
      end
```

The rest of the work is done in **doglob**, which is called (from the main routine) if **ckglob** finds a valid global prefix. **doglob** begins examining lines for marks, starting at **line1**. If one is found **doglob** erases it, sets **curln**, and obeys the command by calling **docmd**. Otherwise, it proceeds around the buffer, keeping careful count of how many lines have been examined since the last success. When it makes a complete pass without seeing a mark (**count > lastln**) it is done.

```
# doglob - do command at lin(i) on all marked lines
      integer function doglob(lin, i, cursav, status)
      character lin(MAXLINE)
      integer docmd, getind, getlst, nextln
      integer count, cursav, i, istart, k, line, status
      include cbuf
      include clines

      status = OK
      count = 0
      line = line1
      istart = i
      repeat {
            k = getind(line)
            if (buf(k+MARK) == YES) {
                  buf(k+MARK) = NO
                  curln = line
                  cursav = curln
                  i = istart
                  if (getlst(lin, i, status) == OK)
                    andif (docmd(lin, i, YES, status) == OK)
                          count = 0
                  }
            else {
                  line = nextln(line)
                  count = count + 1
                  }
            } until (count > lastln | status ¬= OK)
      doglob = status
      return
      end
```

For each marked line, dot is set to that line, then the command is executed with **docmd**. (The **YES** argument indicates that the command is being done under control of a global prefix. Only **a**, **c**, **i** and **q** worry about this.) The command itself can modify dot, access multiple lines, and so forth. For example,

```
g/subroutine/ .,/[  @t]*end$/p
```

prints all subroutines — each time a line containing **subroutine** is found, all lines from there to an **end** statement are printed.

As a more difficult example,

```
g/%/ m0
```

marks *every* line, then goes back and moves each line to the beginning of the buffer. The effect is to reverse the order of the lines. Another example, based on the same operation, is this one which we use from time to time:

```
g/thing/ m0
0;\\=
```

which moves all lines with **thing** on them to the beginning, then finds the last one. The net result is to count the **thing**'s, at the expense of scrambling the buffer. You can also count **thing**'s with

```
x/thing/ d
$=
```

if you don't mind deleting lines from the buffer.

Exercise 6-18: One operation that does not work properly is this attempt to separate even and odd numbered lines in the buffer:

```
g/%/ .+1m$
```

What does it actually do? How would you change **move** so this works right (and no other useful operation gets messed up)? □

Exercise 6-19: Prove that **doglob** cannot loop forever. □

Exercise 6-20: How would you improve the efficiency of **g** processing? Is it worth it? □

6.9 The Main Routine

We are now in a position to present the main routine for **edit**. Before we do, however, here is the entire code for **docmd**, so you can see it all at once and refresh your memory. As we said, though it is long, it is only a **case** statement that selects one of many alternatives.

```
# docmd — handle all commands except globals
      integer function docmd(lin, i, glob, status)
      character file(MAXLINE), lin(MAXLINE), sub(MAXPAT)
      integer append, delete, doprnt, doread, dowrit, move, subst
      integer ckp, defalt, getfn, getone, getrhs, nextln, optpat, prevln
      integer gflag, glob, i, line3, pflag, status
      include cfile
      include clines
      include cpat
```

continued on next two pages

```
pflag = NO              # may be set by d, m, s
status = ERR
if (lin(i) == APPENDCOM) {
        if (lin(i + 1) == NEWLINE)
                status = append(line2, glob)
        }
else if (lin(i) == CHANGE) {
        if (lin(i + 1) == NEWLINE)
          andif (defalt(curln, curln, status) == OK)
          andif (delete(line1, line2, status) == OK)
                status = append(prevln(line1), glob)
        }
else if (lin(i) == DELCOM) {
        if (ckp(lin, i + 1, pflag, status) == OK)
          andif (defalt(curln, curln, status) == OK)
          andif (delete(line1, line2, status) == OK)
          andif (nextln(curln) ¬= 0)
                curln = nextln(curln)
        }
else if (lin(i) == INSERT) {
        if (lin(i + 1) == NEWLINE)
                status = append(prevln(line2), glob)
        }
else if (lin(i) == PRINTCUR) {
        if (ckp(lin, i + 1, pflag, status) == OK) {
                call putdec(line2, 1)
                call putc(NEWLINE)
                }
        }
else if (lin(i) == MOVECOM) {
        i = i + 1
        if (getone(lin, i, line3, status) == EOF)
                status = ERR
        if (status == OK)
          andif (ckp(lin, i, pflag, status) == OK)
          andif (defalt(curln, curln, status) == OK)
                status = move(line3)
        }
else if (lin(i) == SUBSTITUTE) {
        i = i + 1
        if (optpat(lin, i) == OK)
          andif (getrhs(lin, i, sub, gflag) == OK)
          andif (ckp(lin, i + 1, pflag, status) == OK)
          andif (defalt(curln, curln, status) == OK)
                status = subst(sub, gflag)
        }
```

```
else if (lin(i) == ENTER) {
        if (nlines == 0)
          andif (getfn(lin, i, file) == OK) {
                call scopy(file, 1, savfil, 1)
                call clrbuf
                call setbuf
                status = doread(0, file)
                }
        }
else if (lin(i) == PRINTFIL) {
        if (nlines == 0)
          andif (getfn(lin, i, file) == OK) {
                call scopy(file, 1, savfil, 1)
                call putlin(savfil, STDOUT)
                call putc(NEWLINE)
                status = OK
                }
        }
else if (lin(i) == READCOM) {
        if (getfn(lin, i, file) == OK)
                status = doread(line2, file)
        }
else if (lin(i) == WRITECOM) {
        if (getfn(lin, i, file) == OK)
          andif (defalt(1, lastln, status) == OK)
                status = dowrit(line1, line2, file)
        }
else if (lin(i) == PRINT) {
        if (lin(i + 1) == NEWLINE)
          andif (defalt(curln, curln, status) == OK)
                status = doprnt(line1, line2)
        }
else if (lin(i) == NEWLINE) {
        if (nlines == 0)
                line2 = nextln(curln)
        status = doprnt(line2, line2)
        }
else if (lin(i) == QUIT) {
        if (lin(i + 1) == NEWLINE & nlines == 0 & glob == NO)
                status = EOF
        }
# else status is ERR
if (status == OK & pflag == YES)
        status = doprnt(curln, curln)
docmd = status
return
end
```

This is the main routine for **edit**, with its complete declarations. This code also handles the optional file name in **edit** *file.*

```
# edit — main routine
	character lin(MAXLINE)
	integer ckglob, docmd, doglob, doread, getarg, getlin, getlst
	integer cursav, i, status
	include cfile
	include clines
	include cpat

	call setbuf
	pat(1) = EOS
	savfil(1) = EOS
	if (getarg(1, savfil, MAXLINE) ¬= EOF)
		if (doread(0, savfil) == ERR)
			call remark("?.")
	while (getlin(lin, STDIN) ¬= EOF) {
		i = 1
		cursav = curln
		if (getlst(lin, i, status) == OK) {
			if (ckglob(lin, i, status) == OK)
				status = doglob(lin, i, cursav, status)
			else if (status ¬= ERR)
				status = docmd(lin, i, NO, status)
			# else error, do nothing
			}
		if (status == ERR) {
			call remark("?.")
			curln = cursav
			}
		else if (status == EOF)
			break
		# else OK, loop
		}
	call clrbuf
	stop
	end
```

Finally, here is an outline of the subroutine hierarchy for **edit**. As before, a number of low level service routines have been omitted to keep it down to manageable size.

```
edit
        setbuf
                relink
        doread
        getlst
                getone
                        getnum
                                optpat
                                        makpat
                                ptscan
                                        gettxt, match
        ckglob
                optpat, match, gettxt, getind, defalt
        doglob
                getlst, docmd, getind
        docmd
                append
                        inject
                                getind, relink
                defalt
                delete
                        getind, relink
                ckp
                getone
                move
                        getind, relink
                optpat
                getrhs
                        maksub
                subst
                        gettxt, amatch, delete, inject
                getfn
                doread
                        open, inject, close
                dowrit
                        create, gettxt, putlin, close
                doprnt
                        gettxt, putlin
        clrbuf
```

docmd knows about a large number of routines, but this is not as bad as it seems, for on any call to **docmd** we need only concern ourselves with one case. In that light, the hierarchy for **edit** is straightforward.

> *Exercise 6-21:* Complete your editor and test it thoroughly. Do you think it would be better if it told you more about what it is doing? If so, modify **append** to print a prompting * before reading each line, and force a print after every command. Try both versions for a while and see which you prefer. You might consider an *options* command **o**, that lets you run the editor in verbose mode (**ov**) with prompts or in silent mode (**os**). In which state should the editor

start? □

Exercise 6-22: Add a command to turn off the significance of metacharacters like ?, [] and so on. If the metacharacters are turned off, it should be possible to restore the special meaning temporarily by preceding the character with an escape character. Should metacharacters be on or off by default? □

Exercise 6-23: Implement a *list* command **l**, which is identical to the *print* command **p**, except that it prints some visible representation of otherwise invisible characters like backspaces, tabs and non-graphics. □

Exercise 6-24: Some people object to a bald **?** as the sole diagnostic. Implement a **?** command that describes the most recent error. □

Exercise 6-25: How would you specify a global append, so that you only have to enter the text to be appended (or changed or inserted) once? How would you implement it? How would you allow an arbitrary number of commands to be controlled by a global prefix? How would you implement nested global prefixes? Would recursion simplify the job? □

Exercise 6-26: If your system requires or strongly encourages line numbers semi-permanently attached to lines, or if you prefer them on esthetic grounds, modify the editor to handle them. The "absolute" line numbers need to be usable with any command, generated somehow by **a**, **c**, and **i**, treated appropriately by **s** and **m**, and dealt with by **r** and **w**. □

6.10 Scratch Files

Now that we have a working editor, we can concentrate on making it better. Our first concern is the buffer storage, which is admittedly primitive in the current version. We can gain considerable capacity by keeping only the linkage information in memory and maintaining the bulkier text on a *scratch file.*

The main change is to separate the text of the lines from the pointer information, because not all the text will be in memory at once. Most of it is off on a scratch file, stored in a manner we haven't yet described. What we must do is organize the in-memory information so that (with the help of a couple of primitives) we can treat the scratch file as an unlimited extension of memory, albeit with a longer access time.

Consider a substitute command. The text of the line must be accessed, which means it must be found on the scratch file, unless we're lucky and it's already in memory. The current version of the line must be deleted from the scratch file, which can be done by simply forgetting about it — the text remains on the scratch file, but nothing points to it. Then the replacement line is injected, which is most easily done by adding it to the end of the scratch file. Clearly to make all of this work we still require pointer information such as we had with the in-memory version so we can deduce what line follows what; we need to know where the current version of a line is on the scratch file so it can be read; we have to be able to move to that point on the scratch file to access it; and we have to be able to move to the end to write out a new version.

The array **buf** still holds the **PREV** and **NEXT** pointers and the **MARK**. Since **getind** and **relink** use only this information, they do not change with the new organization. But we need two other things for each entry in **buf**: **SEEKADR**, the location of the beginning of the line on the scratch file, and **LENG**, the length of the line.

Rather than restrict ourselves to some specific storage medium such as tape or disk for the scratch file, we introduce two additional primitives to provide a standard interface. One of these primitives is

```
seek(offset, fildes)
```

which positions the specified file for a subsequent read or write beginning at **offset**. (The other is called **readf**; we will return to it shortly.) **fildes** is the internal name returned by **open** or **create**. We maintain **offset** by summing all the line lengths as we call **putlin**, so that a **seek** using **offset** after *n* calls to **putlin** will position the file immediately after the *n*th line of text written. This is clearly character oriented; in a different environment, where lines become records, you might use the number of records as the positioning information. Since **seek** depends very strongly on peculiarities of individual systems, we will not present a version here.

In any case, **seek** does the necessary rewinds and skips (for a tape), or seeks (for a disk file), to find its way back to a line of text written earlier or to find its way forward to the end of the file. The program can thus view a file as a continuous stream of characters, leaving it up to primitives to worry about things like records and blocks. This is as it should be.

inject is much as before, except that we have pushed most of the dirty work into a new sub-module **maklin**.

```
# inject (scratch file) — insert lin after curln, write scratch
      integer function inject(lin)
      character lin(MAXLINE)
      integer getind, maklin, nextln
      integer i, k1, k2, k3
      include clines

      for (i = 1; lin(i) ¬= EOS; ) {
            i = maklin(lin, i, k3)
            if (i == ERR) {
                  inject = ERR
                  break
                  }
            k1 = getind(curln)
            k2 = getind(nextln(curln))
            call relink(k1, k3, k3, k2)
            call relink(k3, k2, k1, k3)
            curln = curln + 1
            lastln = lastln + 1
            inject = OK
            }
      return
      end
```

maklin itself is where most of the interface to our new routines is concentrated.

```
# maklin (scratch file) — make new line entry, copy text to scratch
	integer function maklin(lin, i, newind)
	character lin(MAXLINE)
	integer addset, length
	integer i, j, junk, newind, txtend
	include cbuf
	include cscrat
	include ctxt

	maklin = ERR
	if (lastbf + BUFENT > MAXBUF)
		return			# no room for new line entry
	txtend = 1
	for (j = i; lin(j) ¬= EOS; ) {
		junk = addset(lin(j), txt, txtend, MAXLINE)
		j = j + 1
		if (lin(j - 1) == NEWLINE)
			break
		}
	if (addset(EOS, txt, txtend, MAXLINE) == NO)
		return
	call seek(scrend, scr)		# add line to end of scratch file
	buf(lastbf + SEEKADR) = scrend
	buf(lastbf + LENG) = length(txt)
	call putlin(txt, scr)
	scrend = scrend + buf(lastbf + LENG)
	buf(lastbf + MARK) = NO
	newind = lastbf
	lastbf = lastbf + BUFENT
	maklin = j			# next character to be examined in lin
	return
	end
```

scrend is the offset of the current end of the file, where all new text is added; **scr** is the internal name of the scratch file, returned by **create**. These variables are placed in the **common** block **cscrat**:

```
common /cscrat/ scr, scrend
  integer scr		# scratch file id
  integer scrend	# end of info on scratch file
```

lastbf is the last slot used in **buf**; **BUFENT** is 5, the size of a line entry in **buf**. **buf** and **lastbf** are collected in **common** block **cbuf**, which is unchanged from its previous version, although the structure of a line entry is different.

```
common /cbuf/ buf(MAXBUF), lastbf
  character buf      # structure of pointers for all lines:
       # buf(k+0)  PREV        previous line
       # buf(k+1)  NEXT        next line
       # buf(k+2)  MARK        mark for global commands
       # buf(k+3)  SEEKADR     where line is on scratch file
       # buf(k+4)  LENG        length on scratch
  integer lastbf     # last pointer used in buf
```

gettxt again fetches a line of text; in our implementation, it must **seek** to the proper place on the scratch file, then read the line into **txt**. Reading is done by calling the primitive

```
readf(buffer, count, fildes)
```

which reads **count** characters from **fildes** into **buffer**. This is the second of the two additional primitives that we need to handle scratch files. (**seek** was the first.) **readf** is sufficiently system dependent that again we will not describe any implementation.

```
# gettxt (scratch file) — locate text for line, copy to txt
      integer function gettxt(line)
      integer getbuf, getind
      integer j, k, line
      include cbuf
      include cscrat
      include ctxt

      k = getind(line)
      call seek(buf(k + SEEKADR), scr)
      call readf(txt, buf(k + LENG), scr)
      j = buf(k + LENG) + 1
      txt(j) = EOS
      gettxt = k
      return
      end
```

Our scratch file scheme works with just one line of text in memory at any one time, although this is not very efficient, and we could do much better by keeping more lines around. One of the exercises is concerned with making better use of memory.

Now that we know the steady state workings of the scratch file routines, we can set up the initialization and termination routines. It is usually best to proceed this way, saving initialization and termination to the last, for it is only then that you have a proper appreciation for what has to be done.

```
# setbuf (scratch file) — create scratch file, set up line 0
      subroutine setbuf
      integer create
      integer k
      include cbuf
      include clines
      include cscrat
      string scrfil "scratch"
      string null ""

      scr = create(scrfil, READWRITE)
      if (scr == ERR)
            call cant(scrfil)
      scrend = 0
      lastbf = LINE0
      call maklin(null, 1, k)        # create empty line 0
      call relink(k, k, k, k)        # establish initial linked list
      curln = 0
      lastln = 0
      return
      end

# clrbuf  (scratch file) — dispose of scratch file
      subroutine clrbuf
      include cscrat
      string scrfil "scratch"

      call close(scr)
      call remove(scrfil)
      return
      end
```

Exercise 6-27: Replace the existing buffer control primitives with the scratch file set (plus **seek** and **readf**) and debug them. Measure the mean line length of a sampling of your files (what tools would you use to do this?) and use this data to estimate the relative capacities of the two versions of the editor. □

Exercise 6-28: Verify that if it is not permitted to delete the newline at the end of a line, there is no need for the **LENG** entry in **buf**, and the primitive **readf** can be replaced by **getlin**. □

Exercise 6-29: Is it worthwhile to perform garbage collection on unused pointer blocks in **buf**? Try it. How about reclaiming discarded text space in the scratch file? □

Exercise 6-30: On most systems, **edit** can be made substantially faster by trying to anticipate the lines that will be used in the immediate future and reading several lines at one time. Modify **gettxt** or a subordinate to read a group of lines when **gettxt** is called, unless the line is already present in memory. The challenge is to organize things so that for common editing operations the line *is* already present with high probability. What are the common operations that are worth improving? How much code has to be changed? How much will this speed up various operations? □

Exercise 6-31: Verify that **inject** is an n^2 procedure for adding n lines to the buffer. (That is, the work done is proportional to the square of the number of lines.) Measure **edit** to see whether this matters. If so, what changes would you make to convert it to a linear procedure? □

Exercise 6-32: Magnetic tape has the property that you can never read information past the latest stuff written (i.e., you dare not rewrite patches in the middle). Does our scratch file maintenance scheme work properly with magnetic tape? Why would you want to be able to use tape with the text editor? What are its drawbacks? □

Exercise 6-33: Another possible implementation of the storage management is to keep pointers to the text lines in a contiguous array, so that instead of linkage information all the data about line n is always at the nth position of the array. Re-design the storage management along these lines. What operations are easier than they are with a linked list? Which are harder? □

Exercise 6-34: How would you implement an editor that keeps *all* information on a scratch file, including line linkages? Can you still use magnetic tape? Is garbage collection worthwhile? □

Exercise 6-35: Run various editions of the editor against a standard script of commands and compare response times. Use this information to determine how elaborate your buffer mechanism should be. □

Exercise 6-36: If your system provides a **run** primitive that lets you execute a command from within a running program, implement an "escape" command @ that lets you type an operating system command from within the editor. For instance,

@**edit** *file*

would invoke a fresh instance of **edit** on *file*; when that instance is finished, execution resumes in the current editor. What modifications are necessary in **setbuf** and **clrbuf** if nested editors are to work correctly? □

One aspect of system environment we have not mentioned is handling signals from the outside world, primarily *interrupts.* In an editor it is desirable that the user be able to stop the current command, for example, to terminate a long print command, without losing any information. In general, interrupts arrive at unpredictable and probably inconvenient times, so the editor must be prepared to maintain its integrity as it deals with them. For a print command, this is not much of a problem, but you can imagine the difficulties when an interrupt occurs in the middle of a move command done under a global prefix. The challenge is to stop the current action as soon as possible, yet remain sane so that subsequent editing proceeds properly.

Exercise 6-37: If your system provides a primitive for catching interrupts, modify **edit** so it handles them properly, without losing information or buffer consistency. What can you do if there is no way to intercept an interrupt? □

Once a file gets too big, it may be too much trouble to provide some of the nice features of **edit**, like global commands and reverse searching with \\. But it is still vital to be able to perform most editing tasks on big files. One possibility is to cannibalize **edit** to make a "stream editor," which copies its standard input to its standard output, making a somewhat restricted set of editing transformations on the way. For example, any command that implies backwards or repeated scanning of the file would be disallowed; this includes \\, some aspects of the global prefix, the move command, and minus signs in line number arithmetic (no **/abc/−3**).

The command

/abc/,/def/ *command*

would be taken to mean, "Attempt this command on the first line that matches the first line number, and on all subsequent lines until you find one that matches the second; then begin watching for a match of the first line number again." A single line number would imply doing the command on each line that matched the pattern; a missing line number would perform the command on every line. Multiple commands should be allowed.

If you have a stream editor, **find** and **change** are special cases, respectively

sedit */pattern/***p**

and

sedit */pattern/* **s//***replacement/***gp**

Should **find** and **change** be retained as separate programs nonetheless?

Exercise 6-38: Design and implement a stream editor along these general lines. □

6.11 Summary

It is hard to get a proper perspective on the design or code of anything as large as a text editor, particularly without some experience using it.

One useful approach is to make a list of common editing tasks, then compare how they are expressed in several editors. Here is one example of a task which we do regularly, yet which is far beyond the capabilities of many editors. The text for this book is stored in more than one hundred files in the file system on our computer. From time to time, we need to go through the entire book making some change wherever it occurs in this set of files. Doing each file by hand would be intolerably slow and error-prone, so instead we use **edit**, like this.

First we make a *script* — the set of commands that we want to do on each file. (And of course we make it with **edit**!) One of our scripts, for instance, converted the word **ERROR** to **ERR** globally, so we could avoid a case conflict with the word **error**. The script was

```
f
g/ERROR/ s//ERR/ gp
w
```

The **f** command echoes the name of the file we're editing, in case something goes wrong; the **s** command with global prefix makes the change and prints all affected lines; and the **w** command writes the new version back on the file it came from.

Then we run a program **listcat** ("list catalog") to prepare a list of all our files, one file name per line:

```
listcat >filelist
```

places the file list in a file called **filelist**. (Recall that we discussed the > operation in Chapter 3.)

Next we edit **filelist**. All of the files in our book contain the letters **book** as part of their name, so we first delete all file names that are not part of the book with an **x** command:

```
x/book/ d
```

Then we convert each file name to an **e** command with a substitute:

```
1,$s/?*/e &/
```

This leaves each line in the buffer in the form

e *filename*

Then we read in a copy of the script after each file name:

```
g/?/.r script
```

At this point each of the original book files has been converted into a group of editing commands consisting of **e** *filename* followed by whatever the script specifies.

We write the whole thing into a file called **command**:

```
w command
q
```

Now the single command

```
edit <command
```

invokes the editor with its input coming from the set of editor commands in the file **command**. Thus **edit** does the script, whatever it is, on each of the files in turn.

In practice, this goes far faster than we can describe it. And of course, if you stop to think about it, you will realize that the editing operations to make the **command** file can be placed in another file, perhaps **commandmaker**, and this process run whenever a new file of commands is needed. It is a good test of an editing system to see whether it can accomplish the same function with as little fuss.

Here is a summary of the commands and facilities of **edit**. Text patterns, which are used for context searches, the **s** command, and the **g** and **x** prefixes, are summarized at the end of Chapter 5.

Line numbers are formed from the following components:

17	a decimal number
.	the current line
$	the last line
/*pattern*/	a forward context search
pattern\\	a backward context search

Components may be combined with + or −:

.+1	sum of . and 1
.−1	difference of . and 1

Line numbers are separated by commas or semicolons; a semicolon sets the current line to the most recent line number before proceeding.

Commands may be preceded by an arbitrary number of line numbers (except for **e**, **f** and **q** which require that none be present). The last one or two are used as needed. If two line numbers are needed and only one is specified, it is used for both. If no line numbers are specified, a default rule is applied:

(.)	use the current line
(.+1)	use the next line
(.,.)	use the current line for both line numbers
(1,$)	use all lines

In alphabetical order, the commands and their default line numbers are:

(.)	a	append text after line (text follows)
(.,.)	c	change text (text follows)
(.,.)	dp	delete text
	e *file*	enter *file*, discard all previous text, remember file name
	f *file*	print file name, remember file name
(.)	i	insert text before line (text follows)
(.,.)	m *line3* p	move text to after *line3*
(.,.)	p	print text
	q	quit
(.)	r *file*	read *file*, appending after line
(.,.)	s/*pat*/*new*/gp	substitute *new* for first occurrence of *pat* (g implies repeatedly across line)
(1,$)	w *file*	write *file* (leaves current state unaltered)
(.)	=p	print line number
(.+1)		print one line

The trailing **p**, which is optional, causes the last affected line to be printed.

The global prefixes cause repeated execution of a command, once for each line that matches (**g**) or does not match (**x**) a specified text pattern:

(1,$) g/*pattern*/ *command*
(1,$) x/*pattern*/ *command*

command can be anything but **a**, **c**, **i** or **q**, and may be preceded by line numbers as usual. Dot is set to the matched line before *command* is done.

Bibliographic Notes

The earliest traceable version of the editor presented here is TECO, written for the first PDP-1 timesharing system at MIT. It was subsequently implemented on the SDS-940 as the "quick editor" QED by L. P. Deutsch and B. W. Lampson; see "An online editor," *CACM*, December, 1967. K. L. Thompson adapted QED for CTSS on the IBM 7090 at MIT, and later D. M. Ritchie wrote a version for the GE-635 (now HIS-6070) at Bell Labs.

The latest version is **ed**, a simplified form of QED for the PDP-11, written by Ritchie and Thompson. Our editor closely resembles **ed**, at least in outward appearance.

The article "On-line text editing: a survey," by A. van Dam and D. E. Rice (*Computing Surveys*, September, 1971) discusses several other editors.

CHAPTER 7

FORMATTING

Our next task is to write a text formatter — a program for neatly formatting a document on a suitable printer. Naturally the precise meanings of "neatly," "formatting," and "suitable" will vary according to your aspirations and your budget. Our formatter provides a bare minimum of formatting controls, those which we have observed people actually use when preparing documents. It produces output for devices like terminals and line printers, with automatic right margin justification, pagination (skipping over the fold in the paper), page numbering and titling, centering, underlining, indenting, and multiple line spacing.

A formatter is an important tool for anyone who writes (including programmers describing their programs), because, once correct, material is never re-typed. This has some obvious cost benefits, and helps ensure that the number of errors decreases with time. Machine formatting eases the typing job, since margin alignment, centering, underlining and similar tedious operations are handled by the computer, not by the typist. It also permits drastic format changes in a document without altering any text. But perhaps most important, it seems to encourage writers to improve their product, since the overhead of making an improvement is small and there is an esthetic satisfaction in always having a clean copy available.

Freedom from errors may sometimes be the primary concern. For instance, this book was produced on a phototypesetter driven by a (very) sophisticated big brother of the formatter we are going to write now. The programs are part of the text. To test one, we isolate the code with an editor like the one in Chapter 6, compile it and run it, untouched by human hands. We are fairly confident that what is in the text is what was actually tested.

The **format** program described in this chapter is quite conventional. It accepts text to be formatted, interspersed with formatting commands telling **format** what the output is to look like. A command consists of a period, a two-letter name, and perhaps some optional information. Each command must appear at the beginning of a line, with nothing on the line but the command and its arguments. For instance,

```
.ce
```

centers the next line of output, and

```
.sp 3
```

generates three spaces (blank lines).

Most of the time, however, the **format** user should have to know little about commands and arguments — most formatting happens automatically. This is merely good human engineering. Ideally a document containing *no* commands should be printed sensibly. Default parameter settings and formatting actions are intended to be reasonable and free of surprises. For instance, words fill up output lines as much as possible, regardless of the length of input lines. Blank lines cause fresh paragraphs. Input is correctly spaced across page boundaries, with top and bottom margins.

At the same time the design has to be sufficiently flexible that it can be augmented with more advanced features for sophisticated use. Knowledgeable users should of course be able to change parameter settings as desired. Ultimately it should be possible for users to define new formatting operations in terms of those already provided. We will explore these possibilities in the exercises at the end of the chapter.

7.1 Commands

As we said, all commands consist of a period at the begining of a line, which is an unlikely combination in text, and have two-letter names. It has been our experience that users prefer concise commands in most languages, so this seems a reasonable compromise between brevity and mnemonic value. In any case, the code is written so that some other choice could be made with minimal changes.

By default **format** *fills* output lines, by packing as many input words as possible onto an output line before printing it. The lines are also *justified* (right margins made even) by inserting extra spaces into the filled line before output. People normally want filled text, which is why we choose it as the default behavior. It can be turned off, however, by the *no-fill* command

```
.nf
```

and thereafter lines will be copied from input to output without any rearrangement. Filling can be turned back on with the *fill* command

```
.fi
```

When an **.nf** is encountered, there may be a partial line collected but not yet output. The **.nf** will force this line out before anything else happens. The action of forcing out a partially collected line is called a *break*. The break concept pervades **format**; many commands implicitly cause a break. To force a break explicitly, for example to separate two paragraphs, use

```
.br
```

Of course you may want to add an extra blank line between paragraphs. The *space* command

```
.sp
```

causes a break, then produces a blank line. To get *n* blank lines, use

```
.sp n
```

(A space is always required between a command and its argument.) If the bottom of a page is reached before all of the blank lines have been printed, the excess ones are thrown away, so that all pages will normally start at the same first line.

By default output will be single spaced, but the line spacing can be changed at any time:

```
.ls n
```

sets line spacing to *n*. (*n*=2 is double spacing.) The **.ls** command does not cause a break.

The *begin page* command **.bp** causes a skip to the top of a new page and also causes a break. If you use

```
.bp n
```

the next output page will be numbered *n*. A **.bp** that occurs at the bottom of a page has no effect except perhaps to set the page number; no blank page is generated. The current page length can be changed (without a break) with

```
.pl n
```

To center the next line of output,

```
.ce
line to be centered
```

The **.ce** command causes a break. You can center *n* lines with

```
.ce n
```

and, if you don't like to count lines (or can't count correctly), say

```
.ce 1000
lots of lines
to be centered
.ce 0
```

The lines between the **.ce** commands will be centered. No filling is done on centered lines.

Underlining is much the same as centering:

```
.ul n
```

causes the text on the next *n* lines to be underlined upon output. But **.ul** does *not* cause a break, so words in filled text may be underlined by

```
words and words and
.ul
lots more
words.
```

to get

words and words and <u>lots</u> <u>more</u> words.

Centering and underlining may be intermixed in any order:

```
.ce
.ul
Title
```

gives a centered and underlined title.

The *indent* command controls the left margin:

```
.in n
```

causes all subsequent output lines to be indented *n* positions. (Normally they are indented by 0.) The command

```
.rm n
```

sets the *right margin* to *n*. The line length of filled lines is the difference between right margin and indent values. **.in** and **.rm** do not cause a break.

The traditional paragraph indent is produced with *temporary indent* command:

```
.ti n
```

breaks and sets the indent to position *n* for one output line only. If *n* is less than the current indent, the indent is backwards (a "hanging indent").

To put running header and footer titles on every page, use **.he** and **.fo**:

```
.he this becomes the top-of-page (header) title
.fo this becomes the bottom-of-page (footer) title
```

The title begins with the first non-blank after the command, but a leading quote will be discarded if present, so you can produce titles that begin with blanks. If a title contains the character #, it will be replaced by the current page number each time the title is actually printed. **.he** and **.fo** do not cause a break.

Since absolute numbers are often awkward, **format** allows *relative* values as command arguments. All commands that allow a numeric argument *n* also allow +*n* or −*n* instead, to signify a *change* in the current value. For instance,

```
.rm -10
.in +10
```

shrinks the right margin by 10 *from its current value,* and moves the indent 10 places *further* to the right. Thus

```
.rm 10
```

and

```
.rm +10
```

are quite different.

Relative values are particularly useful with **.ti**, to temporarily indent relative to the current indent:

```
.in +5
.ti +5
```

produces a left margin indented by 5, with the first line indented by a further 5. And

```
.in +5
.ti -5
```

produces a hanging indent, as in a numbered paragraph:

1. Now is the time for all good people
   to come to the party.

A line that begins with blanks is a special case. If there is no text at all, the line causes a break and produces a number of blank lines equal to the current line spacing. These lines are never discarded regardless of where they appear, so they provide a way to get blank lines at the top of a page. If a line begins with *n* blanks followed by text, it causes a break and a temporary indent of +*n*. These special actions help ensure that a document that contains no formatting commands will still be reasonably formatted.

In summary, then, we have the following commands. If a numeric argument is preceded by a + or −, the previous value is *changed* by this amount; otherwise the argument represents the new value. If no argument is given, the default value is used.

command	break?	default	function
.bp *n*	yes	*n*=+1	begin page numbered *n*
.br	yes		cause break
.ce *n*	yes	*n*=1	center next *n* lines
.fi	yes		start filling
.fo	no	empty	footer title
.he	no	empty	header title
.in *n*	no	*n*=0	indent *n* spaces
.ls *n*	no	*n*=1	line spacing is *n*
.nf	yes		stop filling
.pl *n*	no	*n*=66	set page length to *n*
.rm *n*	no	*n*=60	set right margin to *n*
.sp *n*	yes	*n*=1	space down *n* lines
.ti *n*	yes	*n*=0	temporary indent of *n*
.ul *n*	no	*n*=1	underline words from next *n* lines

This is a reasonable set, but others will undoubtedly have occurred to you. We will suggest further possibilities as we go along.

Exercise 7-1: Discuss criteria for which commands should cause a break and which should not. An alternative design is to have two characters that introduce commands, instead of one, so that **.sp** causes a break as before, while **,sp** does not. Discuss this design. □

Exercise 7-2: Write a pipeline to count the words but not the **format** commands in a document. □

7.2 Construction

There is a lot of merit in building a program incrementally — making the minimum amount that will do something useful, and then, with this part operational, fleshing out the skeleton a piece at a time. This divides a big job into smaller and presumably more manageable pieces. Testing the first part is easier because it is smaller. If the design is good, later pieces should not interact much with what has gone before, so for the most part they may be tested independently. There is also a morale boost in having *something* working early.

On bigger projects, friendly users can try out a partial program with limited functions. Their reactions provide vital feedback to evaluate what already exists and what is yet to come. Often you will learn that what the user wants is less ornate than either of you thought at first, so some of the hard work can be postponed indefinitely. Or you may learn that what the user wants is quite different than you thought. It is foolish to build the whole thing in a closet before revealing any part of it. (Innocent users are also marvelous at stumbling into bugs, because they exercise programs in ways you never thought of.)

The text formatter is a case in point. Once a certain minimum capability has been built, additions can be made without affecting previous code very much (assuming sensible design in the first place). We will sketch out how the construction might proceed, now that we know what facilities are to be provided.

There are several choices for program organization, of which two seem promising. One is to handle the input one word at a time, and assemble lines out of words for line-oriented tasks like no-fill and centering. Or we could input a line at a time and break the line into words when filled text is being processed. Given the number of formatting operations that are based on lines — no-fill mode, centering, underlining, and commands themselves — the line-at-a-time structure seems to be easier. It's a good mental exercise to work out details of the word-at-a-time design, however. You will find that neither organization is ideal — each has its awkward parts.

7.3 Command Decoding

The main routine reads input a line at a time and separates it into text and formatting commands. This much we can write before anything else.

```
# format — text formatter main program
	character inbuf(INSIZE)
	integer getlin

	call init
	while (getlin(inbuf, STDIN) ¬= EOF)
		if (inbuf(1) == COMMAND)	# it's a command
			call comand(inbuf)
		else				# it's text
			call text(inbuf)
	stop
	end
```

COMMAND is the character period (.), unless you prefer something else. init sets all parameters to their default initial values; it is sufficiently uninteresting that we will not show it.

We begin with **comand**, the routine that decides what kind of command has appeared, since most of the command interpreting code can be written before anything else is done. Temporarily **text** can be a stub which does nothing more than copy text lines from **inbuf** to the standard output with **putlin**.

The structure of **comand** is a multi-way branch on the command type; we will show it in stages rather than all at once, and explain details as we come to them.

```
# comand - perform formatting command
      subroutine comand(buf)
      character buf(MAXLINE)
      integer comtyp, getval, max
      integer argtyp, ct, spval, val
      include cpage
      include cparam

      ct = comtyp(buf)
      if (ct == UNKNOWN)          # ignore unknown commands
            return
      val = getval(buf, argtyp)
      if (ct == FI) {
            call brk
            fill = YES
            }
      else if (ct == NF) {
            call brk
            fill = NO
            }
      else if (ct == BR)
            call brk
      else if (ct == LS)
            call set(lsval, val, argtyp, 1, 1, HUGE)
      # ...
      # etc.
      # ...
      return
      end
```

Most commands just set the new value of a parameter, perhaps after causing a break. If one is needed, **brk** is called to flush out partially filled lines. For the moment we can write a dummy version which returns without doing anything; since we are currently dealing only with unfilled text, there will never be any partially filled lines anyway.

The majority of the parameters are kept in a **common** block **cparam** since they are needed throughout the program and there are far too many to pass around as arguments. The rest are in **cpage**, to which we shall return.

```
common /cparam/ fill, lsval, inval, rmval, tival, ceval, ulval
  integer fill      # fill if YES; init = YES
  integer lsval     # current line spacing; init = 1
  integer inval     # current indent; >= 0; init = 0
  integer rmval     # current right margin; init = PAGEWIDTH = 60
  integer tival     # current temporary indent; init = 0
  integer ceval     # number of lines to center; init = 0
  integer ulval     # number of lines to underline; init = 0
```

comand calls **comtyp** to decode the command name and **getval** to evaluate any arguments to the command. **comtyp** is so repetitive that we will show only part of it.

```
# comtyp - decode command type
   integer function comtyp(buf)
   character buf(MAXLINE)

   if (buf(2) == LETF & buf(3) == LETI)
         comtyp = FI
   else if (buf(2) == LETN & buf(3) == LETF)
         comtyp = NF
   else if (buf(2) == LETB & buf(3) == LETR)
         comtyp = BR
   # ...
   # etc.
   # ...
   else
         comtyp = UNKNOWN
   return
   end
```

When there are relatively few commands, a direct search with a series of explicit tests is certainly easiest and entirely adequate. Ultimately it might prove desirable to replace the tests by a more general table lookup scheme.

Notice that **comtyp** does not check whether a command is exactly two letters long, only that the first two letters match a known command. This permits users to write **.fill**, **.break**, etc., if they prefer. The drawback is that any new commands introduced must differ in their first two letters from all others, which can lead to some strained mnemonics. You might therefore consider changing **comtyp** to check entire command names.

Since nearly all commands allow a numeric argument with an optional sign, it is best to write a separate routine to get the argument and the sign. **getval** skips over the command, records the presence or absence of a sign and digits in **argtyp**, and converts a numeric argument to an integer with **ctoi**.

```
# getval - evaluate optional numeric argument
      integer function getval(buf, argtyp)
      character buf(MAXLINE)
      integer ctoi
      integer argtyp, i

      i = 1                          # skip command name
      while (buf(i) ¬= BLANK & buf(i) ¬= TAB & buf(i) ¬= NEWLINE)
            i = i + 1
      call skipbl(buf, i)            # find argument
      argtyp = buf(i)
      if (argtyp == PLUS | argtyp == MINUS)
            i = i + 1
      getval = ctoi(buf, i)
      return
      end
```

Even though at the moment all commands consist of a period and two letters, **getval** is written to skip an arbitrary command terminated by a blank, tab or newline. (Recall that **skipbl**, written in Chapter 6, skips blanks and tabs.) Similarly, a separate routine **comtyp** decodes the command type. These choices will make it easier to change the program if it becomes necessary later. Few programs remain static over their lifetime; it is wise to plan ahead so the inevitable changes are not traumatic.

Furthermore, **getval** is called for all commands, even those like **.he** and **.fo** which never have a numeric argument. It just isn't worth making a special case out of them: the formatter may do a microscopic amount of extra work in such cases, but the program is less complicated.

set is a general routine for updating a parameter, relatively or absolutely or to a default value. It also ensures that the resulting value lies within specified bounds. For instance, the line spacing is set with the code in **comand** that reads

```
else if (ct == LS)
      call set(lsval, val, argtyp, 1, 1, HUGE)
```

This call to **set** will set **lsval** to **val** if there was no sign with the **.ls** command, as in **.ls 2**, or to **lsval±val** if there was, as in **.ls −1**, or to 1 if there was no argument at all. In any case the result is forced to lie between the last two arguments, 1 and **HUGE** (a large number).

```
# set — set parameter and check range
      subroutine set(param, val, argtyp, defval, minval, maxval)
      integer max, min
      integer argtyp, defval, maxval, minval, param, val

      if (argtyp == NEWLINE)              # defaulted
            param = defval
      else if (argtyp == PLUS)            # relative +
            param = param + val
      else if (argtyp == MINUS)           # relative -
            param = param - val
      else                                # absolute
            param = val
      param = min(param, maxval)
      param = max(param, minval)
      return
      end
```

We now have enough code to test command decoding, so we can use it and not worry about it while working on the rest of the program.

Exercise 7-3: **format** ignores unknown commands. It could just as well have treated them as normal text to be printed, or as errors to be reported. Discuss the merits of these alternatives. □

Exercise 7-4: Commands begin with a period in column 1, because that occurs infrequently in normal text. What are other plausible choices? How would you arrange to print a line that begins with a period? Suppose you want to mix commands and text on the same line. Is it a good idea? What is a syntax that is easy to type and edit? □

7.4 Page Layout

The next step is to subdivide text handling into reasonable increments. Regardless of whether it fills or not, centers or not, underlines or not, **format** has to get the right number of lines per page. So let us work on that, copying text lines from input to output, but with proper line spacing, titles and page numbers. This will almost dispose of no-fill mode. The code is similar to **print** in Chapter 3, so we can adapt some of the lessons we learned there. The main one is the importance of the boundaries — getting the right number of lines at the right places on each page, and preventing unwanted pages.

The parameters that describe the vertical dimensions of a page are: the page length **plval**; the top margins before and after the header line, **m1val** and **m2val** (**m1val** includes the header); the corresponding bottom margins **m3val** and **m4val**; and **bottom**, the last line upon which text may be placed. The following relationship holds:

```
bottom = plval - m3val - m4val
```

For 11 inch paper and standard six line per inch spacing, **plval** is 66. If each margin is two lines, there are 58 text lines per page and **bottom** is 62.

lineno is the next line to be printed on the output page; a value of zero indicates top of page, and a value greater than **bottom** indicates the end of a page. When **lineno** exceeds **bottom**, it is time to flush the current page. **curpag** is the number of the current page; **newpag** is the number that will go on the next page. All these values are kept in the **common** block **cpage**, which also holds the running titles **header** and **footer**.

```
common /cpage/ curpag, newpag, lineno, plval, m1val, m2val, m3val, m4val,
      bottom, header(MAXLINE), footer(MAXLINE)
  integer curpag    # current output page number; init = 0
  integer newpag    # next output page number; init = 1
  integer lineno    # next line to be printed; init = 0
  integer plval     # page length in lines; init = PAGELEN = 66
  integer m1val     # margin before and including header
  integer m2val     # margin after header
  integer m3val     # margin after last text line
  integer m4val     # bottom margin, including footer
  integer bottom    # last live line on page, = plval-m3val-m4val
  character header  # top of page title; init = NEWLINE
  character footer  # bottom of page title; init = NEWLINE
```

We no longer want to merely copy text lines to the standard output, so we make a small change in **text**, so it calls a new routine **put** instead of **putlin**:

```
# text - process text lines (interim version 1)
   subroutine text(inbuf)
   character inbuf(INSIZE)

   call put(inbuf)
   return
   end
```

Except for header and footer titles, and blank lines produced by **.sp** commands, every line of text that goes out is controlled by **put**. **put** and its subordinates look after top and bottom margins, line spacing, setting the page number, and indenting, which we will get to shortly. The outline of **put** is

```
if (at top or past bottom of page)
     do top margins and top title
put out indent, if any
put out line
increment line number
if (past bottom)
     do bottom margins and bottom title
```

and the code becomes

```
# put - put out line with proper spacing and indenting
      subroutine put(buf)
      character buf(MAXLINE)
      integer min
      integer i
      include cpage
      include cparam

      if (lineno == 0 | lineno > bottom)
            call phead
      for (i = 1; i <= tival; i = i + 1)          # indenting
            call putc(BLANK)
      tival = inval
      call putlin(buf, STDOUT)
      call skip(min(lsval-1, bottom-lineno))
      lineno = lineno + lsval
      if (lineno > bottom)
            call pfoot
      return
      end
```

skip(n) produces **n** empty lines (**NEWLINE** only) if **n** is positive, and does nothing if **n** is less than one. We wrote it for **print** in Chapter 3. We have also included the code for indenting in **put**; all it does is put out the right number of leading blanks and reset any temporary indent, so ignore it for now.

put has to stay sane if handed bizarre parameters. In particular, the line spacing **lsval** could conceivably be larger than the bottom margin values, so after a line is produced, the **skip** that follows skips at most to **bottom+1**. (**put** skips **lsval-1** because **putlin** has already produced one line.) Since each page starts at the top, there will always be at least one output line per page regardless of the line spacing, and we are guaranteed that **format** will always make some progress through a document no matter how strange the parameters.

phead and **pfoot** print the top and bottom margins. **phead** is responsible for updating the current and new page numbers in **curpag** and **newpag**.

```
# phead — put out page header
      subroutine phead
      include cpage

      curpag = newpag
      newpag = newpag + 1
      if (m1val > 0) {
            call skip(m1val-1)
            call puttl(header, curpag)
            }
      call skip(m2val)
      lineno = m1val + m2val + 1
      return
      end

# pfoot — put out page footer
      subroutine pfoot
      include cpage

      call skip(m3val)
      if (m4val > 0) {
            call puttl(footer, curpag)
            call skip(m4val-1)
            }
      return
      end
```

The header title is the last line of the margin **m1val** and the footer title is the first line of **m4val**, so either title, and in fact all pagination, can be turned off by setting the appropriate margins to zero. This is a minor point, but it eliminates what would otherwise be a special case.

phead and **pfoot** call **puttl** to produce the top or bottom title as a single line, inserting the page number with **putdec** if called for.

```
# puttl — put out title line with optional page number
      subroutine puttl(buf, pageno)
      character buf(MAXLINE)
      integer pageno
      integer i

      for (i = 1; buf(i) ¬= EOS; i = i + 1)
            if (buf(i) == PAGENUM)
                  call putdec(pageno, 1)
            else
                  call putc(buf(i))
      return
      end
```

PAGENUM is whatever character is to be replaced by the page number in titles; we use a #, which has some mnemonic value. In the program it has a separate name to keep its function clear and to make it easier to change.

Titles are originally extracted by **gettl**, called from **comand** with

```
else if (ct == HE)
        call gettl(buf, header)
else if (ct == FO)
        call gettl(buf, footer)
```

and **gettl** itself is

```
# gettl - copy title from buf to ttl
      subroutine gettl(buf, ttl)
      character buf(MAXLINE), ttl(MAXLINE)
      integer i

      i = 1                             # skip command name
      while (buf(i) ¬= BLANK & buf(i) ¬= TAB & buf(i) ¬= NEWLINE)
            i = i + 1
      call skipbl(buf, i)               # find argument
      if (buf(i) == SQUOTE | buf(i) == DQUOTE)   # strip quote if found
            i = i + 1
      call scopy(buf, i, ttl, 1)
      return
      end
```

The title is assumed to begin with the first non-blank character, but a leading apostrophe or quote is stripped off, to permit a title to begin with blanks.

Notice that we wrote the calls to **gettl** as

```
call gettl(buf, header)
call gettl(buf, footer)
```

instead of passing the command type to **gettl** and letting it decide where to put the title. The latter way requires **gettl** to know about the format of variables in **cpage**, and increases the data connections in the program. Whenever possible, hide details from routines that don't need them.

space is called directly from **comand** when a **.sp** is seen; if no argument is provided, a single blank line is produced. **.sp 0** is perfectly legal; its only effect is to cause a break.

```
else if (ct == SP) {
        call set(spval, val, argtyp, 1, 0, HUGE)
        call space(spval)
        }
```

space is also called for a **.bp** command, to get to the bottom of the current page.

```
        else if (ct == BP) {
                if (lineno > 0)
                        call space(HUGE)
                call set(curpag, val, argtyp, curpag+1, -HUGE, HUGE)
                newpag = curpag
                }
```

The code for **.bp** has to be exceedingly careful or some unpleasant behavior results. First we must have **.bp** equivalent to **.bp +1**, since this is part of the specification. A **.bp** at the bottom of a page (even the last page) should have no effect except to cause the normal page number increment. You should also verify that beginning a document with any one of **.bp**, **.bp 1**, **.bp +1**, or plain text yields a first page numbered 1. Finally, the **.bp** command allows negative page numbers, not because we think that anyone will ever use them, but because they can do no conceivable harm. Arbitrary restrictions will someday impede someone.

Once **put** works, **space** is written by analogy. **space(n)** does nothing if it occurs at the bottom of a page (**lineno>bottom**). Otherwise it skips **n** lines, or enough lines to get to the bottom of the page, whichever is smaller. If the bottom is reached, the bottom margins are produced.

```
# space - space  n  lines or to bottom of page
        subroutine space(n)
        integer min
        integer n
        include cpage

        call brk
        if (lineno > bottom)
                return
        if (lineno == 0)
                call phead
        call skip(min(n, bottom+1-lineno))
        lineno = lineno + n
        if (lineno > bottom)
                call pfoot
        return
        end
```

It is quite important to distinguish between "bottom of the page" and "top of the next page"; they are not the same place. If a **.sp** occurs at the top of a page the spaces are produced, but normally this can only occur at the beginning of a document. Any blank lines left over at the end of a page are discarded, since this is usually what is wanted. If spaces are actually needed at the top of a page they can be obtained by all-blank lines, which we will treat shortly.

space and **put** are rather similar, and it would be possible to modify **space** to call **put**. This would centralize the output in one place, a desirable goal. The main problem is how to avoid getting **lsval** line spaces each time **put** is called from the proposed new **space**. We certainly don't want to change **lsval** in **space** before calling **put**, then restore it after — this is the worst kind of pathological data connection because it is the least obvious. We don't want to burden each call to **put** with a line-spacing argument, nor do we want leading blanks on each blank line produced by **space** when text is indented. In spite of the apparent repetition of code, it's preferable the way it is.

We now have enough skeleton to test all the permutations of line spacing, blank lines, new pages, and so on. The **.pl** command is particularly useful for testing, since you can shorten the page down to the point where it's easy to count output lines by hand. The code in **comand** for **.pl** is

```
else if (ct == PL) {
        call set(plval, val, argtyp, PAGELEN,
          m1val+m2val+m3val+m4val+1, HUGE)
        bottom = plval - m3val - m4val
        }
```

You might also find it convenient to modify **skip** temporarily to produce a visible character on each skipped line; this makes it easier to interpret output.

What are particularly nasty boundary conditions that might go wrong? There is at least one error — the last page of output is short, because there is no provision to print the extra lines needed to get to the bottom. To repair it we ask for a large number of blank lines in the main routine, after the end of the input has occurred, in exactly the same way the **.bp** command does. Here is the revised version of **format**:

```
# format - text formatter main program (final version)
      character inbuf(INSIZE)
      integer getlin
      include cpage

      call init
      while (getlin(inbuf, STDIN) ¬= EOF)
              if (inbuf(1) == COMMAND)        # it's a command
                      call comand(inbuf)
              else                            # it's text
                      call text(inbuf)
      if (lineno > 0)
              call space(HUGE)                # flush last output
      stop
      end
```

This works (i.e., does nothing) if we are already at the bottom of the last page, because no further spaces will be produced there. It also works for the less common case that we are at the top of a page; in particular, if there is no input, it produces no output.

We could have written special code to handle the end of the last page, but it is much better to use existing mechanisms like this wherever possible. Doing so avoids having two slightly different ways of doing the same thing (one of which is going to be overlooked when the other is improved) and ensures that the standard mechanism is well thought out at an important boundary.

The basic structure of **format** is now pretty well established, so we can show the hierarchy as it currently stands:

```
format
        init
        getlin
        comand
                comtyp, getval, brk, set, gettl, space
        text
                put
                        phead (pfoot)
                                skip
                                        putc
                                puttl
                                        putc, putdec
                        putc
                        putlin
                        skip
                space
                        brk, phead, pfoot, skip
        space
```

phead and **pfoot** call on the same assortment of routines; the hierarchy is shown once for both. Most new subroutines we are going to add will be called from **text**.

Exercise 7-5: Is it really necessary to have the two variables **curpag** and **newpag** to keep track of page numbers? Try to rewrite the code with only one. Make sure that **.bp** and **.bp +1** remain equivalent. □

7.5 Indenting

The next step is to implement settable left and right margins, which are required before we can do filled text properly. For each line of output, we need to know the indent **inval**, the right margin **rmval**, and the temporary indent **tival**. **tival** is the number of blanks to precede a line of output. The code in **comand** that handles the **.in**, **.rm** and **.ti** commands is

```
else if (ct == IN) {
        call set(inval, val, argtyp, 0, 0, rmval-1)
        tival = inval
        }
else if (ct == RM)
        call set(rmval, val, argtyp, PAGEWIDTH, tival+1, HUGE)
else if (ct == TI) {
        call brk
        call set(tival, val, argtyp, 0, 0, rmval)
        }
```

Each line produced by **put** is preceded by **tival** blanks; after each line of output **tival** must be reset to **inval** so that only a single line is temporarily indented. This is done by the code in **put** that reads

```
for (i = 1; i <= tival; i = i + 1)          # indenting
        call putc(BLANK)
tival = inval
```

Leading blanks and empty lines are special cases detected in **text**, where we must add the test

```
if (inbuf(1) == BLANK | inbuf(1) == NEWLINE)
        call leadbl(inbuf)      # move left, set tival
```

before the call to **put**. **leadbl** handles the leading blanks.

```
# leadbl - delete leading blanks, set tival
      subroutine leadbl(buf)
      character buf(MAXLINE)
      integer max
      integer i, j
      include cparam

      call brk
      for (i = 1; buf(i) == BLANK; i = i + 1) # find 1st non-blank
              ;
      if (buf(i) ¬= NEWLINE)
              tival = i - 1
      for (j = 1; buf(i) ¬= EOS; j = j + 1) {    # move line to left
              buf(j) = buf(i)
              i = i + 1
              }
      buf(j) = EOS
      return
      end
```

leadbl moves the entire line to the left so the first non-blank character is in position 1. This ensures that leading blanks in no-fill mode don't get twice as much indent as they should, once from the temporary indent and once from the leading blanks themselves.

7.6 Filled Text

Now that unfilled text and margins work, we can do filled text; that is what will be wanted most of the time. How does it work? Two routines, **getwrd** and **putwrd**, work together almost as co-routines. **getwrd** breaks an input line into words and passes them to **putwrd**. **putwrd** packs them and periodically outputs a filled line. Thus **text** becomes

```
# text — process text lines (interim version 2)
      subroutine text(inbuf)
      character inbuf(INSIZE), wrdbuf(INSIZE)
      integer getwrd
      integer i
      include cparam

      if (inbuf(1) == BLANK | inbuf(1) == NEWLINE)
            call leadbl(inbuf)      # move left, set tival
      if (inbuf(1) == NEWLINE) # all blank line
            call put(inbuf)
      else if (fill == NO)          # unfilled text
            call put(inbuf)
      else                          # filled text
            for (i = 1; getwrd(inbuf, i, wrdbuf) > 0; )
                  call putwrd(wrdbuf)
      return
      end
```

We wrote **getwrd** for the **include** program of Chapter 3. **getwrd** isolates words, that is, strings of non-blank characters. It is called with the index in **inbuf** where it is to start looking for a word; it returns with that index set just beyond the word it found, so it is ready for the next call. **getwrd** returns zero at the end of a line, and a positive word length in the middle.

The other end of the chain is **putwrd**. If the new word does not fit on the current line, **putwrd** flushes the line with a call to **brk** and resets for a fresh line. In any case the new word is tucked onto the end of the line. **putwrd** also adds a blank after the word, so the next word will be separated properly.

The call to **space** after **EOF** in the main routine now serves a double function. Since it causes a break, it will force out any partially completed line collected by **putwrd** before skipping to the bottom of the last page. This is an added benefit of using the high-level function **space** instead of coding an explicit "last page" routine.

```
# putwrd - put a word in outbuf
      subroutine putwrd(wrdbuf)
      character wrdbuf(INSIZE)
      integer length, width
      integer last, llval, w
      include cout
      include cparam

      w = width(wrdbuf)
      last = length(wrdbuf) + outp + 1         # new end of outbuf
      llval = rmval - tival
      if (outp > 0 & (outw+w > llval | last >= MAXOUT)) {   # too big
            last = last - outp                 # remember end of wrdbuf
            call brk                           # flush previous line
            }
      call scopy(wrdbuf, 1, outbuf, outp+1)
      outp = last
      outbuf(outp) = BLANK                     # blank between words
      outw = outw + w + 1                      # 1 for blank
      outwds = outwds + 1
      return
      end
```

The output line is collected in **outbuf**. **outp** is the last character position, **outw** the width of the line, and **outwds** the word count. These are kept in a **common** block **cout**, which is also used by **brk**.

```
common /cout/ outp, outw, outwds, outbuf(MAXOUT)
  integer outp          # last char position in outbuf; init = 0
  integer outw          # width of text currently in outbuf; init = 0
  integer outwds        # number of words in outbuf; init = 0
  character outbuf      # lines to be filled collect here
```

The width of the current line, **outw**, is not the same as **outp**, which points to the last character on the line. Why? What happens if a line typed by some innocent user contains a backspace, perhaps to underline a character by backspacing and underscoring? (We haven't built underlining yet, remember.) Clearly the "width" of

```
a BACKSPACE b
```

is 1 by any reasonable definition — it only occupies one column of output — but its "length" in actual storage space is 3 (characters). The two measures are different.

To handle this (and also looking ahead to underlining) we have separated "width" from "number of characters" and isolated the width computation in a separate function.

```
# width - compute width of character string
      integer function width(buf)
      character buf(MAXLINE)
      integer i

      width = 0
      for (i = 1; buf(i) ¬= EOS; i = i + 1)
            if (buf(i) == BACKSPACE)
                  width = width - 1
            else if (buf(i) ¬= NEWLINE)
                  width = width + 1
      return
      end
```

width has two special characters to worry about: **BACKSPACE** has width −1 and **NEWLINE** has width zero. Everything else has width +1.

We are now in a position to specify **brk**. Actually there isn't much to it — it outputs any text in **outbuf** with **put**, and resets the output pointer, width and word count to zero.

```
# brk - end current filled line
      subroutine brk
      include cout

      if (outp > 0) {
            outbuf(outp) = NEWLINE
            outbuf(outp+1) = EOS
            call put(outbuf)
            }
      outp = 0
      outw = 0
      outwds = 0
      return
      end
```

Exercise 7-6: What characters besides backspaces and newlines have zero width in your environment? Can you think of any characters whose width is not constant? □

Exercise 7-7: If your character set doesn't include a backspace, how would you provide it for **format** users nonetheless? □

7.7 Right Margin Justification

The only remaining loose end is justifying output lines, that is, squaring up the right margin. The best place is in **putwrd**, right before the call to **brk** — at that point we have a full line, we know we're working on filled text, and we know how many words are in the line and what its width is. Thus we modify **putwrd** by calling a separate routine to spread out the line by adding extra spaces.

```
# putwrd — put a word in outbuf; includes margin justification
	subroutine putwrd(wrdbuf)
	character wrdbuf(INSIZE)
	integer length, width
	integer last, llval, nextra, w
	include cout
	include cparam

	w = width(wrdbuf)
	last = length(wrdbuf) + outp + 1		# new end of outbuf
	llval = rmval - tival
	if (outp > 0 & (outw+w > llval | last >= MAXOUT)) {	# too big
		last = last - outp		# remember end of wrdbuf
		nextra = llval - outw + 1
		call spread(outbuf, outp, nextra, outwds)
		if (nextra > 0 & outwds > 1)
			outp = outp + nextra
		call brk			# flush previous line
		}
	call scopy(wrdbuf, 1, outbuf, outp+1)
	outp = last
	outbuf(outp) = BLANK		# blank between words
	outw = outw + w + 1		# 1 for blank
	outwds = outwds + 1
	return
	end
```

spread moves the words on the line to the right, starting with the rightmost. Each time a word is moved, some of the extra blanks are parceled out, as uniformly as possible, until none are left. **nextra** is the number of extra blanks needed to justify the line. Care is necessary in case **nextra** should be negative because of a long input word, or in case there is only one word on the line.

As an esthetic matter, if the extra blanks do not distribute evenly, the surplus ones are spread alternately from the right and from the left on successive lines, to avoid "rivers" of white space down one margin or the other. **dir** alternates between zero and one, selecting the side which gets the extra blanks.

```
# spread — spread words to justify right margin
	subroutine spread(buf, outp, nextra, outwds)
	character buf(MAXOUT)
	integer min
	integer dir, i, j, nb, ne, nextra, nholes, outp, outwds
	data dir /0/

	if (nextra <= 0 | outwds <= 1)
		return
	dir = 1 - dir		# reverse previous direction
	ne = nextra
	nholes = outwds - 1
	i = outp - 1
	j = min(MAXOUT-2, i+ne)		# leave room for NEWLINE, EOS
	while (i < j) {
		buf(j) = buf(i)
		if (buf(i) == BLANK) {
			if (dir == 0)
				nb = (ne-1) / nholes + 1
			else
				nb = ne / nholes
			ne = ne - nb
			nholes = nholes - 1
			for ( ; nb > 0; nb = nb - 1) {
				j = j - 1
				buf(j) = BLANK
				}
			}
		i = i - 1
		j = j - 1
		}
	return
	end
```

This code is tricky (which is not a compliment), but it performs an elaborate function and performs it correctly. The trickery lies in the computation of **nb**, which parcels out the extra blanks as uniformly as possible, while distributing the extras from one end or the other. There is no chance of division by zero even though **nholes** is continually decremented, because the code is executed only when **nextra>0** and **outwds>1**, and the loop exits after **nholes** reaches 1.

By the way, we tested the condition

```
if (nextra <= 0 | outwds <= 1)
```

in **spread**, then repeated the equivalent test

```
if (nextra > 0 & outwds > 1)
```

in **putwrd**. Why not instead write, in **putwrd**,

```
if (nextra > 0 & outwds > 1) {
        call spread(outbuf, outp, nextra, outwds)
        outp = outp + nextra
        }
```

and remove the redundant test from **spread**?

The reason we don't is that this would require the calling program to know about the constraints on the arguments of the called program. This is another form of secret dependency or coupling. From the standpoint of long-term maintenance it is a dangerous practice, because sooner or later someone modifying the caller will violate the constraints and perhaps introduce bugs. Thus we wrote **spread** to check its own arguments instead of relying on **putwrd**. Of course this sort of thing can be carried too far, but here the cost is insignificant, so it's well worth doing.

Exercise 7-8: Demonstrate that **spread** works properly, whether placing extra blanks on the right or on the left. Prove that it does something sane even at the extreme values of **outwds**, **nextra** and **outp**. How could you organize **format** differently so as to make **spread** easier? □

Exercise 7-9: Add the commands **.ju** (justify) and **.nj** (no justify) so justification can be turned on and off separately from filling. Should justification be permitted for unfilled lines? □

7.8 Centering and Underlining

Now that we have most of the formatter formatting, we can start to add bells and whistles.

Centering is a most useful addition, for it mechanizes a tedious and error-prone task that no human should ever have to do. Luckily it's dead easy. When a **.ce** command is seen, **comand** computes the number of lines and places it in **ceval** with the code

```
else if (ct == CE) {
        call brk
        call set(ceval, val, argtyp, 1, 0, HUGE)
        }
```

Each time a centered line is put out, **text** counts **ceval** down by one; when it reaches zero there is no more centering to be done. This code goes into **text**:

```
if (ceval > 0) {                # centering
        call center(inbuf)
        call put(inbuf)
        ceval = ceval - 1
        }
```

Finally, the line itself must be centered before it goes out. This is done by setting a temporary indent that moves the line to the right by the correct amount; when the line is output it will be positioned properly. We put this in a separate routine even though it is only a single line of code, because it seems to clutter up **text** less that way, but you can make a case for the other placement as well.

```
# center — center a line by setting tival
      subroutine center(buf)
      character buf(ARB)
      integer max, width
      include cparam

      tival = max((rmval+tival-width(buf))/2, 0)
      return
      end
```

Underlining is also tedious to do manually; like centering, it's better mechanized. The sequence of events for underlining is essentially the same as for centering. **comand** sets **ulval**:

```
      else if (ct == UL)
            call set(ulval, val, argtyp, 0, 1, HUGE)
```

text decrements **ulval** for each underlined input line:

```
      if (ulval > 0) {                  # underlining
            call underl(inbuf, wrdbuf, INSIZE)
            ulval = ulval - 1
            }
```

Finally, a separate routine **underl** prepares the words to be underlined by converting each character which is not a blank, tab or backspace into

character **BACKSPACE UNDERLINE**

text will then center the line or put it out unfilled or eat it up a word at a time for filling.

```
# underl — underline a line
      subroutine underl(buf, tbuf, size)
      integer i, j, size
      character buf(size), tbuf(size)

      j = 1             # expand into tbuf
      for (i = 1; buf(i) ¬= NEWLINE & j < size-1; i = i + 1) {
            tbuf(j) = buf(i)
            j = j + 1
            if (buf(i) ¬= BLANK & buf(i) ¬= TAB & buf(i) ¬= BACKSPACE) {
                  tbuf(j) = BACKSPACE
                  tbuf(j+1) = UNDERLINE
                  j = j + 2
                  }
            }
      tbuf(j) = NEWLINE
      tbuf(j+1) = EOS
      call scopy(tbuf, 1, buf, 1)   # copy it back to buf
      return
      end
```

Backspaces and underlines are inserted as the line is copied into a temporary array, which is then copied back to the original place. You could also do it in place, but the code is much less clear.

It is important to do all these functions in the proper order in **text**. Underlining and checking for leading blanks must be done first, since all other cases force output. Centering must precede the test for a **NEWLINE**, so a centered blank line will decrement **ceval**. Putting it all together in one place, we get the final version of **text**:

```
# text - process text lines (final version)
      subroutine text(inbuf)
      character inbuf(INSIZE), wrdbuf(INSIZE)
      integer getwrd
      integer i
      include cparam

      if (inbuf(1) == BLANK | inbuf(1) == NEWLINE)
            call leadbl(inbuf)     # move left, set tival
      if (ulval > 0) {             # underlining
            call underl(inbuf, wrdbuf, INSIZE)
            ulval = ulval - 1
            }
      if (ceval > 0) {             # centering
            call center(inbuf)
            call put(inbuf)
            ceval = ceval - 1
            }
      else if (inbuf(1) == NEWLINE)    # all blank line
            call put(inbuf)
      else if (fill == NO)         # unfilled text
            call put(inbuf)
      else                         # filled text
            for (i = 1; getwrd(inbuf, i, wrdbuf) > 0; )
                  call putwrd(wrdbuf)
      return
      end
```

Here is the final subroutine tree of **format**, reflecting the additions we made.

```
format
    init
    getlin
    comand
        comtyp
        getval
        set
        gettl
        space
        brk
            put
    text
        leadbl
            brk
        underl
        center
            width
        put
            phead (pfoot)
                skip
                    putc
                puttl
                    putc, putdec
            putc
            putlin
            skip
        getwrd
        putwrd
            width, spread, brk
        space
            brk, phead, pfoot, skip
    space
```

Exercise 7-10: Investigate the behavior of **format** if a user underlines by backspacing and underscoring. What happens with backspacing across a blank in filled text? What about underlining a word containing backspaces? □

Exercise 7-11: Underlined punctuation characters are often hard to read. Modify **underl** to underline only letters and digits. □

Exercise 7-12: On some video terminals, underlining a character erases it, so it would be better to print in the order

UNDERLINE BACKSPACE *character*

That way you at least get to see the character, even if the underlining is erased. Modify **underl** accordingly. □

Exercise 7-13: Underlining a character at a time is the worst thing we can do to **overstrike** in Chapter 2. (It's also a test to destruction of some terminals.) Should we make **underl** more clever, or improve **overstrike**? □

Exercise 7-14: Another way to do underlining is to surround each string to be underlined with magic "start underline" and "stop underline" characters of zero width. Discuss the merits and demerits of such an organization. □

7.9 Some Measurements

We ran **format** on some large documents, and measured where it spends its time. Here are some measurements for formatting this chapter, which consisted at that time of 2300 lines, or 9200 words, of which 640 lines were formatting commands; it produced 27 pages of single-spaced line-printer output.

As always, most of the CPU time on the system where we did the timing (a Honeywell 6070) was spent processing I/O requests: 70 percent was spent in **getlin** and functions below it (mostly in the latter), 17 percent in **putlin** and its subordinates, and 2 percent in **putch**. These numbers so dominate the run time that until they are improved no other part of the program matters at all. Let us assume, however, that they can be cut down to reasonable size by replacing standard Fortran formatted I/O by routines tailored for efficient character input and output. Then what parts of the program take the time?

The remaining significant routines are

getwrd	3.1%
putwrd	2.3
width	1.7
text	1.6
spread	1.0
put	0.4

After the I/O time has been removed, these routines account for essentially all the time taken by the formatter. The lesson is the same as before, but it is worth repeating. The best procedure for obtaining efficient code is to choose a good algorithm, write a program that implements it as cleanly as possible, then measure it. The measurements will lead you directly to the one or two routines that are worth making as efficient as possible — if they are clearly written and if they hide their information properly, they will be easy to change. Sacrificing readability for efficiency earlier than this, while the bulk of the code is being written, not only results in wasted effort but also leads to code that is hard to improve because it is hard to understand.

7.10 Extensions

As we said, this is not an elaborate formatter, and there are a lot of things that could be added that would make it better without complicating it for unsophisticated users. Extensions to make more parameters settable by users are so straightforward that they don't even qualify as exercises. More involved, but valuable, are these functional enhancements.

Multiple Files

To follow good design principles **format** should read either from a list of files or, if none are specified, from its standard input, like the **print** program of Chapter 3. It should also be possible to include the contents of a file by a formatting command.

Exercise 7-15: Implement multiple files as arguments and a file inclusion command. You might use the name **.so** for "source"; the command

.so *filename*

will interpolate the contents of *filename* in the input at the point it is encountered. If you decided that the name would be better as **.include**, what changes would be needed in **comand** and **comtyp**? Once **.so** is installed, you can use **format** for the same kind of formatting as was done by **print** in Chapter 3. Is it worthwhile to keep **print** around nonetheless? □

Exercise 7-16: Add optional arguments +*m* and −*n* to allow output to begin printing at page *m* and stop printing after page *n*. Thus

format +10 −20

prints pages 10 through 20 inclusive. What is proper behavior if *m* or *n* is outside the range of pages in the document? □

Improved Running Titles

Our top and bottom running titles are sometimes awkward to use. The syntax

.he / *left* / *center* / *right* /

means the heading (top of page title) is to consist of the three parts separated by the (arbitrary) delimiter /. The *left* part is to be left-justified, the *right* part right-justified, and the *center* part centered. As before, any occurrence of the character # in the title is to be replaced by the current page number.

Exercise 7-17: Implement the extended **.he** and **.fo** commands. What right margin and indent values determine placement of the pieces? What should happen if the pieces overlap? How would you permit multi-line titles? Add the commands

.eh .ef .oh .of

to allow different titles on even numbered and odd numbered pages. □

Character Translation

It is often useful to have one character replaced by another upon output. Two obvious cases: first, to have some character translate into a blank, so words in filled text can be kept together; second, to have some character translate into a period in column 1, for writing a document about formatting.

Exercise 7-18: Implement the *transliterate* command **.tr**:

.tr ab cd

translates **a** into **c**, and **b** into **d** on output;

.tr a−z A−Z

translates lower case to upper case;

.tr x

translates **x** into a blank. What happens with variations of

```
.tr a b
.tr b c
```

in your program? Can you borrow any code or design from **translit**? □

'Need' Command

Sometimes it is desirable to force output like a table or a program to appear all on one page; this was done for the programs in this book. Somehow a 'begin page' command must be simulated at the beginning of the table, but only if it would actually fall across a page boundary. The command

.ne *n*

says "I need *n* lines; if there aren't that many on this page, skip to a new page."

Exercise 7-19: Implement the **.ne** command. How would you use **.ne** commands for "widow" suppression? (A widow is an isolated line left at the bottom or top of a page.) □

Exercise 7-20: Forcing people to count lines for a **.ne** command is obviously bad human engineering. Design and implement a mechanism to keep a group of lines together without requiring the user to count them. Extend it to the **.ce** and **.ul** commands, which currently suffer the same deficiency. □

Extra Space after Sentence

Most people prefer an extra space after the period that terminates a sentence; it looks better.

Exercise 7-21: Implement this feature. Make sure it works when the period falls at the end of a line. What other characters and sequences terminate sentences? Is there a reasonable algorithm that doesn't put extra space after people's initials, abbreviations, and so on? □

Automatic Capitalization

Some computer centers have line printers with upper and lower case, but few upper and lower case terminals or keypunches. This need not discourage someone who wants neatly formatted output.

Exercise 7-22: Modify **format** so it detects plausible forms of end of sentence, like a period at the end of a line or followed by two or more spaces, and then capitalizes the next letter. You will also need "escape" characters that override the default action and force the next character to be explicitly lower or upper case. If you are clever about recognizing sentences, however, these will probably be little used. What is the width of these characters? □

7.11 Bigger Things

The suggestions in this closing section are major undertakings if done well, but they should suggest how the formatter may be substantially increased in power. All of these facilities were available in some form in the formatter we used to prepare this book.

Hyphenation

format fills lines by packing as many words onto a line as will fit. Hyphenation increases this number on the average, and thus improves the appearance of the output. The problem is to design a reasonably accurate scheme for hyphenating English words by program.

First make up a list of suffixes that are potentially good hyphenation points, like *-tion*, *-ly*, and so on. (Remember that English hyphenates between syllables, so both suffix and prefix must contain a vowel.) Merely stripping these should provide a useful capability. You might also experiment with prefix-stripping; our experience has been that this is less successful. Next, certain letter pairs ("digrams") should *never* be hyphenated — *qu* is the most obvious example — while others, like double letters, are almost always good bets. Build a 26×26 array (single bits are enough) whose entries show whether or not to hyphenate between particular pairs of letters.

Experiment with these possibilities. Can you think of any other approaches? What programs would you write as tools to help you with this project? What tools have we already written for you in this book?

This book was hyphenated by a more complicated version of the suggested scheme. How many hyphenation gaffes can you find?

Macros

Although the next chapter will be devoted to macro processing, we should mention the possibility of adding macros, even in limited form, to the formatter. As the first step, you could allow a user to define shorthands for frequently occurring sequences of commands. For example

```
.de pp
.sp
.ti +5
.en
```

would *define* a new command **.pp** (for "paragraph"). Thereafter, whenever the "command"

```
.pp
```

occurs, it is replaced by its defining text, everything between the **.de** and the **.en**. In this case, a space and a temporary indent result. And of course it should be possible to redefine any of the built-in names like **.sp**.

This much is easy. The next step is to allow macros to have arguments, so they can produce different results when called with different parameters. For example, you might define a title macro with

```
.de tl
.he 'Chapter $1''
.en
```

The symbol **$1** means that when the macro is invoked, the first argument is to replace the **$1**. Thus you might say

```
.tl 7
```

to create a page title of "Chapter 7."

This syntax limits you to nine arguments, which is probably adequate. As a matter of good human engineering, missing arguments should be replaced by null strings; extra arguments should be ignored. We will return to similar issues in Chapter 8.

Conditionals

A truly powerful formatter needs the ability to alter formatting actions depending on conditions that develop during a run. One possibility is a command like

.if (*condition*) *things*

so you can dynamically test some condition, and take appropriate action if it is true. There is no limit to how complicated this can be made, but as a bare minimum, you will want to be able to test parameter values like output page number, line and page lengths, current position on the page, and whether or not you are in fill mode. You will also need arithmetic, text and arithmetic variables, and string comparison operations. For example, both the section headings and the exercises in this book were numbered automatically by the formatter, using arithmetic variables and operations.

One of the best tests of whether you have enough tools in your formatter is whether you can construct with them a general footnote mechanism, where there can be multiple footnotes per page, and where footnotes are carried forward onto as many pages as are needed. Another test is whether you can do multi-column output. If you can do these cases well, you have enough power for most formatting situations.

These suggestions are intentionally vague, so that they will not bias you too strongly in any particular direction. As always, if you propose to build something, make sure it has some conceptual integrity — it should not be merely a collection of unrelated "features." And build it in increments, not all at once.

Bibliographic Notes

format is loosely based on J. Saltzer's Runoff program on CTSS. Runoff has gone through numerous versions; ours is most closely related to Roff, by M. D. McIlroy. There are many formatting programs available commercially, often as part of a "word processing system." You might find it interesting to compare some of these offerings with **format**.

This book was typeset by a program called Troff, written by J. F. Ossanna for the UNIX system. A typesetter has many more degrees of freedom than a line printer — multiple fonts, several sizes of type, and a much larger character set. A challenging problem is to design a language which permits access to these added facilities without unduly complicating things for naive users. We made extensive use of Troff's macro capabilities to conceal formatting details in macro commands which could be easily changed as necessary without touching the text itself.

CHAPTER 8

MACRO PROCESSING

Macros are used to extend some underlying language — to perform a translation from one language to another. For example, many of our programs contain lines like

```
while (getlin(buf, infile) ¬= EOF)
```

where **EOF** is some unspecified value that indicates end of file. "Symbolic constants" like **EOF** tell you what a number signifies in a way that the number itself could never do: if we had written some magic value like **−1** you would not know what it meant without understanding the surrounding context. Besides, the value of **EOF** may well differ from machine to machine, and it is much easier and safer to redefine the value of a symbolic constant in a single place than it is to go through an entire program finding all the **−1**'s that really mean end of file.

What we want, then, is a program that lets us define symbolic constants like **EOF** so that subsequent occurrences of the name are replaced by the defining string of characters. Such a definition is called a *macro,* the replacement process is called *macro expansion,* and the program for doing it is called a *macro processor.* It reads the source file and writes a new file with the macro definitions deleted and the macro references expanded. This lets us use parameters even in places where a compiler would insist on numbers, as in array size declarations.

Our first step in this chapter is a program **define** for replacement of one string of text by another — the most elementary form of macro processing. This lets us say, for instance,

```
define(EOF, −1)
```

and thereafter have all occurrences of **EOF** replaced by **−1**. Although this is not much of a "language translation," it does make programs easier to read and change. This is the level of macro processing we have used for all programs in this book, and a bit more powerful than the "parameter" statement found in some dialects of Fortran. We didn't need much more than this, and we wanted to stay close enough to Fortran that the code would be recognizable.

The second stage, a much bigger job, is to construct a processor that allows macros to have arguments, so we can say, for example,

```
define(putc(c), putch(c, STDOUT))
```

to have all occurrences of **putc(x)** replaced by **putch(x, STDOUT)** for whatever value the argument **x** might take.

The third stage is to add to the macro processor a handful of other built-in operations that materially assist in writing complicated macro operations. The most important of these is a facility for conditional testing. These last two stages are really luxuries: they are convenient to have, and it is instructive to see how to build them, but you can accomplish a great deal without them.

We should also emphasize that this is not the only way to specify macros. Our notation is *functional*, i.e., it resembles the way function references are written in most programming languages, so macro calls mesh well with such languages. We could have adopted the syntax

```
define EOF -1
```

but that does not extend well to multi-line definitions or to macros with arguments or to some of the other built-in operations we want to add. In Chapter 7 we suggested the form

define *name*
body
endmarker

which is suitable for a language where input is handled a line at a time. Another possibility is a *template* macro processor, in which the macros correspond to operators (like the + and − in arithmetic expressions), and the arguments are the operands. Processors for template macros are sometimes easier to use, but are measurably harder to write. The bibliographic notes at the end of the chapter suggest additional reading.

8.1 Simple Text Replacement

Let us begin with the easiest case. What we want is to copy input to output, except that when certain input strings appear they are to be replaced by previously defined replacement text. In a programming language like Fortran or PL/I, the natural unit of replacement is probably the identifier, that is, a string of alphanumeric characters surrounded by non-alphanumerics. In the text

```
while (getlin(buf, infile) ¬= EOF)
```

EOF is surrounded by non-alphanumerics and is thus a candidate for replacement. Of course so are **while**, **getlin**, **buf** and **infile**, but since they are presumably not defined (to the macro processor anyway), they should be copied unaltered.

The unit of replacement is called a *token*. In other situations, a token might be anything between "white space" (blanks, tabs, newlines) as it was in **format**, or anything between a pair of specified left and right markers. In any case, one part of the processor is a routine that reads input and divides it up into tokens according to some rule.

How are definitions provided? The syntax suggested above is convenient:

define(name, replacement text)

defines **name** to be whatever text follows, up to a balancing right parenthesis; this allows the replacement text to be longer than one line. We will need modules to collect the name and replacement text, and to record new names and definitions as they are encountered.

Some of the implementation details are critical, because the order in which operations are done can make a big difference in the power and convenience of a macro processor. One significant decision is what should happen when one name is defined in terms of another one. For example, after the definitions

```
define(x, 1)
define(y, x)
```

does the input **y** produce **x** or **1**? If the definitions are in reverse order,

```
define(y, x)
define(x, 1)
```

then what is **y**?

These are not academic questions. The **archive** program of Chapter 3, for example, contains two definitions:

```
define(DEL, LETD)
define(LETD, 100)
```

where 100 happens to be the internal representation of the letter **d** in the ASCII character set. It is better to define **DEL** in terms of **LETD** than to wire into the program the representation of a **d** in a particular character set. As we said before, the fewer explicit system dependencies there are in a program, the more readily it can be moved from one system to another, and the better it can survive changes in the current system. Nor do we want users of **define** to have to worry too much about the order in which their definitions appear. Accordingly, **define** is built so examples like this one will work in the more useful way — after a macro has been evaluated, its replacement text is *rescanned.* If it contains any further macros they in turn go through the same expansion process. (This introduces the chance of an infinite loop, of course, so we must be prepared for that eventuality.)

There are also several possibilities for *when* macro calls are evaluated. If we have already defined **x** with

```
define(x, 1)
```

then when

```
define(y, x)
```

is encountered, we can either replace **x** by **1** immediately, or we can ignore the fact that **x** is a macro and replace it later when **y** is invoked. In the example above these two methods produce the same result, but if **x** should subsequently be redefined, there would be a difference. Different choices here lead to somewhat different but equally useful processors. In our **define** processor, definitions are *not* scanned for macro calls while they are being copied into the table of definitions; the interpretation of macros is done as late as possible.

Here is the outline of the no-argument macro processor.

```
while (gettok(token) ¬= EOF) {
        look up token
        if (token == "define")
                install new token and value
        else if (token was found in table)
                switch input to definition of token
        else
                copy token to output
        }
```

Since there are nested sources of input, in principle this is a recursive process. In **define** we will deal with recursion in a different way from the stacks and linked lists that we have used in other programs. We will get back to this shortly.

gettok is analogous to the **getwrd** routine in Chapter 3 and 7, but it must be made somewhat more complicated to handle non-alphabetic characters properly. For example, blanks are now significant and can't be ignored. The call

```
t = gettok(token, maxtok)
```

copies the next token from the standard input into **token**. A token is either a string of letters and digits, or a single non-alphanumeric character. The function value returned by **gettok** is either **ALPHA** for an alphanumeric token, or the single letter itself for a non-alphanumeric. (This implies that **ALPHA** must be distinct from any non-alphanumeric character.) **gettok** uses **type**, which we wrote in Chapter 4, to decide whether a character is a letter, a digit, or something else. Recall that if the type is not alphanumeric, **type** returns the character itself.

```
# gettok — get alphanumeric string or single non-alpha for define
      character function gettok(token, toksiz)
      character ngetc, type
      integer i, toksiz
      character token(toksiz)

      for (i = 1; i < toksiz; i = i + 1) {
            gettok = type(ngetc(token(i)))
            if (gettok ¬= LETTER & gettok ¬= DIGIT)
                  break
            }
      if (i >= toksiz)
            call error("token too long.")
      if (i > 1) {                        # some alpha was seen
            call putbak(token(i))
            i = i - 1
            gettok = ALPHA
            }
      # else single character token
      token(i+1) = EOS
      return
      end
```

Looking for tokens one character at a time, we don't know that we have seen the end of the token until we have gone one character too far. This is a classic example of an undesirable side effect, one that can tremendously complicate a program if we let it. Each time we need another character, we must check whether to read a new character or use the one we already have. Tangling this up with the logic of what to *do* with each character would make an unreadable mess.

Instead we hide the complication by introducing a pair of cooperating routines. **ngetc** delivers the next input character to be considered both in its argument and as its function value. **putbak** puts a character back on the input, so that the next call to **ngetc** will return it again. Now, every time **gettok** reads one character too many, it promptly pushes it back, so the rest of the code does not have to know about the problem.

Ideally **putbak** should be a primitive operation, and **ngetc** can be simply **getc**. We have separated them here to illustrate how the pushback can be done, since in general you will have to provide your own. **putbak** puts the pushed-back characters into a buffer. **ngetc** reads from the buffer if there is anything there; it calls **getc** if the buffer is empty.

```
# putbak — push character back onto input
      subroutine putbak(c)
      character c
      include cdefio

      bp = bp + 1
      if (bp > BUFSIZE)
            call error("too many characters pushed back.")
      buf(bp) = c
      return
      end

# ngetc — get a (possibly pushed back) character
      character function ngetc(c)
      character getc
      character c
      include cdefio

      if (bp > 0)
            c = buf(bp)
      else {
            bp = 1
            buf(bp) = getc(c)
            }
      if (c ¬= EOF)
            bp = bp - 1
      ngetc = c
      return
      end
```

bp is the index of the next character to be returned from **buf**; if **buf** is zero a fresh character is fetched by a call to **getc**. (**bp** must be initialized to zero.) The buffer and pointer used by **ngetc** and **putbak** are kept in the **common** block **cdefio**:

```
common /cdefio/ bp, buf(BUFSIZE)
  integer bp          # next available character; init = 0
  character buf       # pushed-back characters
```

Of course **gettok** never pushes back more than one character between calls to **ngetc**, so **buf** could have been an ordinary scalar variable instead of an array. But pushback is a useful mechanism, well worth generalizing. We can even write **pbstr**, which pushes back an entire string by repeated calls to **putbak**.

```
# pbstr — push string back onto input
      subroutine pbstr(in)
      character in(MAXLINE)
      integer length
      integer i

      for (i = length(in); i > 0; i = i - 1)
            call putbak(in(i))
      return
      end
```

It is of course necessary to push a string back in reverse order.

Only **ngetc** and **putbak** know about the **common** block **cdefio**. **pbstr** could be faster if it also knew about **cdefio** and could avoid the overhead of calling **putbak** for each character, but as much as possible we try to minimize data connections between routines. This is one of the most effective ways we know of to write code that can be easily changed. Certainly if it later proves true that the overhead in **pbstr** is a bottleneck, then we can improve it. The important thing is to start with a good design. It is much easier to relax the standards for something well written than it is to tighten them for something badly written.

Since we can push back something different from what was read, it has probably occurred to you that **putbak** provides an elegant way to implement the rescanning of a macro replacement text. Suppose that after a defined name is found, we push its *replacement text* back onto the input. When that is read, if it in turn contains a defined name, the name will be looked up and translated just as if it had been in the input originally. This pushback is how we handle the recursion implicit in nested sources of input.

Now we can write the main program, **define**:

```
# define — simple string replacement macro processor
      character gettok
      character defn(MAXDEF), t, token(MAXTOK)
      integer lookup
      string defnam "define"
      integer deftyp(2)
      data deftyp(1) /DEFTYPE/, deftyp(2) /EOS/

      call instal(defnam, deftyp)
      for (t = gettok(token, MAXTOK); t ¬= EOF; t = gettok(token, MAXTOK))
            if (t ¬= ALPHA)                # output non-alpha tokens
                  call putlin(token, STDOUT)
            else if (lookup(token, defn) == NO)      # and undefined
                  call putlin(token, STDOUT)
            else if (defn(1) == DEFTYPE) {           # get definition
                  call getdef(token, MAXTOK, defn, MAXDEF)
                  call instal(token, defn)
                  }
            else
                  call pbstr(defn)         # push replacement onto input
      stop
      end
```

If the token returned by **gettok** is not of type **ALPHA**, it cannot be a defined symbol. We test for that right away, to avoid looking up every non-alphanumeric character.

The token is looked up with **lookup**, which also returns the defining text if the name was found. If the name wasn't found by **lookup**, it has no special significance, and can be output immediately. If the name was *define*, the name and replacement text are isolated with **getdef** and installed in the table by **instal**. If the name was found and was not a *define*, the replacement text is pushed back onto the input.

instal is used to place the keyword *define* in the table in the first place, along with the symbolic constant **DEFTYPE** as its translation. This is better than entering it with a **data** statement, because the program doesn't need to know anything about the format of table entries and it is *much* easier to initialize the table to be empty. **lookup** returns the translation when it finds *define*, so we can quickly check whether a name is a *define*. **DEFTYPE** must of course be distinguishable from all other characters. **lookup** and **instal** are the only visible parts of the table-handling mechanism; they are the subject of the next section.

Here is **getdef**:

```
# getdef (for no arguments) — get name and definition
      subroutine getdef(token, toksiz, defn, defsiz)
      character gettok, ngetc
      integer defsiz, i, nlpar, toksiz
      character c, defn(defsiz), token(toksiz)

      if (ngetc(c) ¬= LPAREN)
            call error("missing left paren.")
      else if (gettok(token, toksiz) ¬= ALPHA)
            call error("non-alphanumeric name.")
      else if (ngetc(c) ¬= COMMA)
            call error("missing comma in define.")
      # else got (name,
      nlpar = 0
      for (i = 1; nlpar >= 0; i = i + 1)
            if (i > defsiz)
                  call error("definition too long.")
            else if (ngetc(defn(i)) == EOF)
                  call error("missing right paren.")
            else if (defn(i) == LPAREN)
                  nlpar = nlpar + 1
            else if (defn(i) == RPAREN)
                  nlpar = nlpar - 1
            # else normal character in defn(i)
      defn(i-1) = EOS
      return
      end
```

Most of the task here is coping with balanced parentheses and invalid input.

Notice that we did not need to write most of the **else**'s that we used, since **error** never returns control to the caller. We put them in anyway to emphasize that at most one of each series of actions is to be performed. A reader unfamiliar with the code will grasp it much quicker if it is expressed in a standard form, and the **else if** chain is one of the more important ones.

This particular use of the **else if** closely parallels the way we used **andif** in Chapter 6. There, we wanted to perform a series of steps, checking status after each step and stopping as soon as a test fails. Here, we also do a series of steps, but stop as soon as a test *succeeds*. For that reason we could call this usage an **orif**.

The important thing is to recognize that each test in sequence may well perform some operation as a side effect, that the steps must be done in a particular order, and that we want to perform exactly one of a series of terminal actions depending on how far along the chain of tests we progress. This form appears frequently in our code.

Exercise 8-1: What happens if you say

```
define(d, define)
d(a, b)
a
```

What happens with

```
define(define, x)
define(a, b)
```

□

Exercise 8-2: What happens if you say

```
define(x, x)
```

or

```
define(x, y)
define(y, x)
```

and then ask for **x**? What would you like to have happen? □

Exercise 8-3: If a line contains nothing but a definition, any trailing blanks and the newline are copied to the output, even though it might seem more natural to eliminate them completely. Modify **getdef** or some other part of the program so no output is produced from a line containing only definitions. Is this an appropriate action if the output is fed to a compiler that uses line numbers for diagnostics? □

Exercise 8-4: As an alternate and more general solution to the previous problem, implement a built-in operation **dnl** (for "delete newline") which deletes all characters from its occurrence up to and including the next newline. Thus in the input

```
define(x, 1)dnl
```

the **dnl** deletes all text after the definition, and the line produces no output. □

8.2 Table Lookup

Let us now design **lookup** and **instal**, the routines for handling tables of names and definitions. We have already made one important design decision — *all* information about table format, search strategy, and the like is private, known only by **lookup** and **instal**. All other routines must access the table through them. Information hiding is critical to proper program design: routines which don't need to know about the internal representation of a data structure should not know about it. Not only does this ensure that data is not inadvertently changed, but more important, it breaks the program into independent pieces, where each can be changed without affecting the others. Each piece is a black box, presenting only a well-defined interface to the world. In our case, if we change some aspect of the table — to sort the names, or hash them, for instance — we can do so with impunity, because no other routine knows what the tables look like. Of course the "need to know" has to be genuine. It's all too easy to design routines whose users "need" to know about the data, when with more care the structure could be concealed.

Inside the lookup code, the lookup strategy determines the table structures needed. For now the most important consideration is simplicity. We assume that in general the definitions will arrive at unpredictable times, rather than all at once. This makes it less feasible to sort the entries and use a binary search. Hashing and tree-storage schemes are significantly more complicated than we want to begin with.

Therefore we simply add new entries to the end of a linear table as they arrive, and search the table from one end to the other each time a token must be looked up. In the early stages of a program, fancy search techniques are not worth the extra complexity. Linear search is not always the best thing, but it is an excellent first choice. It is easy to implement and likely to work right the first time. If it later proves to be a bottleneck, it can be replaced with a faster algorithm without affecting the rest of the program.

The linear table is organized like this. One large table contains the names and replacement texts, stored one after another as

```
name EOS definition EOS   name EOS definition EOS  ...
```

A second array holds pointers to the name entries in the first.

```
common /clook/ lastp, lastt, namptr(MAXPTR), table(MAXTBL)
  integer lastp           # last used in namptr; init = 0
  integer lastt           # last used in table; init = 0
  integer namptr          # name pointers
  character table         # actual text of names and defns
```

lastp and **lastt** locate the last used positions in **namptr** and **table** respectively; they must be initialized to zero. We have put all these variables into a **common** block **clook**, because **lookup** and **instal** both have to know about them.

lookup returns **YES** and extracts the definition if the token was found; otherwise it returns **NO**.

```
# lookup — locate name, extract definition from table
	integer function lookup(name, defn)
	character defn(MAXDEF), name(MAXTOK)
	integer i, j, k
	include clook

	for (i = lastp; i > 0; i = i - 1) {
		j = namptr(i)
		for (k = 1; name(k) == table(j) & name(k) ¬= EOS; k = k + 1)
			j = j + 1
		if (name(k) == table(j)) {		# got one
			call scopy(table, j+1, defn, 1)
			lookup = YES
			return
			}
		}
	lookup = NO
	return
	end
```

scopy is the string-copying subroutine we wrote in Chapter 3.

instal adds a new name and definition to the end of the table; it is called when a *define* is encountered. **instal** does not check whether the name is already in the table. Names may be redefined just by giving a new definition; since **lookup** scans its table backwards, the new definition supersedes the old.

```
# instal — add name and definition to table
      subroutine instal(name, defn)
      character defn(MAXTOK), name(MAXDEF)
      integer length
      integer dlen, nlen
      include clook

      nlen = length(name) + 1
      dlen = length(defn) + 1
      if (lastt + nlen + dlen > MAXTBL | lastp >= MAXPTR) {
            call putlin(name, ERROUT)
            call remark(": too many definitions.")
            }
      lastp = lastp + 1
      namptr(lastp) = lastt + 1
      call scopy(name, 1, table, lastt + 1)
      call scopy(defn, 1, table, lastt + nlen + 1)
      lastt = lastt + nlen + dlen
      return
      end
```

Exercise 8-5: Verify that **getdef** and **instal** work correctly if the definition is empty:

```
define(nothing,)
```

defines a string with no replacement text. Why would you want to define such a thing? What is the effect of the macro call

```
nothing(this is a line of text)
```

□

Exercise 8-6: Redefining names without salvaging the old space is obviously profligate if done often. Add an **undefine** command

```
undefine(name)
```

which removes the most recent definition of **name**. What should happen if you **undefine** a name that wasn't defined? □

Exercise 8-7: Measure **define** to find out where it spends its time. Is it worth improving the table-lookup code? One possibility would be to sort the names in **table** as each new definition arrives. (Actually, you would sort the pointers in **namptr**, as we did in **sort** in Chapter 4.) Then change **lookup** to use a binary search. How much faster is the program? How easy is it to do this exercise and the previous one simultaneously? □

Exercise 8-8: Implement a version that does not use pushback in the sense that we have, but instead maintains a stack of current input sources, and switches those appropriately. Which version is easier? Which version is faster? □

Exercise 8-9: How does **define** deal with the comment conventions of common programming languages? Should **define** know about quoted strings? That is, should defined names appearing within quotes be replaced? □

Exercise 8-10: It is often useful to have at least a rudimentary conditional test. Suppose we say that a line like

```
ifdef(name,text)
```

means "if **name** is defined, put **text** in the input, otherwise skip over it." You could parameterize a program for different machines by writing definitions like

```
ifdef(machine1, define(wordsize, 32) define(charsize, 8))
ifdef(machine2, define(wordsize, 36) define(charsize, 6))
```

and so on. Then defining **machine1** with the (empty) definition

```
define(machine1, )
```

sets parameters like **wordsize** correctly for **machine1** when the **ifdef** lines are encountered. Changing this single definition and reprocessing resets the program for **machine2**. Implement this conditional facility. □

8.3 Some Measurements

We timed **define** on some "typical" Ratfor programs (the code in this chapter) to see how it spends its time. Here are some data from one timing study.

	#calls	CPU time
(read)	472	40.3%
(write)	9199	14.4
lookup	1636	13.3
gettok	5263	9.0
getc	9902	6.3
ngetc	12149	4.7
putlin	5092	4.5
define	1	3.6
type	11868	2.7
putbak	2247	0.4
getdef	42	0.2
pbstr	86	0.2
scopy	214	0.2
instal	43	0.1
length	172	0.1

The routine **(read)** reads single lines with Fortran formatted I/O. **(write)** is essentially the **putc** of Chapter 1.

Before we consider the run time percentages, it's worth remarking that there is a lot of information in a measurement as simple as the number of times each subroutine is called, especially if the program is carefully modularized so each routine does only one thing. For example, this data tells us that the input contains 472 lines and 9902 characters (one of which is an **EOF**), that there were 9199 output characters, that there were 42 occurrences of defined tokens out of 1636 (which means that most of the time **lookup** scans through its entire table, then reports failure), and so on. Some of this data provides consistency checking on the operation of the program. We expect one more **instal** than **getdef** (installing the keyword **define** in the first place); if that is not so, something is badly amiss. We can also see that looking up non-alphanumeric tokens would almost quadruple the number of calls to **lookup** and markedly affect the CPU time, so our decision to test for this case separately was justified.

Ideally you should be able to get this kind of information automatically if you need it, but often you will have to arrange for it by yourself. Chapter 9 contains some suggestions on how to go about it.

The CPU time data tells us that as usual with Fortran, the I/O time is the dominant effect, about 65 percent. Of the remaining run time, table lookup is the most significant, but not overwhelming. Of course it grows with the number of table entries, so if there were many more, looking up tokens would eventually swamp the I/O. The pushback mechanism is a modest cost on each character, well worth it for the clarity it brings to the program. Our decision to write **pbstr** in terms of **putbak** is also vindicated.

It is important to justify decisions made in the name of efficiency for one very good reason. Most of the time programmers have no real idea where time is being consumed by a program. Consequently nearly all the effort expended (and the clarity sacrificed) for "efficiency" is wasted. We have found that the best way to avoid too-early optimization is to make a regular practice of intrumenting code. Only from such first hand experience can one learn a proper sense of priorities.

8.4 Macros with Arguments

Macros with arguments add substantially to the power of the macro processor. For example, we said that **getc** and **putc** are equivalent to **getch(c, STDIN)** and **putch(c, STDOUT)** respectively. By defining **getc** and **putc** as macros that expand into references to **getch** and **putch**, we guarantee equivalence, and we eliminate a level of subroutine call, which may improve efficiency. The replacement is not possible without an argument capability.

As a larger instance, in Chapter 6 we wrote a subroutine **skipbl(s, i)**, the entire body of which was

```
while (s(i) == BLANK | s(i) == TAB)
        i = i + 1
```

This is such a short routine that it could readily be a macro instead of a subroutine, expanding into in-line code rather than calling another routine. (This might be worth doing if measurements establish that it consumes excessive space or time as a subroutine.) We could define a macro

```
skipbl(s, i)
```

which would expand into the lines above, with occurrences of the formal parameters **s** and **i** replaced by the actual arguments used when the macro is invoked. For the user, the only difference would be the omission of the **call** statement.

The syntax for specifying macros with arguments is an extension of what we used before:

```
define(name, replacement text)
```

defines **name**. This time, however, any occurrence in the replacement text of **$*n***, where *n* is between 1 and 9, will be replaced by the *n*th argument when the macro is actually called. Thus

```
define(skipbl, while ($1($2) == BLANK | $1($2) == TAB)  $2 = $2 + 1)
```

defines the **skipbl** macro.

Specifying arguments with **$*n*** is not as pleasant as being able to use dummy names for the parameters, as in

```
define(skipbl(s, i), while (s(i) == BLANK | s(i) == TAB) i = i + 1)
```

but it is easier to build. Our rule is always: Write something clean and acceptable that works, then polish it later if necessary.

The restriction to nine arguments is another example of the same philosophy. It is silly to get sidetracked worrying about macros with lots of arguments until the rest of the processor is working. You will find that in practice there is rarely any call for more anyway. Hard cases can wait until the easy ones are well under control.

As another example, many of our programs that deal with files contain lines like

```
fd = open(name, READ)
if (fd == ERR)
        call cant(name)
```

By defining a macro **copen** we can combine these operations into a single line like

```
copen(name, READ, fd)
```

and thus clarify a common construction. The definition is

```
define(copen, {$3 = open($1, $2)
               if ($3 == ERR)
                       call cant($1) } )
```

When

```
copen(name, READ, fd)
```

is encountered, **$1** is replaced by **name**, **$2** by **READ**, and **$3** by **fd**. The braces are included in the definition so we can say

```
if (getarg(1, name, size) ¬= EOF)
        copen(name, READ, fd)
```

and still keep together the statements that **copen** expands into.

It's harder to build a macro processor that allows arguments than to build one that doesn't. Furthermore, we intend to add a small set of "built-in" operations in addition to *define:* a conditional statement, a limited arithmetic capability, and a substring function; and we want these to go in without much change. The main thing is to ensure that any operation — macro call, definition, other built-in — can occur in the middle of any other one. If this is possible, then in principle the macro processor is capable of doing any computation, although it may well be hard to express.

As long as no macro calls are encountered (or built-ins, since they are treated identically), the input is copied directly to the output. When a macro is called, however, its name, its definition, and its arguments (if any) are all collected. Once the argument collection is finished, the macro is evaluated as follows. If it is a built-in like *define,* an appropriate routine is called which does whatever it has to with the arguments. If the macro is not a built-in, the definition text is pushed back onto the input. As it is being pushed back, any **$***n*'s in it are replaced by the corresponding argument that was just collected.

The fun starts when one of the arguments includes a call of another macro or built-in. Although there are various ways to deal with this situation, one of the easiest for a non-recursive language is to interpret the arguments as they are being collected, then push them back onto the input.

When a macro invocation is seen, the name and definition are placed in an evaluation area organized as a stack. Any arguments that follow are copied into this area as well, except that when an argument contains another macro invocation (a nested one) a new stack frame is created, and that inner macro is evaluated *completely* and its translation pushed back onto the input before the stack is popped and we resume working on the outer macro. The outer macro never sees the inner one, just its translation. (Of course the inner macro may in turn call upon other macros; the process is recursive.)

The principle to keep firmly in mind at all times is that arguments are evaluated completely as they are being collected. This is different behavior from the string replacement process we showed earlier in the chapter, but for common uses like replacing symbolic parameters in programs, the two methods produce the same result. (We will also provide for deferred evaluation so we can have the benefits of the earlier method when we need them.) Here are some examples, before we start on the actual code.

Suppose we have

```
define(EOS, 0)
```

When the **define** is seen, **DEFTYPE** and **define** are put in the evaluation stack at positions 1 and 2. (We'll explain the order later.) Now we collect the arguments. **EOS** at this point is nothing special, nor is **0**, so they are put on the stack at positions 3 and 4 respectively. At the end of the **define** we can evaluate, which in this case involves calling a routine to install the name and definition, which are the arguments at positions 3 and 4. Then the top four items on the stack are popped.

If we subsequently see **EOS** in the input, it will be put on the stack with its definition, and no arguments. The definition **0** is pushed back onto the input and the stack popped.

More complicated, here is an example with arguments.

```
define(bump, $1=$1+1)
```

defines **bump** to be a macro that generates code to increment its argument by 1. The input

```
bump(x)
```

causes **bump** and **$1=$1+1** to be copied onto the evaluation stack. **x** is collected as the argument; if it is not a defined name, we reach the end of the invocation of **bump** without incident. The definition is pushed back onto the input, with each occurrence of **$1** replaced by **x**, to yield **x=x+1**.

But imagine for a moment that **x** had earlier been defined to be something else, say **y**. Then **x** is a macro call, so when it is encountered, a new stack frame is formed, and **x** and its definition are copied into that frame. Then the definition **y** is pushed back onto the input, and the frame popped. When argument collection resumes for the previous level (**bump**), the input that used to be **x** has become **y**, and this becomes the actual argument to **bump**. As far as **bump** is concerned, it *was* called with **y** as its argument, and the result is **y=y+1**.

Exercise 8-11: Assuming that **getc** and **putc** have been defined in terms of **getch** and **putch**, walk through the expansion process by hand for the input

```
putc(getc(c))
```

including the processing of values for **STDIN** and **STDOUT**. □

8.5 Implementation

The processing can now be spelled out in more detail.

```
while (gettok(token, maxtok) ¬= EOF)
        if (type == ALPHA)
                if (lookup(token) == NO)
                        copy token to current evaluation stack frame
                          or directly to output
                else
                        make new stack frame
                        copy name and definition to current stack frame
        else if (stack empty)          # not saving arguments
                copy directly to output
        else if (at end of an argument list)
                if (built-in)
                        do appropriate function
                else
                        push definition back onto input,
                          replacing $n's by arguments
                pop stack frame
        else                           # saving arguments
                copy token to current stack frame
```

Of course this skips over a few details like precisely how we know when we're at the end of an argument list, and what the stack looks like. We will get to them in due course.

First the evaluation stack. This is just a long array **evalst**. The first free position in **evalst** is kept in **ep**, which is initially 1. Whenever we are processing a macro, **evalst** contains the strings for the name, definition and arguments. The array **argstk** contains the locations in **evalst** where these strings begin: **argstk(i)** is the beginning of the ith string in **evalst**. **ap** is the first free location in **argstk**; it is also initially 1.

Since macros may be nested, the strings in **evalst** that **argstk** points to are in general associated with different levels of macros. The array **callst** keeps track of each stack frame: **callst(i)** points to the position in **argstk** that in turn points to the defining text of the ith macro. **cp** is the *current* call stack pointer. If **cp** is zero, we are not in any macro. Inside a single level of macro invocation, **cp** is one, and so on. Thus to find the first argument of the third level of macro invocation, we first set **i=callst(3)**. Then **argstk(i)** is the defining text of this macro, **argstk(i+1)** is the name, and **argstk(i+2)** is the first argument.

Argument collection requires keeping track of balanced parentheses independently for each level of macro, so we add another array **plev**, parallel to **callst**, to count parentheses for the corresponding stack frame.

Several routines need to know **cp** and the output buffer, so they are kept in the **common** block **cmacro**:

```
common /cmacro/ cp, ep, evalst(EVALSIZE)
  integer cp              # current call stack pointer
  integer ep              # next free position in evalst
  character evalst        # evaluation stack
```

The other variables, **callst**, **argstk**, **ap**, and **plev**, are used only in the main routine, so we have kept them out of **common**.

There is one last complication. Any macros encountered during argument collection are expanded immediately. But there are times when we must defer the evaluation until later. For example, consider this attempt to make a new macro **d** synonymous with **define**:

```
define(d,define($1,$2))
```

On cursory inspection it should work, because the replacement text of **d** appears to be **define($1,$2)**. But macros and built-ins are evaluated *as soon as they are encountered.* The inner **define** is evaluated before the outer one. Because a **define** has no replacement text, the net effect is to define **d** to be empty, which is hardly what was wanted. To get around the problem of premature evaluation, there must be a quoting convention, so input can be treated as literal text when necessary. In our convention, any input surrounded by [and] is left absolutely alone, except that one level of [and] is stripped off. With this facility we can write the macro **d** as

```
define(d,[define($1,$2)])
```

The replacement text for **d**, protected by the brackets, is literally **define($1,$2)**. Now when we say

```
d(a,bc)
```

everything works and **a** is defined to be **bc**.

Brackets must also be used when it is desired to redefine an identifier:

```
define(x,y)
define(x,z)
```

would define **y** in the second line, instead of redefining **x**. (The first definition is still active, however, so **x** ultimately becomes **y**.) If you do not want to redefine **y**, the operation must be expressed as

```
define(x,y)
define([x],z)
```

which will have the desired effect.

All of these examples look cramped because there are no spaces after commas. Blanks are significant in this macro processor, and we have tried not to put in any spurious ones.

Putting all of these considerations together creates a rather long main program, but it is not really complicated. It follows the outline we gave earlier, except for the addition of brackets. For all its apparent complexity, it is simply a seven-way **case** statement, with the code for each case in-line instead of in a separate routine. We have called it **macro** rather than **define**, because that better reflects what it does.

```
# macro — expand macros with arguments
      character gettok
      character defn(MAXDEF), t, token(MAXTOK)
      integer lookup, push
      integer ap, argstk(ARGSIZE), callst(CALLSIZE), nlb, plev(CALLSIZE)
      include cmacro
      string balp "()"
      string defnam "define"
      integer deftyp(2)
      data deftyp(1) /DEFTYPE/, deftyp(2) /EOS/

      call instal(defnam, deftyp)
      cp = 0
      ap = 1
      ep = 1
      for (t = gettok(token, MAXTOK); t ¬= EOF; t = gettok(token, MAXTOK)) {
            if (t == ALPHA) {
                  if (lookup(token, defn) == NO)
                        call puttok(token)
                  else {                          # defined; put it in eval stack
                        cp = cp + 1
                        if (cp > CALLSIZE)
                              call error("call stack overflow.")
                        callst(cp) = ap
                        ap = push(ep, argstk, ap)
                        call puttok(defn)     # stack definition
                        call putchr(EOS)
                        ap = push(ep, argstk, ap)
                        call puttok(token)    # stack name
                        call putchr(EOS)
                        ap = push(ep, argstk, ap)
                        t = gettok(token, MAXTOK)        # peek at next
                        call pbstr(token)
                        if (t ¬= LPAREN)    # add ( ) if not present
                              call pbstr(balp)
                        plev(cp) = 0
                        }
                  }
            else if (t == LBRACK) {               # strip one level of [ ]
                  nlb = 1
                  repeat {
                        t = gettok(token, MAXTOK)
                        if (t == LBRACK)
                              nlb = nlb + 1
                        else if (t == RBRACK) {
                              nlb = nlb - 1
                              if (nlb == 0)
                                    break
                              }
```

```
                        else if (t == EOF)
                            call error("EOF in string.")
                        call puttok(token)
                        }
                    }
            else if (cp == 0)                   # not in a macro at all
                    call puttok(token)
            else if (t == LPAREN) {
                    if (plev(cp) > 0)
                        call puttok(token)
                    plev(cp) = plev(cp) + 1
                    }
            else if (t == RPAREN) {
                    plev(cp) = plev(cp) - 1
                    if (plev(cp) > 0)
                        call puttok(token)
                    else {                      # end of argument list
                        call putchr(EOS)
                        call eval(argstk, callst(cp), ap-1)
                        ap = callst(cp)         # pop eval stack
                        ep = argstk(ap)
                        cp = cp - 1
                        }
                    }
            else if (t == COMMA & plev(cp) == 1) {        # new arg
                    call putchr(EOS)
                    ap = push(ep, argstk, ap)
                    }
            else
                    call puttok(token)          # just stack it
            }
        if (cp ¬= 0)
            call error("unexpected EOF.")
        stop
        end
```

We want to retain the property of **define** that a macro call without arguments (like **EOF** or **EOS**) does not require parentheses. Thus if a token is a defined name, and it is not followed by a left parenthesis, we push back an empty set of balanced parentheses, so that macro calls without arguments are not a special case for the rest of the program. This is another example of altering some data representation in a minor way to avoid much greater complexity in the code.

You may have noticed that brackets are removed even outside macro definitions. Although this may look like unnecessary meddling on the part of the macro processor, there are good reasons for doing it that way. As the simplest example, if you really want a literal occurrence of the word **define** in your text, you have to protect it with a layer of brackets or it will be interpreted as a call to the built-in **define**. We will see some more substantial instances of this shortly.

puttok and **putchr** put strings and characters respectively either into **evalst** (if we are in the middle of a macro), or directly onto the output with **putc** (if we are not). The test for what destination to use occurs in a single place in **putchr**, not scattered throughout the code.

```
# puttok — put a token either on output or into evaluation stack
      subroutine puttok(str)
      character str(MAXTOK)
      integer i

      for (i = 1; str(i) ¬= EOS; i = i + 1)
            call putchr(str(i))
      return
      end

# putchr — put single char on output or into evaluation stack
      subroutine putchr(c)
      character c
      include cmacro

      if (cp == 0)
            call putc(c)
      else {
            if (ep > EVALSIZE)
                  call error("evaluation stack overflow.")
            evalst(ep) = c
            ep = ep + 1
            }
      return
      end
```

When a new argument is to be put into **evalst** we have to record the current value of the pointer **ep** and increment **ap**; this is done by **push**:

```
# push — push ep onto argstk, return new pointer ap
      integer function push(ep, argstk, ap)
      integer ap, argstk(ARGSIZE), ep

      if (ap > ARGSIZE)
            call error("arg stack overflow.")
      argstk(ap) = ep
      push = ap + 1
      return
      end
```

Once a macro has been identified and all its arguments collected in **evalst** (signalled by the parenthesis level becoming zero), **eval** is called to process a built-in or to push back a definition with the appropriate arguments.

macro pushes the definition onto **evalst** before the name, so when **eval** is called, **args(i)** points to the defining text for the macro and **args(i+1)** points to the name. **args(i+2)** through **args(j)** are the arguments, of which there are **j−i−1**. This organization means that **$0** is the name of the macro itself. Although this will probably be little used, the regularity is nice to have.

```
# eval — expand args i through j: evaluate builtin or push back defn
	subroutine eval(argstk, i, j)
	integer index, length
	integer argno, argstk(ARGSIZE), i, j, k, m, n, t, td
	include cmacro
	string digits "0123456789"

	t = argstk(i)
	td = evalst(t)
	if (td == DEFTYPE)
		call dodef(argstk, i, j)
	else {
		for (k = t+length(evalst(t))-1; k > t; k = k - 1)
			if (evalst(k-1) ¬= ARGFLAG)
				call putbak(evalst(k))
			else {
				argno = index(digits, evalst(k)) - 1
				if (argno >= 0 & argno < j-i) {
					n = i + argno + 1
					m = argstk(n)
					call pbstr(evalst(m))
					}
				k = k - 1	# skip over $
				}
		if (k == t)			# do last character
			call putbak(evalst(k))
		}
	return
	end
```

Most of the subscripted references to **evalst** are actually subarray references, which we discussed in Chapter 4. PL/I users should review that discussion, since several routines in this chapter must use this Fortran facility.

If the type is **define**, **dodef** is called; otherwise the definition is pushed back onto the input, with each **$***n* replaced by the corresponding argument. The symbolic constant **ARGFLAG** is a **$**, defined of course with

```
define(ARGFLAG, DOLLAR)
```

in the Ratfor source code for **macro**.

We haven't said what the macro processor should do when a macro definition asks for an argument that wasn't supplied. The most harmless thing to do is to ignore it — in effect to replace the **$***n* by an empty string — and this is what **eval** does. This is true even if no arguments are present; that way if **x** is defined by

```
define(x, a$1b)
```

the inputs

```
x(+)
x(-,+)
x()
x
```

all produce something sensible: **a+b**, **a−b**, **ab** and **ab** respectively.

dodef is easy: most of the work has already been done for it.

```
# dodef - install definition in table
      subroutine dodef(argstk, i, j)
      integer a2, a3, argstk(ARGSIZE), i, j
      include cmacro

      if (j - i > 2) {
            a2 = argstk(i+2)
            a3 = argstk(i+3)
            call instal(evalst(a2), evalst(a3))   # subarrays
            }
      return
      end
```

One of the first things to try with the macro processor is extending the syntax of our programming language. We have been doing this all along in the limited sense of writing **character** when we actually mean **integer**. For a more sophisticated example, consider

```
define(proc, [integer function $1 $2 define(procname, $1)])
```

The line

```
proc(equal, (str1, str2))
```

produces the output

```
integer function equal(str1, str2)
```

(We enclosed the definition in brackets to prevent the too-early evaluation of the **define**. Bracketing the defining text is almost always a good idea.) As a side effect of invoking **proc**, the function name **equal** is "remembered" by defining **procname** to be **equal**, and this value can be used by other macros. For example, if we define **return** as

```
define(return, [ { procname = $1; [return] } ])
```

then we can write lines like

```
return(YES)
```

to simulate in Fortran a **return** statement that returns a value, as in PL/I. (The extra brackets around the inner **return** prevent it from being evaluated as another call of the **return** macro, which would create a rather long loop. You should walk through this example carefully to be sure you understand the significance of each set of brackets.) Being able to return a value with a **return** statement often clarifies a program, as you can see by comparing this version of **equal** to the one in Chapter 3.

```
# equal — compare str1 to str2; return YES if equal, NO if not
	proc(equal, (str1, str2))
	character str1(ARB), str2(ARB)
	integer i

	for (i = 1; str1(i) == str2(i); i = i + 1)
		if (str1(i) == EOS)
			return(YES)
	return(NO)
	end
```

Exercise 8-12: Re-write the function **filarg** of Chapter 3 with the **return** macro. □

Exercise 8-13: If you use the **skipbl** macro described above, then change your mind and decide to **call** a subroutine instead, do you have to rewrite all the invocations to include a **call**? □

Exercise 8-14: Write the macros that translate **getc** and **putc** into references to **getch** and **putch**, as shown earlier in this chapter. What problems arise with **getc**? □

Exercise 8-15: The definition

```
define(sq, $1 * $1)
```

defines a macro to square an expression. Or does it? What is **sq(x+1)**? What can you do about it? How much should a macro processor know about the language(s) it is used with? □

Exercise 8-16: Invent a syntax that allows macros to have more than nine arguments. Make it compatible with the **$*n*** syntax if $n<10$. How difficult is it to implement? □

Exercise 8-17: Improve **define** to allow the parameters in a macro definition to be specified by dummy names instead of by **$*n***. That is, if **m** is defined by

```
define(m(x,y), replacement text containing tokens x and y)
```

then the invocation **m(a, b)** should replace all occurrences of **x** and **y** in the replacement text by **a** and **b** respectively. How much existing machinery can you use? □

8.6 Conditionals and Other Built-ins

macro has been designed to make it easy to add new built-in functions as the need arises. The next step in the evolution is the addition of a conditional test, with a built-in function **ifelse**. The input

ifelse(*a*,*b*,*c*,*d*)

compares *a* and *b* as character strings. If they are the same, *c* is pushed back onto the input; if they differ, *d* is pushed back. As a rudimentary example,

```
define(compare, [ifelse($1,$2,yes,no)])
```

defines **compare** as a two-argument macro returning **yes** if its arguments are the same, and **no** if they're not. As usual, the brackets prevent the **ifelse** from being evaluated too soon.

More useful, we can now improve our **return** macro, by detecting whether it has arguments or not:

```
define(return, [ifelse($1,, [[return]], { procname=$1; [[return]] })])
```

If **return** is called with an argument as in

```
return(a+b)
```

$1 is not empty, and the result is

```
{ procname=a+b; return }
```

If there was no argument, **$1** is empty, which matches the second argument of the **ifelse**, and a bare **return** is produced. This time we need two levels of brackets around the literal **return** statement, to protect it twice. The first level of protection prevents it from being evaluated during the expansion of the **ifelse**. The second level is necessary, as we mentioned earlier, so that it can appear as a literal **return** in the final output.

While we are adding built-in functions, we will do two more.

incr(*x*)

converts the string *x* to a number, adds one to it, and returns that as its replacement text (as a character string). *x* had better be numeric, or the results may be undesirable.

incr can be used for tasks like

```
define(MAXCARD, 80)
define(MAXLINE, [incr(MAXCARD)])
```

which makes two parameters with values 80 and 81. This is useful when you have to make one number a little bit larger than another, as in **getc** and **putc** in Chapter 1. Rather than write two definitions and remember to update both if one must change, it is better to define one in terms of the other. **incr** also provides a primitive arithmetic capability for writing more elaborate macros.

The final built-in is a function to take substrings of strings.

substr(*s*, *m*, *n*)

produces the substring of *s* which starts at position *m* (with origin one), of length *n*. If *n* is omitted or too big, the rest of the string is used, while if *m* is out of range the result is a null string.

substr(abc, 2, 1)

is **b**,

substr(abc, 2)

is **bc**, and

substr(abc, 4)

is empty.

The changes needed to add **ifelse**, **incr** and **substr** are minor. We modify **macro** to install the new keywords and their values (**IFTYPE**, **INCTYPE** and **SUBTYPE** respectively); each must have a distinguishable value), and change **eval** to look for them as well as for **DEFTYPE**. In **eval** we only have to add the extra tests and subroutine calls.

```
...
t = argstk(i)
td = evalst(t)
if (td == DEFTYPE)
        call dodef(argstk, i, j)
else if (td == INCTYPE)
        call doincr(argstk, i, j)
else if (td == SUBTYPE)
        call dosub(argstk, i, j)
else if (td == IFTYPE)
        call doif(argstk, i, j)
else {
        process normal macro as before
        }
...
```

doif compares the first two arguments, and pushes back the appropriate one onto the input.

```
# doif — select one of two arguments
	subroutine doif(argstk, i, j)
	integer equal
	integer a2, a3, a4, a5, argstk(ARGSIZE), i, j
	include cmacro

	if (j - i < 5)
		return
	a2 = argstk(i+2)
	a3 = argstk(i+3)
	a4 = argstk(i+4)
	a5 = argstk(i+5)
	if (equal(evalst(a2), evalst(a3)) == YES)	# subarrays
		call pbstr(evalst(a4))
	else
		call pbstr(evalst(a5))
	return
	end
```

doinc converts the number, does the arithmetic, and pushes the result back as a character string with **pbnum**. Since characters are produced from right to left, no reversal is needed.

```
# doincr — increment argument by 1
	subroutine doincr(argstk, i, j)
	integer ctoi
	integer argstk(ARGSIZE), i, j, k
	include cmacro

	k = argstk(i+2)
	call pbnum(ctoi(evalst, k)+1)
	return
	end

# pbnum — convert number to string, push back on input
	subroutine pbnum(n)
	integer mod
	integer m, n, num
	string digits "0123456789"

	num = n
	repeat {
		m = mod(num, 10)
		call putbak(digits(m+1))
		num = num / 10
		} until (num == 0)
	return
	end
```

Finally, **dosub** does the **substr** function; it is entirely concerned with getting indices right, particularly in boundary cases where the substring requested is in some way outside the string.

```
# dosub — select substring
      subroutine dosub(argstk, i, j)
      integer ctoi, length, max, min
      integer ap, argstk(ARGSIZE), fc, i, j, k, nc
      include cmacro

      if (j - i < 3)
            return
      if (j - i < 4)
            nc = MAXTOK
      else {
            k = argstk(i+4)
            nc = ctoi(evalst, k)          # number of characters
            }
      k = argstk(i+3)                     # origin
      ap = argstk(i+2)                    # target string
      fc = ap + ctoi(evalst, k) - 1       # first char of substring
      if (fc >= ap & fc < ap + length(evalst(ap))) { # subarrays
            k = fc + min(nc, length(evalst(fc))) - 1
            for ( ; k >= fc; k = k - 1)
                  call putbak(evalst(k))
            }
      return
      end
```

Exercise 8-18: Modify **doincr** to do arbitrary precision arithmetic. □

Exercise 8-19: Add a built-in function for doing arithmetic:

```
arith(operand1, op, operand2)
```

does the operation specified by **op** on the two (numeric) operands. Provide + and − operators at the very least. Multiplication, division, relational testing, and so on are also useful and easy. What do you have to change to handle negative numbers correctly? Modify **arith** for arbitrary precision arithmetic. □

Exercise 8-20: Define an **assert** macro that will cause conditional compilation of assertions in a program: if assertions are turned on,

```
assert(i < j)
```

should expand into something like

```
if ( ¬ (i < j))
      call error("false assertion in ...: i < j.")
```

where "..." is the name of the procedure, saved by the **proc** macro. You will probably also want to define macros that turn assertion checking off and on at desired places. □

8.7 Applications

Let us write macros to handle a variant of the string declaration that we have been using in our programs. Suppose that

```
string(name,"text")
```

is a shorthand for

```
integer name(5)
data name(1) /LETt/
data name(2) /LETe/
data name(3) /LETx/
data name(4) /LETt/
data name(5) /EOS/
```

The task is to convert the **string** declaration into this expanded form.

We need the length of the **text** part, so we begin with a macro **len** which finds the length of a character string. That is, the value of the macro call **len(abc)** is **3**, the length of the argument.

In general, what is the length of a string **s**? If **s** is empty, its length is zero. Otherwise it is one more than the length of the substring of **s** obtained by chopping off one character. This is a recursive definition, which is a natural form of expression if you happen to have a recursive language at hand — and we do. Let's say it with macros:

```
define(len,[ifelse($1,,0,[incr(len(substr($1,2)))])])
```

This is certainly a mouthful, but not hard to understand in the light of the recursive definition above. It is permissible, and indeed usually necessary, to define macros in terms of themselves. It works because conditional testing can be used to prevent an infinite loop. In this case the test is whether all the characters of the string have been chopped away.

The outer layer of brackets prevents all evaluation as the definition is being copied into the table. The inner layer prevents the **incr** construction from being done as the arguments of the **ifelse** are collected.

Now we can do **string** itself. This comes in three parts. First we compute the correct length and generate

integer *name*(*length*)

Then we loop over the characters between quotes, producing lines of the form

data *name*(*i*) **/LET***c***/**

where *c* is the *i*th character of the string. Finally we end with

data *name*(*length*) **/EOS/**

string itself is

```
define(string,[integer $1(len(substr($2,2)))
str($1,substr($2,2),0)
data $1(len(substr($2,2)))/EOS/
])
```

The calls **len(substr($2,2))** compute the effective string length (excluding the quotes but including the **EOS**). **str** creates the intervening **data** statements:

```
define(str,[ifelse($2,",,data $1(incr($3))/[LET]substr($2,1,1)/
[str($1,substr($2,2),incr($3))])])
```

It isolates one character, increments the index, generates the line, and calls itself recursively until it sees the terminating quote. (Why is **LET** enclosed in brackets?)

As you can see this is not the most transparent programming language in the world. It takes some getting used to before you can think of looping in terms of recursion, although with practice you get the hang of it. But beware of becoming too clever with macros. In principle, **macro** is capable of performing any computing task, but it is all too easy to write unreadable macros that cause more trouble than they save work.

It is also the case that complicated recursive macro operations like **string** can be painfully slow. For example, here are some statistics for processing two short **string**'s, of three and nine characters in length:

	#calls	CPU time
gettok	2793	21.7%
macro	1	11.6
puttok	1999	11.6
(all I/O)	...	9.1
putchr	7700	7.5
ngetc	5977	6.4
type	5977	6.1
eval	211	5.4
lookup	648	5.0
putbak	5677	4.8
pbstr	431	3.4

This is a lot of subroutine calls for such a small input; if you did nothing but process **string** macros, it would be intolerable. Fortunately the real use of **macro** as a front end for a language processor tends to involve primarily substituting one string for another, as in **define**. This is much less demanding, so processing an occasional **string** macro is quite practical. The added complexity of **macro** costs very little extra for this kind of application; **macro** takes less than 5 percent longer than **define** on the same input.

The measurements above do indicate where attention can be most profitably directed if it is necessary to speed **macro** up. One possibility is to observe that some of the calls to **gettok** could be replaced by calls to **ngetc**, since only a single character is involved (for example, while processing bracketed text). More generally, there are a number of rather small routines which we wrote to modularize the program properly. Part of the cost of **macro** is the overhead of the subroutine calling mechanism, which can be very inefficient on some machines. We can avoid much of this by replacing subroutine calls by in-line code in these places (although we would do it by defining macros to replace the subroutine bodies, not by writing out the code!). Specifically, since virtually all of the calls to **putchr** originate in **puttok**, **putchr** can be moved into **puttok** with only minor rearrangements. If characters are small positive integers, **type** can be replaced by an in-line reference to an array which contains the type of the corresponding character; this will essentially eliminate the cost of finding character types. And if the **common** block **cdefio** is made more generally known, **ngetc** and **putbak** can also be made in-line operations.

Although care is necessary to keep the program relatively clean, the payoff can be substantial. The original version of **macro**, written in the language C, was speeded up by a factor of about four by such transformations. Similar results could be expected in Fortran on many machines. The procedure should be as we have described several times here, however: write a clean program that implements an appropriate algorithm; measure it to identify the hot spots; refine those as cleanly as possible. Starting from the other end is a sure way to an unworkable mess.

One thing that can be done to make macros faster and more comprehensible is to increase the set of built-ins, so computations like **len** don't have to be spelled out in excruciating detail. Here are some suggestions.

Exercise 8-21: Add **len** as a built-in. □

Exercise 8-22: Add a built-in **index** analogous to the **index** function defined in Chapter 2: **index(s, c)** is the position of **c** in the string **s**, or zero if **c** is not in **s**. Can you do **index** with the existing facilities? Should you? □

Exercise 8-23: The implementation of **string** above is suitable only for strings of letters and digits. Generalize it to cope with strings that contain non-alphanumeric characters. □

Exercise 8-24: Write a macro **err** that converts calls of the form

```
err("message")
```

into the pure Fortran

```
call error(7, 7hmessage)
```

Add the capability to prefix the name of the calling routine to the message. □

Exercise 8-25: Add a macro **count** which counts occurrences of the subroutine by writing the name onto some predefined output file every time the routine is entered. What other tools that we have built would you use to summarize the results for a run? □

Exercise 8-26: What changes would you make to **macro** to adapt it to providing a macro capability for the **format** program of Chapter 7? □

Bibliographic Notes

There is a lot more to macro processing than we have room for here. *An Introduction to Macros* by M. Campbell-Kelly (American-Elsevier, 1973) provides a brief discussion of several different forms of macro processors. *Macro Processors and Techniques for Portable Software* by P. J. Brown (Wiley, 1974) goes into more detail on the subtle aspects of macro processing.

The PL/I macro preprocessor is an attempt to make a macro language that is essentially the same as a compiler language. This is discussed in various PL/I texts and in reference manuals for particular implementations. For example, see *IBM System/360 PL/I Language Specification,* Form Y33-6003, or *Student Text: An Introduction to the Compile-Time Facilities of PL/I,* Form C20-1689.

Macros have been valuable in making "portable" software — programs that move from one machine to another with much less effort than complete re-writing. The program is written in terms of a modest number of macros; nothing but the macros must be written for a particular environment. Snobol is probably the best known example of a major language so implemented. See R. E. Griswold, J. F. Poage and I. P. Polonsky, *The Snobol4 Programming Language,* Prentice-Hall, 1969, or R. E. Griswold, *The Macro Implementation of Snobol4,* Freeman, 1972. The book by Brown discusses other work in this area.

Any number of books on data structures deal with the problems of maintaining tables of information. As usual, one standard reference is D. E. Knuth's *The Art of Computer Programming* (Addison-Wesley). Volume 1 (1968) is concerned with data structures; Volume 3 (1973) discusses searching techniques in great detail.

The **macro** processor described in this chapter was originally designed and implemented in the language C by D. M. Ritchie; we are grateful to him for letting us steal it.

CHAPTER 9

A RATFOR-FORTRAN TRANSLATOR

All of the programs in this book are presented in Ratfor. We are now going to show you how to write a program to translate Ratfor into Fortran. One reason for doing this is to describe in detail a tool which we use extensively, and which we think is of real value to anyone who uses Fortran. As we said in the Introduction, Fortran is certainly not a dead language; its use is widespread and it has many assets to balance its manifold deficiencies. If you use Fortran, you might as well use it as effectively as possible.

The other purpose of this chapter is to demonstrate a preprocessor of significant size. The advantage of a preprocessor is that you don't have to write a compiler to get a better language; instead you build on the work of others. Although you may not need Ratfor *per se,* it is important to appreciate that it is often possible to provide a comfortable interface to some piece of software, or to add missing features, by building a relatively modest intermediate program. The design and construction of Ratfor should suggest useful ideas for analogous tools.

The primary purpose of Ratfor is to make Fortran a better programming language, for both writing and explaining, by permitting and encouraging readable and well-structured programs. This is done by providing the control structures that are unavailable in bare Fortran, and by improving the "cosmetics" of the language.

The control flow structures we will discuss are **if-else**, **while**, **do**, **break**, **next**, and statement grouping with braces. **for** and **repeat-until** are left as straightforward exercises. These structures are entirely adequate and comfortable for programming without **goto**'s. Although we hold no religious convictions about the matter, you may have noticed that there are no **goto**'s in any of our Ratfor programs. We have not felt constrained by this discipline — with a decent language and some care in coding, **goto**'s are rarely needed.

The cosmetic aspects of Ratfor have been designed to make it concise and reasonably pleasing to the eye. It is free-form: statements may appear anywhere on an input line. The end of a line generally marks the end of a statement, but lines that are obviously not yet finished, like extended conditions within **if** and **while** statements and lines ending with a comma, automatically continue onto the next line. Multiple statements may appear on one line if separated by semicolons, although we don't encourage the practice. The comment convention — a sharp # anywhere in a line signaling the beginning of a comment — helps to encourage unobtrusive marginal remarks. Quoted strings are converted into *n***h**'s for old-fashioned Fortran compilers, so that programmers don't have to count characters. Notations like > convey the meaning of code more rapidly than equivalent forms like **.gt.**.

Certainly Fortran is deficient in many ways besides control statements and appearance. As you can see from some of our code, the data structures available (or not available) can seriously complicate programming. Our preprocessor does not try to do anything about these weaknesses, although a more complicated version could. Ratfor is not intended to provide a complete new programming language, but just to help overcome the worst inadequacies of Fortran and convert it into a reasonable language for explication and coding.

There are a number of other widely available Fortran preprocessors. While they differ in superficial ways, most provide facilities analogous to those of Ratfor. If you have access to one, by all means use it — the payoff from any preprocessing is enormous.

9.1 Organization

One convenient way to describe a programming language is the Backus-Naur Form (BNF), which is a formal specification of the grammar of a language, that is, the set of rules by which a legal program in the language is written or recognized. There are several advantages to describing a language with a grammar rather than with an informal description in words. The language specification can be made fairly precise this way, avoiding the vagueness and ambiguities which an English description would probably suffer from. Furthermore, given a grammar, a program called a compiler-compiler can use it to create a program that will analyze or *parse* programs written in that language. For large complicated languages, such automation is invaluable in generating reliable and easy-to-change parsers. Since the parser is at the heart of a compiler, this in turn leads to a higher-quality translator.

Fortunately the Ratfor grammar is sufficiently small and straightforward that a compiler-compiler is not actually needed, although Ratfor was originally implemented with one. In any case, we will use the following grammar to specify the Ratfor language.

```
program   : statement
          | program statement
statement : if ( condition ) statement
          | if ( condition ) statement else statement
          | while ( condition ) statement
          | for ( initialize ; condition ; reinitialize ) statement
          | repeat statement
          | repeat statement until ( condition )
          | do limits statement
          | digits statement
          | break
          | next
          | { program }
          | other
```

The first two lines say that a *program* is a *statement*, or a *program* followed by a *statement*. In other words, a program consists of one or more statements. A *statement* in turn is one of a handful of constructs; the vertical bar | indicates a choice of alternatives. Most statements are straightforward enough, standing for an occurrence of the particular keyword. For instance, a statement can consist of the keyword **if** followed by a parenthesized *condition* and a *statement*. (The definition is recursive, as is the definition of *program*.) A group of statements in braces can be used anywhere a single statement can be, because of the rule

statement : { *program* }

We prefer braces because they are less obtrusive than the more common **begin-end** or **do-end**. Indentation conveys structure more clearly than large keywords. If you have a very restricted character set, however, you might prefer another choice; some possibilities are suggested in the exercises.

digits stands for a string of digits, that is, a standard Fortran statement number or label. Although these are relatively rare in Ratfor programs, the grammar must allow for them.

next is a statement that none of our programs has used, although it is helpful in other applications. Analogous to **break**, instead of exiting from a loop, **next** causes the next iteration of the loop to begin. In a **while**, **repeat** or **do**, it goes immediately to the *condition* part; in a **for**, it goes to the *reinitialize* step.

The last grammatical type is an **other**, which is anything that wasn't recognized as any of the preceding types. This category actually encompasses most of Fortran. For example, the statement

```
i = 1
```

is not an **if** or an **else** or anything else recognizable by Ratfor, and is thus an **other**.

Type **other** is an important simplification, for it frees Ratfor from having to know very much about Fortran. If a statement is encountered which does not begin with one of the keywords (or digits or a left brace), it *must* be an **other**, and no real processing is needed on it. The price of this simplification is that the error-detecting abilities of Ratfor are not as good as they might be with a more comprehensive grammar. This is not a serious drawback, however, since we are translating into Fortran, and Fortran compilers are perfectly capable of detecting any syntax errors that escape the preprocessor.

In principle, associated with each rule of the grammar is a *semantic action* which states what is to be done when that particular construction is recognized in the program being translated. In Ratfor, the semantic actions are usually very simple, involving reformatting the incoming text and occasionally interspersing **if**'s, **goto**'s and **continue**'s to translate the control flow statements.

The preprocessor is organized as follows. The top level is a controlling routine called the *parser*, so called because it controls by analyzing (parsing) the grammatical structure of the input it sees. For instance, when an **if** is seen the parser calls a routine that handles **if** statements. That routine in turn isolates the *condition* part and generates the test, a semantic action. The parser must also remember that an **if** has been seen so that when the end of the *statement* part is reached, the correct terminating code for an **if** can be produced. This may include dealing with an **else** if it is present. Furthermore, all of this is inherently recursive, as the BNF indicates, because constructions can be nested, as in

```
for (i = 1; i <= n; i = i + 1)
        for (j = 1; j <= n; j = j + 1)
                if (m(i, j) < 0)
                        m(i, j) = -1
```

At the beginning of each statement, the parser calls a "lexical analysis" routine to classify it into one of the types specified in the grammar. The lexical routine calls a lower routine to get the first token of the statement, which will determine the statement type. When the statement has been classified, the parser calls the appropriate code generation routine. Some code generation routines also use the token routine to read further parts of the statement being processed.

We will begin by describing the lexical and token code, since these are essentially independent of everything else. Then we can present parsing and code generation more easily.

9.2 Lexical Analysis

Tokens in Ratfor are analogous to those in **define** and **macro** in Chapter 8, with the addition of quoted strings. **gettok** breaks the input into alphanumeric strings, quoted strings, and single non-alphanumerics. It also strips out the blanks, tabs and comments that separate tokens. (Blanks can be discarded because they are not significant in Fortran programs. This is one of several places where the wide latitude permitted in a Fortran program works to our advantage, and makes Ratfor's task easier.) **gettok** returns **ALPHA** if it has found an alphanumeric string; otherwise it returns a single non-alphanumeric character.

```
# gettok - get token for Ratfor
      character function gettok(lexstr, toksiz)
      character ngetc, type
      integer i, toksiz
      character c, lexstr(toksiz)
      include cline

      while (ngetc(c) ¬= EOF)
            if (c ¬= BLANK & c ¬= TAB)
                  break
      call putbak(c)
      for (i = 1; i < toksiz-1; i = i + 1) {
            gettok = type(ngetc(lexstr(i)))
            if (gettok ¬= LETTER & gettok ¬= DIGIT)
                  break
            }
      if (i >= toksiz-1)
            call synerr("token too long.")
      if (i > 1) {                       # some alpha seen
            call putbak(lexstr(i))       # went one too far
            lexstr(i) = EOS
            gettok = ALPHA
            }
      else if (lexstr(1) == SQUOTE | lexstr(1) == DQUOTE) {
            for (i = 2; ngetc(lexstr(i)) ¬= lexstr(1); i = i + 1)
                  if (lexstr(i) == NEWLINE | i >= toksiz-1) {
                        call synerr("missing quote.")
                        lexstr(i) = lexstr(1)
                        call putbak(NEWLINE)
                        break
                        }
            }
      else if (lexstr(1) == SHARP) {    # strip comments
            while (ngetc(lexstr(1)) ¬= NEWLINE)
                  ;
            gettok = NEWLINE
            }
      lexstr(i+1) = EOS
      if (lexstr(1) == NEWLINE)
            linect = linect + 1
      return
      end
```

gettok uses the same I/O pushback routines that we wrote for **define** and **macro** in Chapter 8: **putbak** puts one character back on the input; **ngetc** reads one character from the input, including the pushed back characters. **type** is from Chapter 4; it returns **LETTER** or **DIGIT** if its argument is a letter or digit, or the character itself for a non-alphanumeric argument.

As a safety measure, quoted strings may not extend across a line boundary. An end of line encountered inside a quoted string almost always indicates a missing quote, and if it's not detected, a single unbalanced quote can turn an entire program inside out. If **NEWLINE**'s were permitted inside quotes, **gettok** could be less complicated, but a valuable error check would disappear and other parts of the program would have to be much more careful about checking *their* data. It is best to head off potential trouble as early as possible.

Since **gettok** uses blanks to separate tokens, blanks are significant in Ratfor when they are not in Fortran. Keywords like **if** must not contain blanks, or they won't be recognized. Although Fortran ignores blanks essentially everywhere, this freedom is more often abused than used. We can certainly live without the added complexity of allowing imbedded blanks in Ratfor keywords.

synerr is called from several places to print syntax error messages, like the two in **gettok**. **gettok** and **synerr** share one data item in common, the source line count **linect**, so offending lines can be tagged with their position in the input. **linect** is passed via the **common** block **cline**. Even though **gettok** and **synerr** are the only two routines that use this data area, it must be a **common** block, or nearly every routine would have to carry the line number around so it would be available when needed. This is a case where a hidden data connection is actually used to advantage in reducing the overall coupling in a program.

```
common /cline/ linect
  integer linect      # line count on input file; init = 1
```

The code for **synerr** is

```
# synerr - report Ratfor syntax error
      subroutine synerr(msg)
      character lc(MAXLINE), msg(MAXLINE)
      integer itoc
      integer junk
      include cline

      call remark("error at line .")
      junk = itoc(linect, lc, MAXLINE)
      call putlin(lc, ERROUT)
      call putch(COLON, ERROUT)
      call remark(msg)
      return
      end
```

itoc, from Chapter 2, converts the line number to a character string suitable for printing.

Although lexical analysis for Fortran is difficult, it is easy in Ratfor. The only types to be identified are literal characters like semicolons and braces, keywords like **if** and **else**, labels (all digits), or unrecognized tokens. This identification is done by **lex**:

```
# lex — return lexical type of token
      integer function lex(lexstr)
      character gettok
      character lexstr(MAXTOK)
      integer alldig, lookup
      integer ltype(2)

      while (gettok(lexstr, MAXTOK) == NEWLINE)
            ;
      lex = lexstr(1)
      if (lex==EOF | lex==SEMICOL | lex==LBRACE | lex==RBRACE)
            return
      if (alldig(lexstr) == YES)
            lex = LEXDIGITS
      else if (lookup(lexstr, ltype) == YES)
            lex = ltype(1)
      else
            lex = LEXOTHER
      return
      end
```

First we discard empty lines. If the first token is a semicolon or brace or **EOF**, it is returned as the lexical value. If the token contains only digits it must be a Fortran label, because it is the *first* token encountered in a statement. In typical Ratfor programs labels appear only on **format** statements, although they are accepted on any statement. The lexical value returned for a label is **LEXDIGITS**.

If the token isn't a label, it is looked up in a table containing the keywords **if**, **else** and so on. If it is found, **lex** returns the corresponding keyword type; otherwise it returns the value **LEXOTHER**. The table searching routine **lookup** is the one we used in Chapter 8. The parser initializes the symbol table with the keyword names and type values which will be returned by **lex**. The types are single-character strings with values **LEXIF**, **LEXDO**, and so on, returned in **ltype** (which must be a two-element array to hold the type and an **EOS**). The types need to be distinct from **EOF**, semicolon and braces since these are also returned by **lex**, but there are no other constraints.

alldig tests a string to see if it contains only digits.

```
# alldig — return YES if str is all digits
        integer function alldig(str)
        character type
        character str(ARB)
        integer i

        alldig = NO
        if (str(1) == EOS)
                return
        for (i = 1; str(i) ¬= EOS; i = i + 1)
                if (type(str(i)) ¬= DIGIT)
                        return
        alldig = YES
        return
        end
```

9.3 Code Generation Rules

In Chapter 1 we gave a brief indication of how the Ratfor control flow statements could be mechanically translated into Fortran. In this section we will make that informal description more precise.

if *Statement:*

The translation of

if (*condition* **)** *statement*

is essentially

if (*condition* is not true **)** go around *statement*

Thus when an **if** is encountered, we must

isolate the *condition* part
generate and save some unique label **L**
output " **if (.not. (** *condition* **)) goto L** "

(In Fortran, the construction

.not. (*condition* **)**

inverts the truth value of the *condition.*) When we get to the end of the statement that follows the **if**, there are two possibilities. If there is no **else** following, we need output only

```
L       continue
```

If an **else** follows, however, we must generate another label **L1** and output

```
        goto L1
L       continue
```

to branch around the **else** part, and then, after whatever statement follows the **else**,

```
L1      continue
```

to terminate the **if-else** construction. In summary, the code generation for

if (*condition* **)** *statement*

is

```
        if ( .not. ( condition ) ) goto L
                statement
L       continue
```

and for

if (*condition* **)** *statement1* **else** *statement2*

is

```
        if ( .not. ( condition ) ) goto L
                statement1
                goto L1
L       continue
                statement2
L1      continue
```

Since labels are "free," in the sense that we will never run out of legal statement numbers in any program, the easiest thing to do is *always* to generate two consecutive labels when an **if** is seen: **L1** is just **L+1**. If one of them turns out to be unnecessary because there is no **else**, it doesn't cost anything. And because we know that the labels are always **L** and **L+1**, only one of them need be remembered; the other is deduced by adding 1.

do *Statement:*

The Ratfor **do** is a Fortran **do** without a label. When **do** is seen, we

isolate the *limits*
generate a label **L**
output " **do L** *limits* "

Then at the end of the statement associated with the **do**, we output

```
L       continue
```

Thus the Ratfor

do *limits statement*

is translated into

```
        do L limits
                statement
L       continue
L+1     continue
```

The second **continue** is produced in case the loop contains a **break** statement; the **break** generates

```
        goto L+1
```

while a **next** generates

```
        goto L
```

In this case we generate the second **continue** regardless of whether or not there is a **break**; it is simply too much effort to check. To make our code generation task easier, we take advantage of the fact that Fortran compilers are usually quite clever about dealing with unreferenced **continue**'s.

while *Statement:*

The **while** statement combines aspects of **if** and **do** in an obvious manner. The code for

```
    while ( condition ) statement
```

is

```
        continue
    L   if ( .not. ( condition ) ) goto L+1
            statement
            goto L
    L+1 continue
```

L+1 also serves as the **break** label; **next**'s merely go to **L**. The **continue** before the **if** is there for the unlikely circumstance that the **while** has been labeled, as in

```
    10  while (i > 0) ...
```

In this case, Ratfor will put the **10** in the statement number field of the first line of code generated for the **while**, which is the **continue**. You should rarely have to write a statement number in Ratfor, but it is a basic principle of good design that you should be allowed to say anything that makes sense.

Labels and Others:

When a label is seen (lexical type **LEXDIGITS**), the label is output, beginning at column 1, and followed by enough blanks that the next character will come out in column 7, the standard place for a Fortran statement to begin. Input of type **LEXOTHER** need only be copied from input to output with appropriate formatting to adhere to Fortran requirements, usually that it lie between columns 7 and 72 of the line.

As you can see, Ratfor generates straightforward code for all of its constructs; there is no attempt to optimize special cases. The **if** statement is a case in point. The code generated for

```
    if ( condition ) statement
```

(without an **else**) is *always*

```
        if ( .not. ( condition ) ) goto L
                statement
L       continue
```

This is true even if *statement* is a single Fortran construction which need not be translated, as in

```
if ( condition ) return
```

This is a viable approach because in most circumstances the "optimization" will have negligible effect. For the several compilers we use, the only additional cost is typically one unnecessary **goto**, with an imperceptible effect on running time. It is rare that tinkering with the code will make any significant difference. (Measure it before you make it more complicated!) Algorithm and data structure changes are by far the most effective way to improve performance.

One drawback to this simplistic code generation, which should not go unmentioned, is that a few constructions can cause diagnostics from a Fortran compiler. The code generated for

```
if ( condition )
        return
else
        a = b
```

is

```
        if ( .not. ( condition ) ) goto L
                return
                goto L+1
L       continue
                a = b
L+1     continue
```

Some compilers trouble to check whether all statements are reachable, decide that **goto L+1** is not, and produce a warning. The same message will be produced if **return** is replaced by **break**, **next**, **goto** or **stop**.

The fix is easy: omit the **else**. It is unneeded, in the strictest sense, and it is responsible for generating the unreachable code. Still, this is regrettable, because it denies us the use of an important standard form and hence can interfere with readability. Whenever we see an **else**, we *know* that only one of two statements will be executed. But an **if** followed by a second statement implies that the second statement *will* be obeyed. The context may assure us otherwise but the form is misleading.

Throughout the book we have used **else**'s and **else if**'s whenever possible to emphasize that only one of a set of statements is to be performed. But we have also avoided the **else** in any situation that might generate unreachable code, to make the programs as portable as possible.

Exercise 9-1: Why is it not correct to follow a label by a **continue** in all cases? (Hint: What Fortran statement always has a label, yet is not executable?) □

9.4 Parsing

We come now to parsing, which ensures that the code generation operations are done at the right time with the right values. The basic organization is this. When the beginning of a statement (**if**, **else**, **while**, **do**, left brace, digits) is encountered, the corresponding type is pushed onto a stack and the code generation routine for that type is called if there is one (for instance, **ifcode** is called when **if** is seen). The routines for keywords **if**, **do** and **while** generate and return a unique label, which is placed on a parallel stack of label values.

When the end of a statement is encountered (types **other**, **break**, **next**, right brace, and semicolon), an appropriate code generation routine is called if there is one. Because it has found the end of a statement, the parser may also be able to pop one or more things off the stack. For instance, in

```
if ( a )
        if ( b )
                i = i + 1
j = j + 1
```

when **i = i + 1** is seen (type **other**), it can pop both stacked **if**'s; because there is no following **else**, both **if** statements are finished.

The parsing routine is by far the most complicated part of the program but its general outline is straightforward enough.

```
while (token ¬= EOF)
        if (token == if, else, while, do, left brace, digits) {
                do corresponding code generation routine
                stack type of token and label returned by code gen
                }
        else {
                do code generation for corresponding type
                   (must be other, break, next, semicolon, right brace)
                while (stack not empty) {
                        if (stack == left brace)
                                break
                        if (stack == IF & next token == ELSE)
                                break
                        do code generation for end of stacked type
                        pop stack
                        }
                }
```

Leaving aside some defenses against invalid input, the main complication is the necessity of looking ahead one token to see whether there is an **else** associated with an **if**. Consider the construction

```
if ( a )
        if ( b )
                c
        else
                d
```

To which **if** does the **else** belong? This is an ambiguity in Ratfor (as in many other languages); logically it could go with either. We have chosen the widely used and more useful interpretation, that the **else** goes with the nearest previous "un-**else**d" **if**. Thus, if the current top of the stack is an **if** and the next input is an **else**, the parser must not pop the stack any further; instead it must stack the **else** and later pop the **if** and **else** together.

As an example of the parsing process, let us translate the input

```
if ( a ) {
        if ( b )
                c
        while ( d )
                e
        }
else
        f
g
```

First,

```
        if (.not.(a)) goto L1
```

is generated, and an **if** is stacked at stack position 1, along with the generated label L1. The left brace is stacked at 2. Another **if** is stacked at 3 and

```
        if (.not.(b)) goto L2
```

is generated. c is encountered; when the code for c is produced,

```
        c
```

the top of the stack is an **if**, and the next token is a **while**, so the **if** can be popped and the code

```
L2      continue
```

generated. Now the stack pointer is 2 and the top is a left brace. The **while** is stacked at 3 and code for the start of the **while** is output:

```
        continue
L3      if (.not.(d)) goto L3+1
```

When e is encountered, it is output:

```
        e
```

Then the **while** can be unstacked and its termination code

```
        goto L3
L3+1 continue
```

generated. This leaves a left brace on the stack at 2 and a right brace as the next input. The left brace is popped; this leaves an **if** at stack position 1, and an **else** on the input, so the **else** is stacked at position 2 and

```
        goto L1+1
L1      continue
```

are produced. After **f** is output,

```
        f
```

we have an **else** stacked, so *two* items are unstacked — the **else** and the **if** — and

```
L1+1 continue
```

is output. Finally

```
        g
```

is produced.

It is important to carry out several such hand simulations, to be sure that in principle the mechanism does what it is supposed to, and to be sure that you understand what *should* happen.

We are now in a position to present the code for the parser. This is a sizable routine at first sight, but it follows closely the outline we gave above.

```
# parse — parse Ratfor source program
      subroutine parse
      character lexstr(MAXTOK)
      integer lex
      integer lab, labval(MAXSTACK), lextyp(MAXSTACK), sp, token

      call initkw      # install keywords in table
      sp = 1
      lextyp(1) = EOF
      for (token = lex(lexstr); token ¬= EOF; token = lex(lexstr)) {
            if (token == LEXIF)
                  call ifcode(lab)
            else if (token == LEXDO)
                  call docode(lab)
            else if (token == LEXWHILE)
                  call whilec(lab)
            else if (token == LEXDIGITS)
                  call labelc(lexstr)
            else if (token == LEXELSE) {
                  if (lextyp(sp) == LEXIF)
                        call elseif(labval(sp))
                  else
                        call synerr("illegal else.")
                  }
            if (token==LEXIF | token==LEXELSE | token==LEXWHILE
             | token==LEXDO | token==LEXDIGITS | token==LBRACE) {
                  sp = sp + 1                   # beginning of statement
                  if (sp > MAXSTACK)
                        call error("stack overflow in parser.")
                  lextyp(sp) = token            # stack type and value
                  labval(sp) = lab
                  }
            else {            # end of statement — prepare to unstack
                  if (token == RBRACE) {
                        if (lextyp(sp) == LBRACE)
                              sp = sp - 1
                        else
                              call synerr("illegal right brace.")
                        }
                  else if (token == LEXOTHER)
                        call otherc(lexstr)
                  else if (token == LEXBREAK | token == LEXNEXT)
                        call brknxt(sp, lextyp, labval, token)
                  token = lex(lexstr)           # peek at next token
                  call pbstr(lexstr)
                  call unstak(sp, lextyp, labval, token)
                  }
            }
      if (sp ¬= 1)
            call synerr("unexpected EOF.")
      return
      end
```

initkw places the keywords in the table for later lookup, using **instal** as in **define**.

As we said, if the token returned by **lex** is one of those that mark the beginning of a statement, the corresponding code generation routine is called. The type and any generated label are stacked. We will return to the code generation routines momentarily.

If the input token marks the end of a statement, appropriate code generation is done, and then as much as possible is unstacked. This task is performed by **unstak**.

```
# unstak — unstack at end of statement
      subroutine unstak(sp, lextyp, labval, token)
      integer labval(MAXSTACK), lextyp(MAXSTACK), sp, token

      for ( ; sp > 1; sp = sp - 1) {
            if (lextyp(sp) == LBRACE)
                  break
            if (lextyp(sp) == LEXIF & token == LEXELSE)
                  break
            if (lextyp(sp) == LEXIF)
                  call outcon(labval(sp))
            else if (lextyp(sp) == LEXELSE) {
                  if (sp > 2)
                        sp = sp - 1
                  call outcon(labval(sp)+1)
                  }
            else if (lextyp(sp) == LEXDO)
                  call dostat(labval(sp))
            else if (lextyp(sp) == LEXWHILE)
                  call whiles(labval(sp))
            }
      return
      end
```

After calling the right code generation routine, **unstak** pops the stack. If the top is an **else**, *two* things must be removed — the **else** and its **if**.

The main program for Ratfor calls **parse**. Depending on your environment, it might then call the local Fortran compiler to complete the translation. Ours simply exits.

```
# ratfor — main program for Ratfor
      call parse
      stop
      end
```

One of the major problems in designing a language translator is deciding what to do for each of the myriad syntactic errors that can occur in the input. It is seldom acceptable merely to report the first error and quit; even if there is no possibility that the output will be usable, it is still desirable to detect as many errors as possible on a given run. This requires that the translator recover from every error quickly, reporting as few spurious errors as possible in the process of resynchronizing.

This is not an easy task. Although **parse** and **unstak** contain some defense against syntactically illegal inputs like missing **if**'s and braces, they are not perfect. In particular, one error may leave the parser in a state where successive inputs appear invalid even though they aren't, and a cascade of messages appears. This is common to many parsers, but undesirable nonetheless. One of the exercises is concerned with improving the error recovery process.

You should realize that our parser is in no sense the state of the art. Although parsers can be written by hand for quite substantial languages, the task is not an easy one, and the resulting parsers are often hard to change, and may well contain significant errors and anomalies. We are fortunate that the Ratfor grammar is so small.

If a language is formally specified by a grammar (as most should be), it is an essentially mechanical task to construct a parser for it. As we mentioned, this is the function of a compiler-compiler, a tool too big and technical to talk about here. (See the bibliographic notes at the end of the chapter.) The original version of our parser was developed with a compiler-compiler; the parser presented here was derived from it, once we were satisfied with the language design.

Exercise 9-2: Modify **parse** to respond better to fatal syntax errors. You might consider skipping over input until you find a safe place to resume. (Where would that be?) Or you could try to *insert* tokens you think were left out. What are the dangers of this approach? □

Exercise 9-3: An interesting view is to think of error recovery as an *editing* process that converts unacceptable input to valid by making a series of insertions, replacements and deletions. One school of thought is that the best recovery is that which can be made with a minimum number of editing steps. Discuss the implications of this criterion. Specify minimum editing sequences for the errors detected in **parse**. □

9.5 Code Generation

parse and **unstak** call upon a fair number of code generation routines; these are described in this section.

if *Statement:*

When an **if** is encountered, we must collect the condition part (a string in balanced parentheses), generate a pair of consecutive unique labels **L** and **L+1**, output

```
if ( .not. ( condition ) ) goto L
```

and return **L**. This is accomplished by **ifcode**:

```
# ifcode - generate initial code for if
      subroutine ifcode(lab)
      integer labgen
      integer lab

      lab = labgen(2)
      call ifgo(lab)
      return
      end
```

labgen creates the labels; we will return to it shortly.

ifgo generates the construction

if (.not. (*condition* **)) goto lab**

It exercises most of our output routines; for now their names and the brief comments should be sufficient explanation until we are able to return to them.

```
# ifgo - generate "if(.not.(...))goto lab"
      subroutine ifgo(lab)
      integer lab
      string ifnot "if(.not."

      call outtab                   # get to column 7
      call outstr(ifnot)            # " if(.not. "
      call balpar                   # collect and output condition
      call outch(RPAREN)            # " ) "
      call outgo(lab)               # " goto lab "
      return
      end
```

balpar collects and outputs the condition part of an **if**, which is a string enclosed in balanced parentheses. If this is spread over several lines **balpar** handles the continuations by ignoring newlines.

```
# balpar — copy balanced paren string
      subroutine balpar
      character gettok
      character t, token(MAXTOK)
      integer nlpar

      if (gettok(token, MAXTOK) ¬= LPAREN) {
            call synerr("missing left paren.")
            return
            }
      call outstr(token)
      nlpar = 1
      repeat {
            t = gettok(token, MAXTOK)
            if (t==SEMICOL | t==LBRACE | t==RBRACE | t==EOF) {
                  call pbstr(token)
                  break
                  }
            if (t == NEWLINE)          # delete newlines
                  token(1) = EOS
            else if (t == LPAREN)
                  nlpar = nlpar + 1
            else if (t == RPAREN)
                  nlpar = nlpar - 1
            # else nothing special
            call outstr(token)
            } until (nlpar <= 0)
      if (nlpar ¬= 0)
            call synerr("missing parenthesis in condition.")
      return
      end
```

As we said before, Ratfor doesn't really know much Fortran. **balpar** does nothing but collect a string; it performs no syntax checks except some elementary but effective precautions against one of the most common errors, unbalanced parentheses.

The actions for the beginning of an **else** and for the end of an **if** or an **else** are only a few lines each. If an **else** is seen and the top element on the stack is an **if**, the parser calls **elseif** to produce the output

```
      goto L+1
L     continue
```

where **L** is the value on the stack. Here is **elseif**:

```
# elseif - generate code for end of if before else
      subroutine elseif(lab)
      integer lab

      call outgo(lab+1)
      call outcon(lab)
      return
      end
```

outcon generates a labeled **continue** statement; **outgo** generates a **goto** to a label.

At the end of an **else**, or an **if** that doesn't have an **else**, the output is produced by the lines in **unstak** that read

```
if (lextyp(sp) == LEXIF)
      call outcon(labval(sp))
else if (lextyp(sp) == LEXELSE) {
      if (sp > 2)
            sp = sp - 1
      call outcon(labval(sp)+1)
      }
```

These both produce a labeled **continue**; the appropriate label is picked out of the stack. The test on **sp** is part of error recovery; it prevents popping the stack too far if there is an **else** without an **if**.

labgen generates a group of distinct, consecutively numbered labels, and returns the first as its function value. The generated labels begin arbitrarily at 23000, a sufficiently unlikely value that collision with a label used by a Ratfor programmer is improbable.

```
# labgen - generate  n  consecutive labels, return first one
      integer function labgen(n)
      integer label, n
      data label /23000/

      labgen = label
      label = label + n
      return
      end
```

Labels:

When a label is seen (lexical type **LEXDIGITS**), the label is output along with enough spaces to get to column 7.

```
# labelc — output statement number
        subroutine labelc(lexstr)
        character lexstr(ARB)
        integer length

        if (length(lexstr) == 5)      # warn about 23xxx labels
                if (lexstr(1) == DIG2 & lexstr(2) == DIG3)
                        call synerr("warning: possible label conflict.")
        call outstr(lexstr)
        call outtab
        return
        end
```

Since labels are not needed in Ratfor programs except for **format** statements, a label beginning with 23000 will probably never occur. Just in case, however, **labelc** warns about input labels in the 23000 range. We can't silently ignore this pathological case, but carefully checking every input label to see whether it matches some generated label will make the preprocessor much more complicated but not much better. The warning is a reasonable compromise. Notice that only **labgen** and **labelc** know the range of label values to be generated, since there is no good reason why any other part of the preprocessor should care.

do *Statement:*

Code generation for a **do** is straightforward. We collect the **do** limits, generate a pair of consecutive labels **L** and **L+1**, output

```
        do L limits
```

and return **L**.

Since Ratfor knows no Fortran to speak of, the *limits* part can be anything which is legal for the local brand of Fortran, typically a construction like **i = 1, n**. If this part should be illegal for any reason, the error will be detected by the Fortran compiler.

At the end of the statement associated with the **do**, we output

```
L       continue
L+1     continue
```

The **continue** statement labeled **L+1** is a target for any **break**'s that might occur within the **do**. (**L** serves as the target for **next**'s).

docode is called when **do** is encountered:

```
# docode - generate code for beginning of do
      subroutine docode(lab)
      integer labgen
      integer lab
      string dostr "do"

      call outtab
      call outstr(dostr)
      lab = labgen(2)
      call outnum(lab)
      call eatup
      call outdon
      return
      end
```

eatup collects the rest of the input statement — the part that follows the token isolated by **lex**. **eatup** also handles the continuation convention for ordinary statements — a line ending with a comma is continued. Like **balpar**, it looks for unbalanced parentheses, but it does not look across multiple lines for the balancing parenthesis — in an ordinary statement, a missing parenthesis is more likely to be an error than an intentional continuation.

```
# eatup — process rest of statement; interpret continuations
      subroutine eatup
      character gettok
      character ptoken(MAXTOK), t, token(MAXTOK)
      integer nlpar

      nlpar = 0
      repeat {
            t = gettok(token, MAXTOK)
            if (t == SEMICOL | t == NEWLINE)
                  break
            if (t == RBRACE) {
                  call pbstr(token)
                  break
                  }
            if (t == LBRACE | t == EOF) {
                  call synerr("unexpected brace or EOF.")
                  call pbstr(token)
                  break
                  }
            if (t == COMMA) {
                  if (gettok(ptoken, MAXTOK) ¬= NEWLINE)
                        call pbstr(ptoken)
                  }
            else if (t == LPAREN)
                  nlpar = nlpar + 1
            else if (t == RPAREN)
                  nlpar = nlpar - 1
            call outstr(token)
            } until (nlpar < 0)
      if (nlpar ¬= 0)
            call synerr("unbalanced parentheses.")
      return
      end
```

dostat is called at the end of a **do** to output two appropriately labeled **continue**'s.

```
# dostat — generate code for end of do statement
      subroutine dostat(lab)
      integer lab

      call outcon(lab)
      call outcon(lab+1)
      return
      end
```

while *Statement:*

When a **while** is seen, the condition is isolated with **ifgo** and labels for **next**'s and **break**'s are generated. The output code, if you recall, is

```
        continue
L       if ( .not. ( condition ) goto L+1
                statement
                goto L
L+1     continue
```

This is produced by **whilec** and **whiles**.

```
# whilec — generate code for beginning of while
        subroutine whilec(lab)
        integer labgen
        integer lab

        call outcon(0)    # unlabeled continue, in case there was a label
        lab = labgen(2)
        call outnum(lab)
        call ifgo(lab+1)
        return
        end
```

whiles is executed after the end of the statement part of a **while**:

```
# whiles — generate code for end of while
        subroutine whiles(lab)
        integer lab

        call outgo(lab)
        call outcon(lab+1)
        return
        end
```

break *and* **next** *Statements:*

Code generation for **break** and **next** relies on the fact that **do** and **while** have carefully stacked the correct labels — the stacked value is always the **next** label, the **break** label one number higher. **brknxt** searches down the stack until it finds the enclosing **do** or **while**, then outputs a

```
        goto L
```

with the correct label.

```
# brknxt — generate code for break and next
      subroutine brknxt(sp, lextyp, labval, token)
      integer i, labval(MAXSTACK), lextyp(MAXSTACK), sp, token

      for (i = sp; i > 0; i = i - 1)
            if (lextyp(i) == LEXWHILE | lextyp(i) == LEXDO) {
                  if (token == LEXBREAK)
                        call outgo(labval(i)+1)
                  else
                        call outgo(labval(i))
                  return
                  }
      if (token == LEXBREAK)
            call synerr("illegal break.")
      else
            call synerr("illegal next.")
      return
      end
```

Type **other**:

otherc outputs code for a statement which isn't any of the others, using **eatup** to copy it through.

```
# otherc — output ordinary Fortran statement
      subroutine otherc(lexstr)
      character lexstr(ARB)

      call outtab
      call outstr(lexstr)
      call eatup
      call outdon
      return
      end
```

Exercise 9-4: **eatup** ensures that a line ending with a comma is continued. Add the convention that a line ending in an underscore is also continued, but with the underscore deleted. This provides a way to continue any line at an arbitrary point. Would it also be desirable to continue lines automatically after operators like +, − and so on? What about after / ? □

Exercise 9-5: If there is no **break** in a **do** loop, the second **continue** statement generated by **dostat** is unnecessary. How would you eliminate the unneeded ones? Is it worth it? What does your Fortran compiler do with excess **continue**'s? What does it do with unlabeled ones? □

9.6 Output Routines

Output lines are collected a character at a time in an array **outbuf**; a pointer **outp** is the index of the last character put into **outbuf**. These data are kept in a **common** block called **coutln**.

```
common /coutln/ outp, outbuf(MAXLINE)
  integer outp              # last position filled in outbuf; init = 0
  character outbuf          # output lines collected here
```

outdon flushes **outbuf** and resets **outp** to zero. It is called at the end of various statements, and is also called by **outch** to flush a line prior to starting a continuation. **outdon** is the only Ratfor routine that actually produces output.

```
# outdon - finish off an output line
      subroutine outdon
      include coutln

      outbuf(outp+1) = NEWLINE
      outbuf(outp+2) = EOS
      call putlin(outbuf, STDOUT)
      outp = 0
      return
      end
```

outch enters characters into **outbuf**; it is responsible for handling continuation lines according to local conventions. Lines are 72 characters long, as is usual with standard Fortran. A non-blank, non-zero character in column 6 of a line signals that it is a continuation of the previous line; we use a star.

```
# outch - put one character into output buffer
      subroutine outch(c)
      character c
      integer i
      include coutln

      if (outp >= 72) {    # continuation card
            call outdon
            for (i = 1; i < 6; i = i + 1)
                  outbuf(i) = BLANK
            outbuf(6) = STAR
            outp = 6
            }
      outp = outp + 1
      outbuf(outp) = c
      return
      end
```

outtab is used by several routines to force **outp** past column 6.

```
# outtab — get past column 6
        subroutine outtab
        include coutln

        while (outp < 6)
                call outch(BLANK)
        return
        end
```

There are a handful of other output routines for generating common constructs, but they all call on **outtab** to start a new statement, **outch** to build it, and **outdon** to finish it off. *Only* these three routines need to know the particular format of Fortran statements, so all the magic numbers like 6 and 72 can be confined here. Even **outtab** calls on **outch**, despite the fact that it could store blanks in **outbuf** directly.

Here are the remaining output routines. **outstr** outputs a string by repeated calls to **outch**. It also converts quoted strings into the standard Fortran *n*h construction, although you may not need this with your Fortran compiler. **outstr** is also the place to do any other character translations that might be desired, such as converting > to **.gt.**, etc; these are left as exercises.

```
# outstr — output string
        subroutine outstr(str)
        character c, str(ARB)
        integer i, j

        for (i = 1; str(i) ¬= EOS; i = i + 1) {
                c = str(i)
                if (c ¬= SQUOTE & c ¬= DQUOTE)
                        call outch(c)
                else {
                        i = i + 1
                        for (j = i; str(j) ¬= c; j = j + 1)   # find end
                                ;
                        call outnum(j-i)
                        call outch(LETH)
                        for ( ; i < j; i = i + 1)
                                call outch(str(i))
                        }
                }
        return
        end
```

outnum converts numbers from internal representation into characters with **itoc** and outputs them with **outch**.

```
# outnum - output decimal number
      subroutine outnum(n)
      character chars(MAXCHARS)
      integer itoc
      integer i, len, n

      len = itoc(n, chars, MAXCHARS)
      for (i = 1; i <= len; i = i + 1)
            call outch(chars(i))
      return
      end
```

Finally, **outcon** and **outgo** output **L continue** and **goto L** respectively, then call **outdon** to flush out the line in **outbuf**.

```
# outcon - output "n   continue"
      subroutine outcon(n)
      integer n
      string contin "continue"

      if (n > 0)
            call outnum(n)
      call outtab
      call outstr(contin)
      call outdon
      return
      end

# outgo - output "goto  n"
      subroutine outgo(n)
      integer n
      string goto "goto"

      call outtab
      call outstr(goto)
      call outnum(n)
      call outdon
      return
      end
```

The subroutine tree for **ratfor** is not especially complicated. Here are the essential parts, with all of the output routines removed, since they contribute no complexity.

```
ratfor
        parse
                initkw
                        instal
                lex
                        gettok
                                ngetc
                                        getc
                                putbak
                        alldig
                        lookup
                ifcode
                        labgen
                        ifgo
                                balpar
                                        gettok
                elseif
                docode
                        labgen
                        eatup
                                gettok
                whilec
                        labgen, ifgo
                labelc
                otherc
                        eatup
                brknxt
                unstak
                        dostat, whiles
```

9.7 Extensions

These are obviously many things that can be done to the basic tool once it is available. Not all of these are worth the effort involved, but here is a list of possibilities, phrased as exercises. Most are easy enough, and require only straightforward additions to the basic program.

Exercise 9-6: Add a translator for these operators:

```
>     .ge.
>=    .ge.
<     .lt.
<=    .le.
==    .eq.
¬=    .ne.
¬     .not.
&     .and.
|     .or.
```

□

Exercise 9-7: If your character set is so restrictive that you cannot use braces or brackets for statement grouping, modify Ratfor to use some other notation. **begin-end**, **do-end** and **do-od** are forms that have been used in other languages. You might also consider shorter character strings like << and >> or **$(** and **$)**. □

Exercise 9-8: Integrate the **include** and **define** or **macro** processors into this program. What are some good reasons for doing so? Are there good reasons for *not* doing so? □

Exercise 9-9: Add the **for** and **repeat-until** statements. A **repeat** without an **until** should be an infinite loop. Don't forget that since **until** is optional, **repeat-until** has the same ambiguity as **if-else**. Resolve it the same way. □

Exercise 9-10: In a few of our programs it would be convenient to exit from several loops all at once (see **expand** in Chapter 2, for instance). Invent a syntax for multi-level **break** and **next** and implement it. What are the good and bad points of your statements for writing readable, modifiable code? □

Exercise 9-11: We mentioned the logical operator **andif** in Chapter 6, and a corresponding **orif** in Chapter 8. These force a left to right evaluation of logical expressions, and guarantee termination as soon as the truth value is known. Implement **andif** and **orif**. (**&&** and **||** are convenient abbreviations.) □

Exercise 9-12: Add the **string** declaration. ANSI Fortran requires **data** statements to follow all declarations. How does this complicate matters? □

Exercise 9-13: The gravest deficiency in Ratfor, as in Fortran, is the restricted set of data types supported. How would you add character variables, strings, structures, pointers? □

Exercise 9-14: Many of our identifiers are strained because we adhered to the Fortran limit of six character identifier names. Modify Ratfor to truncate all longer names to six characters. Does Ratfor now have to know about Fortran keywords? More involved, but safer, modify Ratfor to generate unique internal names for truncated identifiers which happen to be identical in the first six characters. □

Exercise 9-15: Measure some programs to find out how often transfer of control statements like **return**, **goto**, **break**, **next** and **stop** occur after an **if**. Measure running programs to see how frequently these statements are executed. If your measurements indicate that it is worthwhile, rewrite the parser to optimize these special cases. Do you think it is worth doing anyway, to avoid the possibility of generating unreachable code? What aspects of your Fortran compiler would you investigate before rewriting anything? Why are constructions like

```
if ( condition )
        i = 0
```

harder? Did you think they were? Are they worth doing? □

Exercise 9-16: Improve Ratfor's error *recovery* by making the parser recover better from invalid inputs like **else**'s without **if**'s, missing or excessive braces, and the like. Improve error *detection* capabilities by careful checking of Ratfor source programs for obvious blunders like unbalanced parentheses, adjacent operators, etc. Improve error *reporting* by tagging each output line with some sequencing information determined by the input line that created it, so that messages which come from the Fortran compiler can be more readily associated with their Ratfor source. (Remember that this is inherently system-dependent, although columns 73-80 of Fortran source lines are often available in a card environment.) If you integrate the **include** processor into your version, how do you report line numbers for errors within included files? □

Exercise 9-17: Improve the readability of the generated code by indenting appropriately, retaining blanks, eliminating unnecessary **continue**'s, and converting Ratfor comments into Fortran comments. Is it worth it? □

Exercise 9-18: Write a "beautifier," i.e., a program that converts an unformatted Ratfor program into one that is neatly indented and spaced. Is it better to use a beautifier or to maintain programs neatly yourself? Should Ratfor itself produce a neat source listing? How does your computing environment affect the answers? □

Exercise 9-19: A much harder job than a preprocessor is a *structurer* — a program to take an existing Fortran program and convert it into a structured language like Ratfor. Carry out the design of such a program, for several degrees of perfection. How complete a job should a structurer do? □

Exercise 9-20: Other programming languages can benefit from preprocessing. (If no examples spring to mind, you might consider various flavors of Algol, APL, assembly language, Basic, Cobol, PL/I, Snobol, and your local job control language.) Is a preprocessor for your language possible at all in your operating system environment? Define and implement a preprocessor for a reasonable set of improvements, bearing in mind that it is much more useful to do part of the job well than the whole thing badly (or not in time). □

Exercise 9-21: If your system permits, write a preprocessor to read the job control language that we have been using — file redirection with < and >, and pipelines — and generate a file of job control language to be run as a subsequent step. Implement pipes with temporary files. How much help do you need from your operating system? How much would you have to change the preprocessor to make it into the command interpreter for an interactive environment? □

9.8 Some Measurements

If you use a preprocessor like Ratfor, it costs you more to compile programs. How much? That depends on your system, but as a rough estimate it will double the cost of each compilation merely because the program is read twice, once in Ratfor and once in Fortran, instead of just once in Fortran.

We feel strongly that this cost is absolutely immaterial in comparison to the benefits of the preprocessor. Even though a single compilation may cost twice as much, our experience has been that many fewer compilations are needed, because the code *works* sooner. If you can find a bug in a few minutes instead of a few hours it pays for a lot of compiling. The other saving is in the much reduced cost of modifying a program after it's been in service for a while. Every program in this book has been extensively revised several times. We honestly believe that this amount of revision wouldn't have been possible in standard Fortran.

Still, it's worth finding out where the preprocessor spends its time, to see if it can be speeded up. We measured the Ratfor presented in this chapter while it was compiling 900 lines of code. 65 percent of its time was spent doing input and output at the lowest level — below **getc** and **putlin**. On the system we were using, **getc** and **putlin** both use Fortran formatted I/O, which is notoriously slow.

The remaining 35 percent of Ratfor's run time is distributed like this:

gettok	11.1%
ngetc	5.2
outstr	3.2
getc	2.5
type	2.4
outch	2.0
eatup	1.5
putbak	1.4
lookup	1.1

and everything else under one percent. The moral? Once again, you might as well write the program as cleanly as you can, for until you've got truly fast I/O, nothing else matters. After that, the token routine is the place to look.

We also measured a production version of Ratfor, containing **define** and **include** and character translations. This one spent 60 percent of its time in input-output, and 15 percent looking up tokens in its table of definitions (there were 60 symbolic constants). This reinforces our conclusions about the dominance of I/O time, and also supports our contention that a linear table search is often adequate.

The general observation is that many programs don't do much processing compared to the amount of work needed merely to get the characters in and out. Even with efficient I/O routines, most of the tools presented in this book spend most of their time doing I/O. (Some uses of **find** and **macro** are exceptions.)

Timing measurements are often hard come by, at least not without a lot of special pleading with your operating system. A valuable measurement tool which doesn't require nearly as much system facility is a *profiler* — a program which counts the number of times each statement in the program is executed, by adding counting statements to source statements before compilation, then neatly listing the accumulated information alongside the original source program after the modified program has run. Just knowing the number of times each statement has been executed tells you what parts of the program are most often executed and are thus most likely to dominate the execution time. You can see what parts of the program have never been executed, which may indicate useless code, inadequate testing, or just plain errors. And you can detect performance bugs — regions which are executed more than they should be, such as computations inside loops when they don't have to be.

Exercise 9-22: Having built a preprocessor for a language, you now have most of the tools needed for a profiler. Build as simple a profiler as you can. Is a profiler easier for Ratfor than for Fortran? □

9.9 Some Usage Statistics

We also made some measurements to find out how Ratfor is actually used. We counted the occurrences of the various statement types in 5400 lines of Ratfor (the programs in this book), to see how often they occur, and whether they are worth the effort of putting into the preprocessor. Here are the results.

	total	followed by { }	
if	556	161	
else	229	81	(132 **else if**'s)
for	154	55	
while	45	15	
repeat	22	21	
until	14		
do	0		
break	55		
next	0		

Naturally we used our tools to get these numbers — **find** to pick out interesting lines, and various combinations of **translit**, **charcount**, **linecount** and **edit** to distill and count them.

Taken together, the control flow statements add up to only twenty percent of the lines; the rest is plain old Fortran. But you must agree by now that Ratfor is a lot easier to read than Fortran; those twenty percent make a difference. The number of loops and compound statements gives a crude measure of how many **goto**'s and statement numbers have been avoided.

Most of our loops test at the top — **for** and **while** outnumber **repeat** by nine to one. (Make sure you "do nothing" gracefully!) **break** seems to be necessary, but **next** is much less important; although we had originally used a handful, they disappeared quite naturally as the code was refined.

As you can see, **do** is hardly vital, at least to us. In fact, since there weren't any, we looked at **for**, **while** and **repeat** statements to see if any could have been be replaced by **do**'s. About one quarter of the **for**'s could be, *if* we occasionally added extra statements to set up the limits, *and if* we nearly always added a test to ensure that the loop could be done zero times. Another quarter of the **for**'s could probably be contorted into **do**'s, but only by sacrificing clarity. The rest of the **for**'s and essentially all of the **while**'s and **repeat**'s simply aren't **do**'s at all. They loop, but they don't progress arithmetically.

The lesson is clear. Few of the loops in this collection of code are best expressed with the **do** statement (which is the only looping construct in Fortran). If you persist in using **do**'s, most of the time you must twist your logic to meet the restrictions of the **do**. And twisted logic is not the most pleasant kind to work with.

Bibliographic Notes

Fortran preprocessors have become very popular recently, probably because they give so much benefit for so little effort. Most provide improved control flow structures; fewer address cosmetic issues. (We think that the appearance of a language is also important, but that puts us in a minority.) Three widely available preprocessors, capable of running on almost any Fortran system, are Flecs, by T. Beyer (University of Oregon); Mortran, by J. Cook and C. Zahn (Stanford Linear Accelerator); and Iftran, by E. Miller (General Research). Mortran is based on a macro processor, and is thus more easily changed and extended than implementations based on a compiler. Ratfor itself is also available; the version distributed with the machine-readable code of this book includes **for**, **repeat-until**, **include** and **define**.

If you are serious about compiling techniques, including compiler-compilers, there is an extensive literature. You might look at A. V. Aho and S. C. Johnson, "LR parsing," *Computing Surveys,* June, 1974, or A. V. Aho and J. D. Ullman, *The Theory of Parsing, Translation, and Compiling* (Prentice-Hall, 1972).

Preprocessors are not restricted to enhancing conventional programming languages, of course. We have built several for the typesetting language used to set this book; one of the most successful implements a language for typesetting mathematics (B. W. Kernighan and L. L. Cherry, "A system for typesetting mathematics," *CACM,* March, 1975).

For a fascinating study of what can be learned with a profiler, and for some intriguing statistics on how Fortran is used in real life, read "An empirical study of Fortran programs," by D. E. Knuth, *Software—Practice and Experience,* April, 1971. (The term "profile" to describe a statement frequency count for a program was coined by Knuth in this article.)

C. A. R. Hoare once said, "One thing [the language designer] should not do is to include untried ideas of his own." We have followed that precept closely. The control flow statements of Ratfor are shamelessly stolen from the language C, developed for the UNIX operating system by D. M. Ritchie. Our measurements of Ratfor (and of other programs in this book) were obtained on a Honeywell 6070 with a timing package developed by A. D. Hall.

EPILOGUE

We have come a long way. Nine chapters stuffed with code is a lot to negotiate. If you didn't assimilate all of it the first time through, don't worry — you weren't really expected to. Even the best of code takes time to absorb, and you seldom grasp all the implications until you try to use and modify a program. Much of what you learn about programming comes only from working with code: reading, revising and rereading.

Reading and *revising* are the key words. No program comes out a perfect work of art on its first draft, regardless of the techniques you use to write it. We rewrote every routine in this book several times, yet we still would not claim that any one is flawless. Extensive revision may sound like a costly and time-consuming luxury, but when the programs are clean and the modules small, it is not. Moreover you will find that with practice in reading and revising, your first versions get better and better, since you soon learn what to use and what to avoid, what is good style and what is not. Even so, rewriting will always remain an important part of the programming process.

The purpose of most rewriting is to simplify a program, to make it easier to understand, to keep its complexity within manageable bounds. *Controlling complexity* is the essence of computer programming. We will always be limited by the sheer number of details that we can keep straight in our heads. Much of what we have tried to teach in this book is how to cope with complexity.

At the lowest level, we were careful in our choice of control structures and in how we used the ones we chose. We found no need for the **goto** statement, for instance, nor for the **do**. **if**'s are seldom nested more than two levels deep, save in the restricted form of **else if**'s for multi-way decisions. Loops generally are tested at the top, before it's too late. Subroutines and functions rarely spread over more than one page; most are much shorter. As a result the code is readable. It is easy to convince yourself that a module is probably correct, because it is broken up into pieces that you can grasp one at a time and read in sequence.

Each module is also *cohesive:* it has good reasons for being a separate entity. It is not a tangle of multiple functions lumped arbitrarily, nor is it a displaced fragment of some other module. This means that we can describe the function of each routine in a line or two. Further, the routine is written to *meet* this specification, a discipline far superior to writing a subroutine that might be useful, then describing how it does what it does.

Several programs in this book comprise five hundred to a thousand lines of source code, yet none is conceptually "big." Each can be understood a module at a time, a section at a time. This is because the hierarchy of subroutines was designed so that no one module has to know about much of the total problem, nor deal with more than a handful of immediate neighbors. There is little fear that a change in one part of the hierarchy will cause unexpected repercussions in another part, because the modules are kept as uncoupled as possible, and the coupling that exists is kept visible.

We tried to make the programs easy to modify, by hiding design decisions and data structures so that routines that don't need to know about them don't. We built checks and firewalls into the code so that errors and inconsistencies are detected quickly. We expressed details of character set, parameters and flags in terms of symbolic constants so that only one change is needed to alter a value throughout a program. We were also careful to isolate as much as possible of the operating system interface in a small set of primitives, so the bulk of the code is independent of the local environment.

Finally, at the highest level, we wrote programs so they could work together, so complex tasks could be implemented by *combining* existing programs instead of by writing new ones. Each program so used is just a module, with a particularly simple interface to others.

This is "structured programming" in the best sense of the term. It is clear that the method works, and works well, for real programs. The rewards are substantial: we can write comprehensible, reliable, robust code and remain relatively unaffected by major changes in implementation strategies and even by changes from one computer to another. Proper structure, at all levels, is not just nice, it is vital to the successful control of a complex job.

Besides these considerations of structure, we tried to convey some helpful guidelines for attacking a programming task. Like all questions of judgment, they are subject to debate, but we have found that they work well.

Principle 1 is the most important: *keep it simple.* At all levels, be as clean as possible, and write the simplest, clearest thing that will do the job. You can't be utterly naive, of course; common sense is still needed. When you choose an algorithm, there has to be some hope that it will be economical. But if implementation details and strategies are concealed, an inadequate algorithm can be changed without affecting much else. Since you are building tools, you also have to remember the people who will use your program, and make *their* task lighter, even at the expense of complicating your own. Fortunately, a uniform and regular design is often reflected in a clean interface for users.

Principle 2 is related: *build it in stages.* Undertake a complex task only in manageable steps. Concentrate on the central, most important aspects first; don't get sidetracked on frills. If your basic plan is good, later additions will fit in smoothly. In the meantime, people can use what you already have produced, and their advice and experience should help you decide what comes next. You may even find that the part already built is adequate by itself. Ninety percent of the right job done well and available today is a lot more valuable than ninety-nine percent promised for sometime next month.

Principle 3 is intuitively appealing: *let someone else do the hard part.* Build on what you or others have already done, instead of starting from scratch each time. If you write a routine for something, make it general enough that it can be used again for a related job. In a larger context, you can often get a great deal of leverage by interfacing a small program to a large one — the Ratfor preprocessor is a good example. And of course, whenever you can, let the machine do the work, for that is the ultimate purpose of building tools.

One complication you probably have no control over is your local computing environment. But even if it's horrible, as many are, you don't have to suffer stoically. Even a modest improvement of frequently used parts, like your programming and job control languages, is well worth while, and there's no excuse for not trying to conceal the worst aspects.

Keep these thoughts in mind as you look back over the code. Although our suggestions were made during the development of specific programs, the lessons they contain are applicable in general. The design principles and guidelines summarized here are an effective way to produce tools that work properly, and that work well with people and with other programs. That should be your goal for every program you write.

APPENDIX

PRIMITIVES AND SYMBOLIC CONSTANTS

The primitives are routines needed to interface the programs in this book to the operating system upon which they run. Most programs need only **getlin** and **putlin** or **getc** and **putc**, and of course one of these pairs can be implemented in terms of the other. **getch** and **putch** fall into the same category. Similarly, **error** and **cant** can be written using **remark**. **remark** is called a primitive only because there is no implementation-independent way in Fortran to detect the end of a quoted string passed to a subroutine.

Many of the programs need **getarg**; an adequate temporary version can be made by reading arguments from a file, since all of the programs read the arguments in order and only once.

File system interactions are handled by **open**, **close**, **create** and **remove**. These are needed by the file programs of Chapter 3, **sort** in Chapter 4 and **edit** in Chapter 6. **edit** also requires **seek** and **readf** for the scratch file version.

The following routines, which were not presented in the text, are needed to complete certain programs. Some are available in Fortran, usually under an alias. These are **abs (iabs)**, **max (max0)**, **min (min0)**, and **mod**. The logical functions **and**, **or** and **not** are used only by **xor** in **crypt**. The routines **init** (for **format**) and **initkw** (for **ratfor**) initialize parameters as specified in the text.

The following is a list of consistent values for the symbolic constants used throughout the book. *n* stands for an unspecified numeric value, typically the size of an array used for a stack or a string of characters. The list omits names beginning with **MAX**, which are also numeric values. Also omitted are constants of the form **LET***x* and **DIG***n*, which indicate the internal representation used for the corresponding letter *x* or digit *n*, respectively. It is assumed that characters are encoded internally as small positive integers.

Printable characters are used as much as possible for parameter values to improved the readability of code and of diagnostic printouts inserted while debugging. Non-printing characters are indicated in italic and actual numeric values are in Roman.

Name	Value
ALPHA	a
AND	&
ANY	?
APPENDCOM	a
ARB	*n*
ARGFLAG	$
ARGSIZE	*n*
BACKSCAN	\
BACKSPACE	*backspace*
BACKWARD	−1
BLANK	*blank*
BOL	%
BOTTOM	62
BP	5
BR	3
BUFENT	5
BUFSIZE	*n*
CALLSIZE	*n*
CCL	[
CCLEND	]
CE	10
CHANGE	c
CHAR	a
CLOSIZE	4
CLOSURE	*
COLON	:
COMMA	,
COMMAND	.
COUNT	1
CURLINE	.
DASH	—
DEFTYPE	−4
DEL	d
DELCOM	d
DIGIT	0
DITTO	−3
DOLLAR	$
DQUOTE	"
ENTER	e
EOF	−1
EOL	$
EOS	−2
ERR	−3
ERROUT	7
ESCAPE	@
EVALSIZE	*n*
EXCLUDE	x
EXTR	x
FI	1
FO	13
FOLD	$
FORWARD	1
GLOBAL	g
HE	12
HUGE	1000
IFTYPE	−5
IN	7
INCTYPE	−6
INFILE1	1
INFILE2	2
INSERT	i
INSIZE	*n*
LASTLINE	$
LBRACE	{
LBRACK	[
LENG	4
LETTER	a
LEXBREAK	−8
LEXDIGITS	−9
LEXDO	−10
LEXELSE	−11
LEXIF	−12
LEXNEXT	−13
LEXOTHER	−14
LEXWHILE	−15
LINE0	0
LOGPTR	*n*
LPAREN	(
LS	4
MARGIN1	2
MARGIN2	2
MARK	2
MERGEORDER	7
MERGETEXT	*n*
MIDDLE	40
MINUS	−
MOVECOM	m
NAMESIZE	*n*
NCCL	n
NEXT	1
NEWLINE	*newline*
NF	2
NFILES	*n*
NO	0
NOSKIP	+
NOSTATUS	0
NOT	¬
OK	−2
PAGELEN	66
PAGENUM	#
PAGEWIDTH	60
PERIOD	.
PL	14
PLUS	+
PREV	0
PREVCL	2
PRINT	p
PRINTCUR	=
PRINTFIL	f
QUIT	q
RBRACE	}
RBRACK	]
RCODE	0
READ	0
READCOM	r
READWRITE	2
RM	8
RPAREN	)
SCAN	/
SEEKADR	3
SEMICOL	;
SHARP	#
SKIP	*blank*
SP	6
SQUOTE	'
STAR	*
START	3
STDIN	5
STDOUT	6
SUBSTITUTE	s
SUBTYPE	7
TAB	*tab*
TBL	t
TEXT	3
THRESH	5
TI	9
UL	11
UNDERLINE	_
UNKNOWN	0
UPD	u
WRITE	1
WRITECOM	w
YES	1

INDEX OF FIRST LINES

This index contains an alphabetical list of the comment lines that introduce each routine, with the page number where the final version of the routine occurs.

INDEX

This index was prepared in large part with the tools described in the book, including **sort**, **find**, **translit**, **edit**, and only two small, special-purpose programs. The first, a variant of **kwic**, accepts lines of the form

self reference:331

and generates the permutations

self reference:331
reference, self:331

These lines were sorted, by dictionary order before the colon and numerically after, then delivered to a variant of **unique** that changes occurrences such as

self reference:331
self reference:337

into

self reference:331, 337

find was used extensively to locate references to indexed terms.

In this index, page numbers in italics refer to *definitions* of routines and **common** blocks.